Dominic Selwood was awarded his masters in history from the Sorbonne in Paris and his doctorate from Oxford. He is a Fellow of the Royal Historical Society and a Fellow of the Royal Society of Arts. His previous books include *Knights of the Cloister*, a university textbook on the Knights Templar, and *The Sword of Moses*, an Amazon bestselling historical crypto-thriller.

SPIES, SADISTS AND SORCERERS

THE HISTORY YOU WEREN'T TAUGHT IN SCHOOL

DOMINIC SELWOOD

CRUX
PUBLISHING

First published in the United Kingdom in December 2015
by Crux Publishing Ltd.

ISBN: 978-1-909979-34-5
Copyright © Dominic Selwood, 2015

Also available as an ebook:
eISBN: 978-1-909979-33-8

Requests for permission to reproduce material from this work
should be sent to hello@cruxpublishing

Though a good deal is too strange to be believed,
nothing is too strange to have happened.

Thomas Hardy
The Personal Notebooks of Thomas Hardy
1871

FOREWORD

Winston Churchill once explained that history would be kind to him, because he intended to write it himself. Behind the joke, he understood a simple truth. So did Adolf Hitler, who insisted that people would believe anything if it was repeated often enough. Yet another European soldier-politician, Napoleon Bonaparte, was also aware of it when he defined history as a series of untruths people have agreed upon.

What all three knew was that history is not a hard science. It is much more soft and yielding, capable of being defined and shaped—or distorted and falsified—by those who live it, or those who tell it.

There are, of course, fixed historical facts. For instance, in 1215, the barons forced King John to agree Magna Carta. In 1533, King Henry VIII broke from Rome. No one is going to dispute these dates. However, scratch deeper into the surrounding events, and things become less certain.

Take Magna Carta. It is one of the world's most famous documents—the West's charter of liberty and democracy. Except it wasn't. John and the barons disowned it within nine weeks and threw it in the bin, where it lay unused and irrelevant for centuries. Our modern image of its significance was only invented in the 1600s, when it was resurrected and dubiously hoisted as a battle standard for the will of the people against tyranny.

Or take Henry's break from Rome, and the transformation of English religion finished by his children, Edward VI and Elizabeth I. We now know many of the changes were implemented with state terror and violence—the Tudors effectively massacred their people into a new religion. And yet, the Tudor spin machine constructed its story of Henry the benign Renaissance spiritual liberator so well that it is still taught in schools around the world.

In fact, a lot of the history we learn turns out to be only half the picture. Worse, some of it is just plain wrong. There are so many examples. People learn that Constantine the Great made Christianity the state religion of the Roman Empire in AD 313. He didn't. Theodosius I did in AD 380. Everyone knows that Christopher Columbus discovered North America. Except he didn't. He never even set foot there. He found a few islands in the Caribbean, parts of Central America, and the eastern tip of Venezuela, but had no idea North America even existed.

The list of myths we honour as history is enormous. Sometimes we are being purposefully misled. Other times we mislead ourselves, seeing only what we want.

My first history teacher fought in the Battle of Britain. Dozens of lovingly-assembled and painted model Spitfires, Hurricanes, Messerschmitts, Stukas, and the rest hung on invisible cotton threads from the ceiling of his classroom. Looking up instantly transported me to sunny rural airfields in 1940, where gangs of young men puffing pipes were scrambled into the air for the dogfights of their lives. Only in later life did I find out that he had been a flight instructor. It wasn't his fault we all thought he was a fighter ace. We simply saw what we wanted.

Many of the stories in this book are about setting the record straight. Or, at least, presenting another perspective. They first appeared in *The Daily Telegraph* and *The Spectator*, designed to give historical context to contemporary events or anniversaries.

I have rewritten some of the titles, and there is a list at the back of where and when each article first appeared. I have left the content of the stories unchanged.

I hope you enjoy them, and that—in their own way—they show history to be so much more than we think.

DKS

London

December 2015

CONTENTS

THE ANCIENT
WORLD

1

Flavius Josephus, the Roman destruction of Jerusalem, and two millennia of bloodshed in the Middle East

Flavius Josephus, the famous Jewish historian, saw the Roman armies smash Jerusalem to dust in AD 70. With the Middle East entering another round of profound destruction, this piece explores the Jewish-Roman wars, and the endless conflicts that have plagued the wider region ever since.

Joseph ben Matthias of Jerusalem was one of history's survivors. When he was born into a privileged, royal, priestly family in AD 37/38 (only a few years after Jesus' crucifixion), Jerusalem was a thriving—if somewhat edgy—city at the heart of Roman Judaea. By the time he died in AD 100, all of Jerusalem, barring a few sections of wall, had been wiped off the face of the earth so comprehensively that, as he later said, no one would ever know that anyone had lived there.

Joseph, or Josephus as be became known, lived through the most turbulent period of the Jewish-Roman wars, and—to the joy of later historians—loved writing as much as he enjoyed talking about himself. He had a very high opinion of everything he did, and clearly saw himself at the centre of events. That said, his boastful personality is inextricably linked to the extraordinary life he led, and to his unique closeness to the decision makers on both sides of the war. Whatever one thinks of his character or actions, his eye for detail and his fascination with the politics driving Rome and Jerusalem make him one of the most immediate and exciting writers of the first century.

As a young man, Josephus saw three main groups around him in Jewish society: Pharisees, Sadducees, and the ascetic Essenes (who produced the Dead Sea Scrolls). He had an inquiring mind, and so spent three years in the desert with an Essene master named Banus, before coming back to civilization and joining the Pharisees, whom he later described as Jewish Stoics. His choice to become a Pharisee speaks volumes about what was to happen later, as the Pharisees were notable for their willingness to live peacefully under Roman rule.

Josephus was known for his memory and knowledge of the Law (i.e., religious practices). Being from an elite family, he was soon drawn into Jerusalem's political life. Aged 26, he was dispatched on a sensitive mission to Rome to negotiate the release of some Jewish priests being held hostage. Once there, he managed to arrange an introduction to the beautiful and political Poppaea Sabina, Nero's second wife, with whom he made friends, and through whose intervention he succeeded in freeing the prisoners. The whole affair left a deep mark on him—especially the wonders of the Eternal City and its indomitable politico-military machine.

But back in Judaea, things were becoming increasingly tense.

When the Roman consul Pompey had first conquered Judaea in 63 BC, the Romans had been happy for the territory to be ruled by puppet kings (Hasmonean then Herodian). But when the Jews revolted against Herod Archelaus for contracting a bigamous marriage and for his ongoing cruelties, Rome banished him to the south of France and pulled Judaea fully into the empire as an official province.

Factions within Jewish society opposed the direct rule from Rome. Their resentment began to escalate, resulting in increasingly frequent rebellions. For instance, in his later writings, Josephus would mention the famous uprising led by Judas of Galilee in AD 6/7 around the time of the tax census ordered by Quirinius, the Roman governor of Syria. Interestingly, this is the same census referred to in the Bible:

> *In those days a decree went out from Emperor Augustus that all the world should be registered. This was the first registration and was taken while Quirinius was governor of Syria. All went to their own towns to be registered. Joseph also went from the town of Nazareth in Galilee to Judea, to the city of David called Bethlehem, because*

he was descended from the house and family of David. He went to be registered with Mary, to whom he was engaged and who was expecting a child. (Luke, 2:1–5)

Unfortunately, this Gospel account is historically problematic as Rome never ordered a global census. Also, the Gospel of Matthew says Jesus was born in the reign of King Herod the Great, who died in 4 BC. Moreover, most scholars reject the idea that any Roman tax census ever required people to travel to their ancient ancestral homes in order to register, as it makes no economic sense. (It is most likely that the author of the Gospel of Luke was using entirely standard artistic licence of the day to tie Jesus more firmly to the royal house of David.)

Most importantly in this context, in his later writings Josephus cites Judas of Galilee's rebellion as the start of the rise of the Zealots, or the *Kanna'im*, an 'aggressive and fanatical war party' sworn to overthrow the Romans.

The members of this party bore also the name Sicarii, from their custom of going about with daggers ('sicae') hidden beneath their cloaks, with which they would stab anyone found committing a sacrilegious act or anything provoking anti-Jewish feeling. ('Zealots', Jewish Encyclopedia, 1906)

By this or any other any definition, the Zealots/*Sicarii* were religious fundamentalists. Josephus describes them as a 'seditious' group, 'fond of war', and filled with 'madness', and he puts the blame for everything that was to happen squarely on their shoulders. 'They were the tyrants among the Jews who brought the Roman power upon us', he laments.

Interestingly, the Bible corroborates the identity of Judas:

After him Judas the Galilean rose up at the time of the census and got people to follow him; he also perished, and all who followed him were scattered. (Acts, 5:37)

Following Judas's failed revolt in AD 6/7, relations between the Judaean Jews and Rome remained fractious throughout the first half of the century.

A flare-up was narrowly avoided in AD 40 when the Emperor Caligula ordered a statue of himself to be set up in the Jerusalem Temple. The local governor, Petroius, realized how inflammatory it would be, and delayed. The inevitable riots were only finally averted when Caligula was assassinated early the following year.

Another flashpoint came a few years later, in AD 46–8, when Simon and Jacob of Galilee revolted, but the Romans crushed their uprising swiftly, executing both.

Throughout this time, the Zealots were growing as a group, intent on seizing the 'kingdom of heaven' by force, as alluded to in Bible:

> From the days of John the Baptist until now the kingdom of heaven has suffered violence, and the violent take it by force. (Matthew, 11:12)

By the time Josephus returned from his Roman mission, the Zealots had become dangerous. They wanted war with Rome, and were ready to provoke it.

Herod Agrippa II (a regional Roman-appointed Jewish governor) tried to appeal for calm and urge the Zealots to cease provoking the Romans to war. He reasoned that dozens of proud and warlike people, such as the Greeks, Germans, and Gauls, were all subject to Rome, and there was therefore no shame in it. But the Zealots did not listen. Josephus quotes Agrippa's further appeal to them:

> Have pity, therefore, if not on your children and wives, yet upon this your metropolis, and its sacred walls; spare the temple.

But to no avail. In AD 66, when relations with Gassius Florus, the Roman governor, were at an all-time low, the Zealots seized their opportunity. First they stormed the desert outpost of Masada, an imposing fortress built high on top of a vast rock in the Judaean desert, where they slaughtered the Roman garrison. Then they turned on the

Roman forces in Jerusalem, killing the troops before ousting Florus and setting up a revolutionary government.

Josephus summarized the Zealots' motives, none of which he had any sympathy with:

> *Some are earnest to go to war because they are young, and without experience of the miseries it brings ... some are for it out of an unreasonable expectation of regaining their liberty ... and others hope to get by it.*

The Zealots were now in charge, and strategic parts of Jerusalem were in their hands. But it was only the start of what was to come.

Their rash coup horrified the majority of Judea's Jews, and provoked bloody confrontations among an increasingly factional Jewish society. Civil war erupted, with family turning on family. For instance, one of the main rebel leaders was Eleazar, and one of the earliest casualties to be summarily executed was Ananias, his father, the High Priest most famous to Christians for overseeing the trial of St Paul (*Acts*, 22–3). In no time, the rebels began fighting among themselves and blood started to flow freely when Menahem, one of the Zealots' leaders and son of Judas the Galilean (the original Zealot), fell out with Eleazar. Their rivalry for power began to spill over into violence in wider society. 'They agreed in nothing', Josephus lamented, 'but this, to kill those that were innocent'.

In response to the rebels' power grab, Cestius Gallus, the Roman legate in Syria, brought a small army to re-establish order, but left defeated. Meanwhile, in the wider eastern Mediterranean region, the coup provoked scattered waves of anti-Jewish violence. However, when Nero heard about the loss of Roman control in Judaea, he unleashed hell in the form of a vast imperial army led by the battle-hardened generals Vespasian and his son, Titus.

In the build-up to the revolt, Josephus had done his best, as a senior citizen of Jerusalem, to oppose the Zealots. He understood that they were fuelled by the fervour of their youth and 'vehemently inflamed to fight'. With his experiences of Rome, he tried to convince them of the folly of picking a fight with the world's foremost military empire, but to his surprise he was sucked directly into the conflict when the Jerusalem Sanhedrin appointed him military commander of Galilee. It was technically not part of Roman Judaea, but still a separate client state of the Roman Empire, just as Judea had been until AD 6. That is why, in the Gospels, Pontius Pilate (governor of Jerusalem in Judaea) says he has no jurisdiction over Jesus, and packs him back up north to Galilee's ruler, Herod Antipas, who also features in the Bible as Salome's stepfather, who had John the Baptist beheaded (*Mark*, 6:21–9; *Matthew*, 14:6–11).

The Romans decided to invade Judaea from Syria through Galilee, so before long, Josephus faced the unenviable task of defending the fortress of Jotapata (modern Yodfat in Galilee) against Vespasian and his legions. To his credit, Josephus managed to hold out for 47 days, but when the city finally fell he hid in a cistern-cave with a bunch of 40 diehards who were convinced suicide was better than surrender. Josephus tried to argue that taking their own lives was immoral, but he made no headway. Finally, he agreed to their suicide plans, and suggested they draw lots to see who would kill whom in pairs. 'Whether we must say it happened by chance, or whether by the providence of God' (in other words, he rigged it), he ensured he was one of the final pair alive, at which point he succeeded in convincing his lone companion to surrender.

As a senior captive, Josephus was then dragged before Vespasian and Titus, where he had something of a brainwave. He declared himself to be a prophet, and foretold in front of the gathering that Vespasian would soon be emperor, followed by Titus. Vespasian must have been tickled by it, because he spared Josephus's life. When Nero died the following year and Vespasian then became emperor, Josephus was freed in recognition of his gift of foresight (or his brassiness and good luck).

Seeing clearly which way the wind was blowing, Josephus now took the single biggest decisions of his life. Instead of going back and rejoining his countrymen, he swapped sides, becoming a close friend and confidant of Vespasian, and even adopting the emperor's family *nomen*, calling himself Flavius Josephus.

Josephus travelled with Vespasian to Alexandria, and then returned to Judaea with Titus to set about besieging Jerusalem. As the siege unfolded, Titus sent him into the city as a messenger several times to convince the Zealots and other defenders to surrender, but no one wanted to listen. In truth, Josephus's life was now fairly uncomfortable—the Jews loathed him for his desertion, while many of the Roman officers assumed that every smallest setback was owing to his treachery.

After a brutal seven-month siege, Titus finally took Jerusalem. In the chaos of the hand-to-hand battle, the truth of how the Temple was destroyed has been lost. The Roman consul Cassius Dio says Titus gave orders for it to be levelled, whereas Josephus maintains that Titus forbade its destruction but the soldiery torched it anyway. Whichever, the triumphal arch later erected to Titus's victory at the entry to the Roman Forum shows in detail the Romans carrying off the most precious artefacts from the Temple. Like Pompey before him, Titus then entered the Temple, but whereas Pompey had penetrated into the forbidden Holy of Holies, Titus was beaten back by the smoke.

In victory, the Romans showed no mercy in culling the Zealots. The fate of Jerusalem was sealed. Josephus recorded what happened next:

> *Caesar gave orders that they should now demolish the entire city and temple ... that there was left nothing to make those that came thither believe it had ever been inhabited.*

Even after the loss of Jerusalem, the war raged throughout Judaea. The Zealots' last stand was at Masada, the fortress they had taken at the beginning of the conflict. Unable to scale it, the Romans built a monumental earthen ramp up to the summit. To avoid capture, the 960 Zealots defending it killed each other. Only two women survived by hiding in the complex together with five children.

With the revolt crushed, Josephus looked around his wrecked country, packed his bags, and resettled in Rome—where he was granted citizenship, a very healthy tax-free income from land in Judaea, and a permanently warm welcome at the courts of Emperors Vespasian, Titus, and Domitian. With the benefit of their patronage and the money, he dedicated the remaining 30 years of his life to writing history.

From AD 75–9 he composed *The Jewish Wars*, chronicling the bloody conflict he had lived through. His original Aramaic text is long lost, but the eloquent Greek version he supervised survives. It is the most comprehensive source of information for the war, and contains an amazing amount of priceless military detail. The book began to circulate as a clear warning to anyone who opposed Caesar, but it soon won praise from many corners for its detailed accuracy.

In AD 93, Josephus published his masterpiece, *The Antiquities of the Jews*—a highly successful attempt to tell selected stories of the Jewish people in a way his Romano-Hellenic audience would warm to. Even though his account of the Jewish-Roman wars was uncompromising in its criticism of the Zealots and 'seditious' factions he blamed for the loss of his country, he remained firmly wedded to his religion and culture, keen to present it in a rational, Hellenistic light. *Antiquities* is without doubt one of the greatest books of the classical world, and demonstrates an extraordinary and rich breadth of knowledge of Jewish and classical authors. St Jerome (who famously later translated the Bible into Latin) called him 'the Greek Livy'.

Josephus was very aware that he lived in brutal times and that life was cheap. Both *Jewish Wars* and *Antiquities* make for pretty gruesome and depressing reading in places. His friend Titus was cruel beyond normal—inflicting ghastly punishments on those he captured. However, Josephus knew that rulers of all cultures committed atrocities. He recounted with horror how the Jewish King Alexander Jannaeus ('King Yannai' in the Talmud), king of Judah from 103–76 BC:

> *... as he was feasting with his concubines, in the sight of all the city, he ordered about eight hundred [Pharisees] to be crucified; and while they were living, he ordered the throats of their children and wives to be cut before their eyes.*

No one reading Josephus's works can be in any doubt about the fact that the power politics of the classical-era Mediterranean were brutal.

Although things ended well for Josephus in Rome, over in Judaea the dramatic endgame was about to be played out.

In AD 131, the Emperor Hadrian went on a tour of the east. He had been fighting off minor Jewish rebellions for a decade, but something seismic was about to happen to reignite the passions of the war Josephus had lived through.

The truth is lost, but either Hadrian provoked a war by a series of restrictive religious declarations, or he published the harsh orders after the war as revenge. Either way, he reached a decision to Hellenize the Jews in order to integrate them into the Empire and remove their separate identity that he saw as the cause of their incessant rebellions. He therefore forbade circumcision and ordered a new city, Aelia Capitolina, to be built on the rubble of Jerusalem. It was named after Aelius, his *nomen*, and Jupiter Capitolinus, to whom he built a temple on the site of the destroyed Jewish Temple. The implication was clear—Jerusalem, the Jewish capital, was gone.

Opposing Hadrian was a Jewish army under Simon, whom his followers revered as a Messiah—a Davidic figure who would deliver them from their troubles and lead them back to God, hence they began calling him 'bar Kokhba', or Son of the Star, a Messianic title. As the uprising spread, bar Kokhba appointed himself a prince, seized large amounts of territory, and began minting coins stamped with triumphant texts such as 'To the freedom of Jerusalem'.

Unlike previous emperors, Hadrian was a man who believed in decisive action, and he reacted to the 'Bar Kokhba Revolt' (as it is now known) with crushing force, summoning his greatest general, Julius Severus, then in Britain, to march on Judaea with a vast army.

A vicious war of over 50 individual battles ensued, leaving bar Kokhba and a reported 580,000 of his men slaughtered (not including those who died of hunger and disease). The Romans then grimly laid waste to the whole of Judaea, annihilating virtually the entire Jewish population.

After so many rebellions for as long as anyone could remember, Hadrian decided that prevention was better than cure. Aelia Capitolina was completed in order to obliterate all trace of Jewish Jerusalem. The regional name Judaea was scrapped as sounding too Jewish, and replaced by 'Syria Palaestina'. All Jewish religious rites and rituals in Judaea were forbidden. And Jews were banished forever from Aelia Capitolina, except for one day a year, on *Tisha B'Av*, the Jewish day of mourning to commemorate the anniversary of the destruction of the Second Temple by Nebuchadnezzar II of Babylon (587 BC) and the final destruction of the rebuilt Second Temple by Titus in AD 70. As the 1906 *Jewish Encyclopedia* comments laconically: 'the end of the Jewish Nation had come'.

As it turned out, the price had been heavy on all sides. The Romans had also suffered major losses, and Cassius Dio reported that Hadrian's victory message back to the Senate did not start with the usual airy greeting, 'The army and I are well'.

Hadrian's retribution was, historically, one of the most profound events in the history of the Jewish people. They were permanently uprooted from the city they had conquered and made theirs just over a thousand years earlier. It was far worse than the Babylonian captivity of 500 years earlier, which had come to an end after 50–60 years.

When Hadrian's city of Aelia Capitolina rose from the rubble of Jerusalem, Josephus had been dead for 35 years. But he had already made his decision to live at the heart of the Roman Empire rather than on its troubled eastern border. He may even have suspected that something as dramatic as Hadrian's revenge would one day be inevitable. Yet what neither he nor Hadrian could have foretold was that Aelia Capitolina would eventually pass from Roman hands into a variety of others for almost two millennia before again becoming Jewish in 1948.

History is a witness that the land has belonged to many rulers. Before King David conquered Jerusalem around 1020 BC it had already been a Jebusite Canaanite city for around 2,000 years. During 'biblical' Jewish control (*c.* 1020 BC–AD 135) Jerusalem was sacked five times according to Josephus, most seriously by Nebuchadnezzar and Titus.

After the Jews came the Romans (AD 135–325), then Constantine and the Byzantine Christians (AD 325–637), Muslims (AD 637–1099), Christian crusaders (AD 1099–1187), Muslims (AD 1187–1516), Turks (AD 1516–1917), the British (AD 1917–48), and finally the Jews again (1948–present), with dozens of short-lived minor conquests breaking the sequence.

The eastern Mediterranean seaboard is—and has always been—a troubled region that has seen too much blood spilled for one reason or another, all of which seemed important at the time. As Churchill noted, so bluntly but accurately, the first casualty of war is truth. And the truth of the land is that the various competing webs and roots of nationhood, identity, and memory that have flourished for millennia are thick and run deep into its dust and soil.

As Josephus observed, 'as for war, if it be once begun, it is not easily laid down again'. History may not repeat itself exactly, but it does teach us lessons. One thing is certain: in 1,000 years' time, the Near East will look different. And perhaps the lesson for the troubled land is that throughout history extreme military force has been used there time and time again—but, in over five millennia, it has never yet brought lasting peace for anyone.

2

Theodosius I: the forgotten man who turned Christianity into a global religion

In 380, the Roman Emperor Theodosius I proclaimed Christianity to be the official religion of the Roman Empire. This piece celebrates the proclamation's anniversary, and tells the story of how Rome adopted Christianity.

Who founded Christianity?

It is an age-old debate.

Christ? Well, yes. Of course. Obviously.

St Peter? Also yes. Christ built his church upon the rock—so the faithful believe, following the Gospel of St Matthew.

St Paul? Yes again. In first century Galilee, there were no schools for those who farmed, fished, or worked with their hands. St Peter was a simple worker from an agrarian community, and there is no reason to suppose he could read, write, or speak any language other than his native Aramaic. By contrast, St Paul was a highly educated and literate intellectual. He was a Roman citizen of Cilicia (south-eastern Turkey), and his native language was Greek—which enabled his letters and public speaking to be understood across the vast reaches of the empire. His indefatigable thinking, preaching, and writing unquestionably defined great swathes of Christianity.

Yet in some senses, asking who founded Christianity is a fatuous question. The Greek honorific title *Christos* (meaning the Anointed One) and the word *Christianos* (Christian) would have meant nothing to Yeshu'a, which was the Aramaic name Jesus would have answered to. The words were never used in his life time. The first recorded occasion was years later, miles to the north-west in Antioch.

Beyond the words, how many of Christianity's reported 41,000 denominations would they recognize today? Would any of the buildings, activities, liturgies, theologies, vestments, ecstatic glossolalia, and all the rest be familiar?

Whatever the answer, there is, in fact, one more person to add to this list—and he definitely would recognize the 1.5 billion Catholics and Orthodox Christians alive today. He was not a founder of Christianity. But he was definitely one of its most important figures. Ever.

Flavius Theodosius was born in Spain in AD 347, and one of his two most memorable achievements was to be the last man to rule over both the Western and Eastern Roman Empires.

But his truly lasting achievement was perhaps one of the ten decisions that have most shaped the post-Roman world.

Today, the 27th of February, in AD 380, Theodosius proclaimed Christianity as the official religion of the Roman Empire.

> *It is our desire that all the various nations which are subject to our clemency and moderation should continue in the profession of that religion which was delivered to the Romans by the divine Apostle Peter, as it has been preserved by faithful tradition, and which is now professed by the Pontiff Damasus .... We authorize the followers of this law to assume the title of Catholic Christians. (Theodosius I, Cunctos populos)*

At the time, the empire heaved with colourful temples to everything you can think of. Cicero called the Romans 'the most religious people' (*religiosissima gens*), and the sheer variety of popular cults proves it. Worshippers could find everything from traditional Graeco-Roman deities, the Egyptian cults of Isis, Osiris, and Serapis, the ubiquitous near-eastern mystery religions of Mithras, Cybele, and Attis, and hundreds of others—all spiced up with the usual sacrificial fare and traditional temple prostitutes.

But enough was enough. To reinforce the status of Christianity as the sole imperial religion, Theodosius outlawed all pagan practices.

It was a highly controversial move, and he must have been aware of its enormity.

Even the Serb, Emperor Constantine I (AD 305 to 337), had not gone that far.

It is true that Constantine is reported to have fought and won the decisive battle of the Milvian Bridge with the *Chi Rho* daubed onto his men's shields. He had apparently seen a vision of the Christian symbol in the sky, along with the Greek words ἐν τούτῳ νίκα (*en touto nika*, 'In this, conquer'), and it had inspired him. Once emperor, in AD 313 he promptly enacted the Edict of Milan to guarantee freedom of religion throughout the empire.

> *Of the things that are of profit to all mankind, the worship of God ought rightly to be our first and chiefest care. Christians and all others should have freedom to follow the kind of religion they favour. We therefore announce that all who choose Christianity are to be permitted to continue therein, without any let or hindrance, and are not to be in any way troubled or molested. At the same time, all others are to be allowed the free and unrestricted practice of their religions; for it accords with the good order of the realm and the peacefulness of our times that each should have freedom to worship God after his own choice. (Constantine, The Edict of Milan)*

Perhaps the drafters of the First Amendment to the American Constitution had this edict in mind, although they expressed their version significantly less eloquently:

> *Congress shall make no law respecting an establishment of religion, or prohibiting the free exercise thereof.*

Constantine did not stop with freeing everyone from religious persecution. In AD 325 he convened, presided over, and paid for the first ecumenical Church council. He held it at Nicaea (modern-day Iznik in Turkey), where it oversaw the resolution of numerous key decisions regarding the early Church and its structure. Yet Constantine did it all while still a pagan and *pontifex maximus*, or head of Rome's pagan priesthood—a role he officially retained until his death, even after his personal conversion to Christianity late in life. Theodosius was, unsurprisingly, the first emperor to abandon the priestly title, which in time migrated across to the pope.

Today, Christianity has 2.2 billion followers (32 per cent of the world's population), making it by far the largest, and most evenly spread, religion on the planet. Islam is next at 1.6 billion (23 per cent), followed by Hinduism at 1 billion (15 per cent).

Theodosius is perhaps more responsible for the massive spread of Christianity than either St Peter or St Paul, for the simple reason that religions and their denominations benefit from political backing to light the afterburners and tear free from the pack. This should come as no real surprise—it is how human society generally works.

We have even seen it in England. In the Late Middle Ages, Lollards and the occasional disgruntled theologian grumbled on and off. But it took almost a century of the sheer absolutist power and political resolve of the Tudor monarchs to carve a new church into the ages-old landscape of England.

The same union of religion and politics can be seen elsewhere, too.

Muhammad ibn Abd al-Wahhab (1703–92) was an Islamic preacher and reformer who wished for a simpler form of Islam that better reflected early practice. In many ways, he was the equivalent in Islam of those medieval Catholics who sought the apostolic life of the early desert fathers, or the later Protestant reformers of Europe who strove to take the Church to a perceived former simplicity. Abd al-Wahhab's ideas were powerful, but they truly became globally significant after they were endorsed and promulgated by Muhammad ibn Saud, whose legacy has shaped the modern state of Saudi Arabia, and whose influence can be felt throughout the Arab world.

Therefore, when Theodosius adopted Nicene Christianity as the imperial religion in AD 380, he set a precedent whose impact is now felt globally. For as the Roman Empire in the West fell, the monarchs who were to fill the void in Europe for the next millennium and a half largely kept Christianity as their state religion. And when they conquered and colonized, they took their religion with them.

Unlike ancient Rome, we no longer exterminate those who profess other religions.

So as Prince Charles ponders becoming Defender of the Faith (a title first given to Henry VIII by Pope Leo X, but then revoked and now conferred by Parliament instead), he has a few questions to consider.

What does it mean, historically, to defend the faith? Henry VIII was given the title in recognition of his most Catholic written refutation and execration of what he saw as Luther's pernicious heresies. Henry wrote up his passionate arguments in a book he nattily entitled *Defence of the Seven Sacraments*, which he dedicated to the pope.

That is what it meant to defend the faith in the early 1500s. But what does it require now? In the twenty-first century, is Defender of the Faith an honorific title, or does it mean something more?

And equally as important, should the Defender of the Faith choose to be a Constantine or a Theodosius? Should he rule over a realm in which he protects his subjects' freedom to practise a religion of their choice, or should he defend only the state religion?

Prince Charles has made his position clear. He will be the Defender of Faith. Happily the Latin, *fidei defensor*, does not change with the loss of the definite article.

He has history on his side. For it is interesting to note that everyone has heard of Constantine the Great's religious toleration—but, for all his seismic historical importance, how many remember Theodosius I?

THE MEDIEVAL
WORLD

3

Rome was not civilized and the 'Dark Ages' were not dark

The immense success of George R R Martin's saga A *Song of Ice and Fire* (televised as *Game of Thrones*) has again made the 'Dark Ages' a byword for barbarity, but this view is largely based on Victorian prejudices. This piece sets out some of the beauties of the Early Middle Ages (the period's proper name), and compares it favourably with some of Rome's less civilized aspects.

In the epic 1982 swords-and-sorcery film *Conan the Barbarian*, when the massively muscled hero is asked what is best in life, he memorably decrees: 'To crush your enemies, see them driven before you, and to hear the lamentation of their women'.

Conan, like *Game of Thrones* (its modern progeny), is set in a fictional age, but the saga's look and feel is a hundred per cent Dark Ages Europe.

The Dark Ages. The thousand years that filled the void from the fall of the Roman Empire to the start of the Renaissance—a period of blood, conflict, destruction, and ignorance.

Educated people of the Enlightenment shunned it as an aberration. Edward Gibbon famously dismissed the entire epoch as 'the triumph of barbarism and religion'.

Even today, the phrase the 'Dark Ages' effortlessly conjures up images of pelt-clad Visigoths and Vandals smashing up Rome and torching it, filling the sky with clouds of billowing smoke that would smother the heavens for a millennium.

Schoolchildren know it well—how the 'glory' of Rome was ruthlessly snuffed out, trampled under hooves that sought only plunder. As the Empire's marbled temples and libraries fell to the boorish hordes, the light of Graeco-Roman learning was forever extinguished, plunging Europe into a long dark night of tumult and oblivion.

With Rome aflame, the continent retreated into huts of wood and mud. Greek was forgotten, and Latin was bastardized into the primary Romance languages of Italian, Spanish, French, and Provençal. Rome's poetry and literature were effaced, along with the arts of engineering, building, sculpture, metalwork, glass, enamelling, mathematics, geometry, law, rhetoric, and the rest.

The Empire officially died on the 4th of September AD 476—and so 'civilization' ended, until awoken in 1401, when the contest to cast the bronze doors of Florence's Baptistery of St John sparked the Renaissance.

Okay. I'll stop now. You get the picture.

This is Victorian pseudo-history at its judgmental worst—a tragically emotionalized and simplistic view of the past with all the historical accuracy of Errol Flynn playing Robin Hood. It may have been good enough for a child's history primer in the mid-1800s, but these days we know it to be wrong in so many key ways.

First, it assumes that the barbarians overwhelmed Rome by force, bringing civilization to an abrupt and violent end. That may be how it happens in Hollywood, but it's not remotely accurate.

The Western Roman Empire had been disintegrating for centuries (just as the wheels had come off from under the Roman Republic before it). The Western Empire was old, tired, and coming apart at the seams. It was in a state of terminal decline. The emperors had long ago even done the unthinkable and abandoned Rome—choosing instead to rule from Trier, Milan, and especially Ravenna. As the map changed, they also realized they needed to shift power eastwards, which is why the Emperor Constantine eventually built his magnificent new Rome at Constantinople (Istanbul). There, where Europe meets Asia, the ever-philhellenic Romans continued to flourish as the Byzantine Empire for another thousand years.

So, barbarian hordes may have picked over the carcass of the fading Eternal City in the 400s, but imperial Rome continued largely uninterrupted on the shores of the Bosphorus until AD 1453 (give or take the odd Crusader *coup d'état*).

Next, the notion of Rome giving way to a 'Dark Age' presupposes that the Roman Empire shimmered in light, wonder, and glory.

To an extent, it did. How can you not be impressed with a culture that gave us Catullus and Christianity, stone arenas of up to 50,000 seats, the stunning temples at Baalbek, the unsupported concrete dome of the Pantheon, and armies of almost living marble statues (largely in the Greek style), depicting everything from megalomaniacal emperors to callipygous goddesses? There is no doubt it was an impressive culture.

But beyond these achievements, there was also a distinctly less glamorous side.

The Romans were, and made no bones about being, an aggressively militaristic and expansionist society. The *pax romana* was built and governed the old fashioned way—by hardened soldiers armed with bronze and steel. You need only read Tacitus's account of how the legions met the druids of Anglesey to appreciate that Roman rule was not a soft, fluffy, inclusive proposition.

> *Reassured by their general, and inciting each other never to flinch before a band of females and fanatics, they charged behind the standards, cut down all who met them, and enveloped the enemy in his own flames. (Tacitus, Annals)*

If the Romans were coming, subjugated people either opened their doors and welcomed them or faced annihilation. Whichever Roman spin-doctor put the '*pax*' in *pax romana* certainly earned his keep.

Existence could be harsh in the farther reaches of the Empire. Yet even in the glittering city of Rome itself, life for half of its million inhabitants left a lot to be desired.

If you happened to be born female, you probably had a very different experience of Rome. Unless you were highborn from an aristocratic patrician family, the chances are you had no education, no influence and no role outside the home—a significantly less glorious and civilized existence than the one offered to the city's male shakers and movers.

And then there were the slaves—those endlessly resourceful characters who steal the show in every beginner's Latin grammar textbook, where they mischievously play pranks on each other to the hilarity of the assembled household, before their fidelity and industry eventually wins them a well-deserved manumission.

Honestly? I doubt it. Throughout history slaves have been there to be bought, sold, used, misused, and abused in the privacy of their owners' homes. One needs only look at countries where slavery has been legal or normal in the last hundred years to know what the ghastly and vulnerable exploitative reality usually is.

In an age when opinion shapers from Mel Gibson to George W Bush have trumpeted the universal imperative of 'freeeedom', can we really, uncritically, admire a culture that denied millions their names, families, and backgrounds, giving wealthier citizens largely unchecked powers of life, sadism, and death over them?

The answer is: no. Slavery is a form of institutionalized violence, and there is nothing 'light' or 'glorious' about it.

In fact, violence and ruthlessness were fundamental building blocks of imperial Rome's DNA—a fact constantly reinforced by the emperors.

Everyone knows how Nero burned Christians as 'Roman candles' to illuminate his gardens. But he was not alone. There were the persecutions under Domitian, Trajan, Decius, Diocletian, and the others. There was also a more personal violence, too. For instance, on one occasion Caligula was so bored at the games that, to liven things up, he had an entire section of the crowd rounded up by his troops and dumped into the arena to be torn apart by the wild animals. The Emperor Commodus took the bloodmania even further. He loved the idea of being a heroic gladiator (but only in rigged fights). To satisfy his craving, he would have the city's cripples tethered to stakes in the arena so he could dress as a gladiator, pretend they were giants, and enthusiastically club them to death in front of the delighted crowd

For all the literary and artistic wonders of ancient Rome, we also need to recognize that Roman imperial society was complex, and it is difficult to ignore a deep element of what was definitely 'dark'.

So, if Rome was unenlightened and barbaric in certain ways, then what did Gibbon & Co find so abhorrent about the European tribes that succeeded them?

It certainly wasn't the brutality of their conquest—because the fall of Rome was all relatively civilized.

When Alaric the Visigoth entered Rome in AD 410 for a three-day sack, his men did a good deal of pilfering, but there was not much bloodshed. And 45 years later, in June 455, when Gaiseric the Vandal sacked Rome definitively for 14 days—one of the many dates regularly touted as the end of the Roman Empire—he heeded Pope Leo I's request not to murder the inhabitants or raze the buildings. Instead, he focused on the real priority of stripping the Eternal City of all remaining valuables.

The restraint shown by Alaric and Gaiseric—who were both Christians—would have been unrecognizable to the Roman legions who had slashed and bludgeoned their way across the Empire.

Nevertheless, it is a fair question to ask whether darkness descended as the 'Dark Ages' got under way.

In a manner of speaking, it did. Writing and record keeping fell off sharply in the early medieval period (no one says 'Dark Ages' any more), leaving us with a lot less information to pick over.

But there was still plenty of learning and nib-scratching going on. Early medieval chroniclers wrote up what they saw, heard, and read, and their works were every bit as sophisticated as anything that came before.

Take the Venerable Bede (born AD 672), the sage of Sunderland. His history of the English people, written in excellent clear Latin of the day, is one of the great works of English history. No one can criticize him for ignorance. His opening stands as a classic:

Britain, an island in the ocean, formerly called Albion, is situated between the north and the west, facing, though at a considerable distance, the coasts of Germany, France, and Spain, which form the greatest part of Europe. It extends 800 miles in length towards the north, and is 200 miles in breadth, except where several promontories extend further in breadth, by which its compass is made to be 3,675 miles. (Bede. Ecclesiastical History of the English People)

Not long after Bede, Europe bore one of its greatest ever kings—Charlemagne (Charles the Great, born 740s). As well as being the first European ruler since the fall of Rome to be crowned emperor, he was passionate about education and literacy. Not content with fully educating himself and his court, he sponsored the 'Carolingian Renaissance', encouraging the highest standards of learning in his kingdom, taking scholars from all over (under the direction of the mighty Alcuin of York), tasking them with overseeing a fresh burst of education throughout his lands.

For although correct conduct may be better than knowledge, nevertheless knowledge precedes conduct. Therefore each one ought to study what he desires to accomplish that so much the more fully the mind may know what ought to be done. And may this be done with a zeal as great as the earnestness with which we command it. (Charlemagne, On the Study of Letters)

Just over a century later, England found its own Charlemagne in King Alfred the Great (born 849). He was quite happy translating theological and moral texts from Latin into English himself, for the betterment of his people. In the preface to his most famous translation he was clear about his priorities:

Therefore it seems better to me that we also [like the Greeks and Romans] translate certain books which are most needful for all men to know into that language that we can all understand, so that all the youth of free men now in England who have the means to apply themselves to it be set to learning until they know how to read English writing well. (King Alfred, Pastoral Care)

With this kind of approach to learning, it is hard to see the 'barbarity' in these kingdoms. It is simply plain wrong to categorize the early medieval period as an age of bovine ignorance.

And then there is the art.

Ruskin famously remarked that great nations write their most trustworthy autobiographies in the books of their art (well, he would). But it is worth testing his theory by looking at the art of the early medieval period.

As far as anyone can tell, finely skilled craftsmen continued to flourish, just as they had in Rome. The statues were no longer marble, and they depicted the holy family and saints rather than pagan deities, but the skill of the sculptor was undiminished.

In terms of the decorative arts, our museums burst with incomparable early medieval wonders—the Alfred Jewel, the Sutton Hoo treasures, the Lindisfarne Gospels, the Book of Kells, the Cross of Lothair, the list is endless. Archaeologists have dug up a mass of items attesting to the artistic genius of the period.

Turning to buildings, the scale was diminished, but the quality was not. Take Charlemagne's Palatine chapel, now at the heart of Aachen cathedral. It is far from being a mud hut, wooden shack, stone bunker, or anything else one might expect from the 'Dark Ages'. As you gaze around its undulating polychromed stonework, you see a Roman/ Byzantine chapel built with all the skill of the inheritors of Rome. It makes clear, if there were any lingering doubts, why our European neighbours have no concept of the 'Dark Ages'. The expression is simply alien to them. And for a very good reason.

It never existed.

So far we have only looked at the Early Middle Ages (AD 476–1000). But for Gibbon and the Victorians, the Dark Ages carried on through the High Middle Ages (AD 1001–1300), and even the Late Middle Ages (AD 1301–1500). In their eyes, civilization did not return until the Renaissance.

But that is simply untenable. The High Middle Ages burned with knowledge and creativity. The twelfth-century Renaissance saw a quantum leap in human understanding and achievement as cathedrals, universities, scholars, mystics, scientists, and philosophers pushed the boundaries of their minds. And it is a rank absurdity to denigrate the Late Middle Ages of Dante, Marco Polo, Chaucer, Petrarch, and the many others, whose outlook seems closer to our own modern experiences than to life in Rome.

So, for all the Victorians' wondrous achievements in industry, machinery, railways, architecture, and a host of other areas, they built on Gibbon and both romanticized and distorted the past unrecognizably, leaving a legacy we are still battling to undo.

In fact, if we shine a light closely into the gloomy underbelly of Victorian society, with its Jack-the-Ripper slums, gin-sodden destitution, workhouses, debtors' prisons, and not always fragrant imperial administrations, it may be that they are among the last people who should be pejoratively labelling any age 'dark'.

But finally back to Gibbon, perhaps the first and greatest detractor of the Middle Ages. He summed up his hostile view of the period clearly:

> *The clergy successfully preached the doctrines of patience and pusillanimity; the active virtues of society were discouraged; and the last remains of the military spirit were buried in the cloister. (Gibbon, Decline and Fall)*

Aside from his well-known hostility to Christianity, his main problem with the Middle Ages was therefore not that they were filled with conflict—which they were, just like today and every other period in history. But rather he was aghast that the Middle Ages had turned people soft, killing off the Roman martial spirit and zeal for war.

That's my day sorted out then. I can clear that one up once and for all. I'll nip down to Fletching parish church this lunchtime and drop him off a box set of *Game of Thrones*.

4

The Vikings were no worse than the Anglo-Saxons

This Vikings get a bad press, and are a byword for looting and slaughter. But it is not really fair. This piece looks behind the cinematic myths to the Vikings' many contributions to world culture, and was prompted by a major Viking exhibition at London's British Museum.

For the last few centuries, the Vikings have been enjoying a European revival.

The composer Richard Wagner was in the vanguard, burying his unfathomably brilliant head deep into the Norse Eddas, mining the stories for material to build the Ring Cycle.

Around him, at the same time, fledgling neo-pagan groups surfaced in smoky upper-rooms, dusting the centuries of abandon off Thor's great hammer, *Mjöllnir*.

Following directly in this tradition, in Scandinavia today, armies of forked-bearded fans of Viking heavy metal can be found chanting along to thundering music hyping the axe-wielding heroes of Norse myths and sagas.

And along the way, we have seen almost everything in between—from the elite *Wiking* Fifth Panzers of the *Waffen SS* to modern light relief like *Hägar the Horrible* and *How to Train Your Dragon*.

In March this year, the British Museum is hosting its first major Viking exhibition for 30 years: *Vikings. Life and Legend*, spotlighting many exhibits never before seen in the UK, and drawing on the vast amount of more recent Viking scholarship.

Although the Vikings are at times increasingly presented as slightly comical figures, no one was laughing in late 700s England.

Take Alcuin. He was a Yorkshireman. Perhaps he is not so well known now. But he was, once.

At a time when there was not a great deal of learning about, his brilliance shone out, winning him an invitation to set up a school for Charlemagne, king of the Franks.

Once at Charlemagne's court in Aachen, he ripped up the dreary text books and started his royal pupils studying English humanism.

In AD 793 he wrote a letter to his friend, Bishop Higbald, in Northumbria:

> *The pagans have contaminated the sanctuaries of God, and have poured out the blood of the saints round about the altar. They have laid waste the house of our hope, and have trampled upon the bodies of the saints in the temple of God like dung in the street.*

Surprisingly, he was not sending Higbald news of some distant calamity, although the language is almost identical to that used on the eve of the First Crusade three centuries later.

No. Alcuin was describing something that had happened in his native England—in Bishop Higbald's own diocese.

The Anglo-Saxon Chronicle also described the event, but preceded it with some quality harbingers of doom:

> *This year dire forwarnings came over the land of the Northumbrians, and miserably terrified the people; these were excessive whirlwinds, and lightnings; and fiery dragons were seen flying in the air. A great famine soon followed these tokens; and a little after that, in the same year ... the ravaging of heathen men lamentably destroyed God's church ... through rapine and slaughter.*

It was the 8th of June AD 793. And the Vikings had arrived.

Longboats from Scandinavia beached on the small two-mile-square Northumbrian island of Lindisfarne and sacked the world-famous priory that had painstakingly produced the exquisite Lindisfarne Gospels less than a century earlier.

There had been Viking raids to England before, of course. But nothing on this scale.

And from that moment on, it was only going to get worse. For the next 300 years, the history of Britain and of the marauding Scandinavian seafarers would be inseparably intertwined.

Nowadays, everyone calls them Vikings. But it is not, in fact, a racial description. The Scandinavians of Denmark, Norway, and Sweden were farmers. But when the men—and it was only ever men—went off looting, they were 'going on a viking' (*farar i vikingr*). In other words: pirate raiding.

After some 70 years of harrying Britain in amphibious hit-and-run raids, the Vikings stepped up a gear and decided to invade properly, sending armies from Norway and Denmark to conquer parts of England, Ireland, and Western Scotland.

As the Vikings never did anything by halves, their conquests were so successful that the legacy can still be felt tangibly today—in social structures, in place names like Cawdor, Fishguard, Grimsby, Keswick, Thurso, and hundreds of others, and even in first names like Eric, Garth, Howard, and Ivor.

But perhaps their biggest contribution was linguistic. Many modern everyday English words come directly from the Old Norse: anger, berserk, birth, cake, club, crawl, die, dregs, egg, fellow, fog, guest, haggle, Hell, hit, husband, ill, knife, knot, law, loose, mistake, muck, muggy, outlaw, plough, ransack, rotten, shirt/skirt, slaughter, steak, troll, ugly. And even the word 'gun', amazingly, is Norse—from a 1330 inventory of weapons in the Tower of London listing a spectacular balista called 'Lady Gunilda' (the name Gunnhildr means war or battle).

But Viking expansionism was not just about Britain. The indefatigable wanderers went virtually everywhere on the map. And beyond.

American schoolchildren still sing, 'In fourteen hundred ninety-two, Columbus sailed the ocean blue'. But what the classroom ditty misses is that in *c.* AD 1000, the Icelander, Leif Ericson, was off on a spot of *vikingr* when he stumbled into the New World. Newfoundland in Canada, to be precise, which he named Vinland.

Having rooted around a bit, it seems he was largely unimpressed with his discovery, perhaps at modern-day L'Anse-aux-Meadows. Anyway, he soon packed everything up and headed home, where he did not make a great deal out of his voyage once he got back.

Columbus, in fact, never even reached North America—he only found the Caribbean and northern Venezuela.

Leif Ericson's low profile in the history books is a spectacular injustice. He was happily running around in North America a full five centuries before Zuan Chabotto (sponsored by King Henry VII of England), who is widely credited as the 'first' European to set foot there.

But the Scandinavians did not only go on vikings to the west. They struck east, too—where they soon set up lucrative trading routes with Russia, and even found good money as bodyguards to the emperor of Constantinople.

Yet perhaps the most extraordinary of all Viking adventurers was Sigurd I Magnusson *Jórsalafari* (Jerusalem-farer), king of Norway. On pondering the news that Latin Crusaders had seized Jerusalem in 1099, Sigurd jumped into his longboat and led a flotilla to join in. After a winter stop in England, he set sail properly. Pausing only to loot in Spain, al-Andalus, Formentera, Ibiza, and Minorca, he made his final landfall in Sicily before drawing up his longboats at the crusader port of Acre. King Baldwin I of Jerusalem was mightily impressed, and Sigurd willingly accepted a royal invitation to join in the successful siege of Sidon (now in Lebanon). Baldwin was so thrilled with his new best friend that he had a piece hacked off his favourite relic, the True Cross, which he presented to a delighted Sigurd in thanks.

Needless to say, Sigurd was never one to take the easy option. When he again felt restless, he left King Baldwin and sailed to Cyprus, then caught the winds up through the Aegean and on to Constantinople. Maybe tired of sailing, or perhaps merely looking for a new adventure, he gifted the emperor all his boats, then rode and walked the two thousand miles home to tell the astonishing tale of 'Sigurd the Crusader'.

Alcuin, I suspect, would have approved.

Yet, thanks largely to the heavy dollop of romanticism accompanying the 1800s revival in Viking studies, the roving Scandinavians are universally now seen as barbarous savages—good for nothing but *rannsaka* and *slátr*.

In fact, this view could not be more wrong.

It cannot be denied that they were quite spectacularly violent. But they did not have a monopoly in treating life cheaply. The British Museum's exhibition will highlight a recently excavated mass grave in Dorset where a group of Vikings had been summarily executed by the locals. And anyone who wants to read the medieval chronicles will quickly find good old British warriors also looting monasteries and villages, mutilating and hacking apart anyone who got in their way. Extreme and random violence was part of day-to-day life. Even allowing for exaggeration in the chronicles, no one can overlook the many mangled, brutalized, and decapitated bodies in early medieval graves, or even the poor souls it seems were buried alive.

But leaving bloodlust aside, the Vikings were far from being ignorant, unclean, and boorish. In fact, they were rather advanced.

For a start, they were highly literate. Great stones carved with jagged Tolkienesque runes (called futhark) carpet Scandinavia, some going back as far as the AD 300s.

There is more traditional writing, too—especially in the Eddas and Skaldic poetry, whose sophisticated forms record and preserve the wondrous mythology of the Nine Worlds hinging around the cosmic tree, *Yggdrasil*.

As for the idea the Vikings were unkempt and unwashed, the truth is the polar opposite. Archaeology reveals endless combs, tweezers, razors, earwax scrapers, and other grooming items. They used special strong soap for cleaning and bleaching their hair blond. And the grubby Anglo-Saxons, for whom an annual wash was excessive, could not believe that the Vikings bathed religiously every weekend. (The Old Norse word for Saturday literally meant 'washing day'.)

Finally, anyone who thinks that all the Vikings did was get *Mjöllnired* on mead and break things needs to pay an urgent visit to the Gold Room at Stockholm's Swedish History Museum, where the eye-popping complexity of the silver- and gold-work is up to the highest standards of anything made by anyone in any period.

So, it is time to rehabilitate the Vikings.

Their classic warrior brew of tribal loyalty and vengeance for wrongs was no more nor less barbaric than that of the contemporary residents of Britain.

Back in the 700s, on the eve of the Viking sack of Lindisfarne, the Anglo-Saxons in England were still praising the Vikings to the rafters of their wooden halls. One needs look no further than the highpoint of Anglo-Saxon epic poetry, *Beowulf.* It is a paean to Danish and Norwegian warrior values: 3,182 lines of celebration extolling the heroic deeds and hearts of their Viking cousins.

The truth is that there was not a lot separating the Anglo-Saxons and the Vikings. Their backgrounds and warrior cultures was very similar, not least because many of the original Anglo-Saxon invaders came from the exact same lands—'beyond the whale-road', as the North Sea is so magically described in *Beowulf.*

The Viking invasions only strengthened these ancient ties.

In the 1000s, England had four Danish monarchs. The last Anglo-Saxon king to follow them, Harold II, was half-Danish. And William the Conqueror, who defeated Harold at Hastings and changed everything again, was himself more Viking than French. He was directly descended from Rollo the Danish Viking, who had invaded and settled northern France with his Norsemen, whom the centuries had not-so-quietly turned into the Normans.

So, one way or another, it is time to give the Vikings back their magnificent and rich history, their unparalleled adventurousness, their beautiful runes and writing, their exemplary hygiene, and their preeminent place in our national history. They are clearly one of our many minority groups who need a bit more understanding.

So, roll on the British Museum's exhibition. Let's hope it's a barnstormer the Vikings would have been proud of.

5

Alfred the Great, king of Wessex, was a Roman Catholic

An ancient piece of hipbone languishing in Winchester's City Museum hit the headlines when an expert suggested it might be part of King Alfred, one of England's greatest Saxon kings. This piece explores Alfred's world, highlighting the inherent contradiction in the modern idea of 'White Anglo-Saxon Protestants'.

Royal archaeology is again all over the news, and excitement is mounting.

A piece of male hip bone (the right *os coxa*, to be precise) is no longer languishing in a dreary cardboard box in Winchester's City Museum, but is suddenly in the spotlight.

Experts are now saying that it might be the only known fragment of one of England's wisest, most dynamic, and illustrious kings—Alfred the Great.

Unlike the recent unearthing of Richard III, the Winchester hip bone was not triumphantly prised from the ground in front of the world's media. Instead, it was quietly excavated 14 years ago by a community dig. But, owing to a predictable lack of funds, it was boxed up alongside a mixed bag of human and animal fragments, and ignored.

Now two things have recently catapulted it onto the front pages.

The first is the result of carbon dating. The people in white coats have said that the hip's owner died around AD 895–1017. In other words, he was an Anglo-Saxon.

The second is where the bone was found.

Winchester's famed Hyde Abbey was razed to the ground in the Reformation. The agents of Thomas Cromwell, wrote to him in

September 1538 to say they were successfully ripping the place up with their own hands. Thomas Wriothesley reported that he had looted around 2,000 marks of silver, and was happily engaged in smashing up the altar and sweeping away 'the rotten bones'.

In fact, he and his band did such a comprehensive job of levelling the place that when the antiquarian John Leland visited the following year, he found nothing left. All he could laconically record was, 'in this suburb stood the great Abbey of Hyde'. Unsurprisingly, by then the abbey's annuities were flowing nicely into Wriothesley and Cromwell's pockets. (Just so there's no mistake, Wriothesley's star was on the rise, and plundering Hyde Abbey was a super career move for him. He was a loyal Cromwellite, duly repaid for his efforts with large chunks of land stretching from Winchester to Southampton. At court, he was noticed and even given a spin as Lord Chancellor, a position which allowed him to enjoy personally turning the handle during the vicious racking of the early English poet Anne Askew, the only woman ever to be tortured in the Tower. I digress.)

In the succeeding centuries, any bodies at Hyde Abbey lucky enough to have survived Wriothesley's ransacking were despoiled and scattered as the remaining coffins were ripped open and stripped of their lead and anything else of value.

But, despite all the desecration and grave-robbing, Winchester's Anglo-Saxon hip bone was nevertheless dug from the area of the abbey's great High Altar, where Alfred and his son, Edward, were known to have been buried and honoured until the arrival of Wriothesley and his hired pick axes.

No one can say for sure whether the Winchester bone belongs to King Alfred, King Edward, or someone else. DNA testing requires a relative, and that is a significant problem.

Queen Edith (Eadgyth, AD 910–46) is undoubtedly the best match. She was Alfred's granddaughter by Edward, and went off to marry Otto I, Holy Roman Emperor. Her bones, the oldest known English royal remains, are still buried at Magdeburg Cathedral some 70 miles west of Berlin. Although recent tests have proved the entombed body is almost certainly her (the tooth enamel shows regular quaffing of chalky Wessex water as a girl), the remains are sadly not well enough preserved for DNA analysis. So the search is still on for DNA that could confirm whether the Winchester bone is a match for Anglo-Saxon Wessex royalty.

Which brings us back to the main challenge. If the Winchester hip is shown to be King Alfred, then where and how do we rebury it, along with any other parts of him that surface? What would be an appropriate setting for the reinterment of one of England's most accomplished kings?

The current tug of love over Richard III's remains is instructive. Leicester has him, but York is making a serious late bid, putting the whole thing through a rather sensational High Court judicial review. Meanwhile, quietly in the background, an Oxford medieval musicologist is painstakingly building a liturgy from a 1475 reburial service.

So where does this leave Alfred?

Well. Here's the thing. The royal house of the West Saxons was traditionally laid to eternal rest in their capital, Winchester.

However, although reinterring Alfred in Winchester Cathedral alongside some of his family (not to mention Cnut, Harthacnut, Emma, William Rufus et al) would ring all the bells of that ultra-historic royal city, the centuries have elevated Alfred into a bigger figure. He is now celebrated as a king 'of England' (despite the large independent Viking kingdom militarily occupying everything east of Watling Street). And, quite uniquely among English monarchs, he glories under the qualifier: 'the Great'.

There's no doubt he has become a national treasure.

Realistically, what this all adds up to for his reburial, what with national pride, tourism, and everything else, is London.

But if we're going to do it properly this time and honour his remains, then why don't we do it right in all aspects and respect his faith as well?

It would be all too easy, and a splendidly English fudge, to lay him to rest in an imposing Anglican cathedral to the accompaniment of soft dreamy Reformation motets and a movingly poetic Elizabethan Church of England liturgy.

But it would just be plain wrong on so many levels.

Alfred wasn't a White Anglo-Saxon Protestant, which is a historical absurdity. He was, like all his kin, a White Anglo-Saxon Roman Catholic.

Alfred was old school. He went on pilgrimage to Rome when he was four, where Pope Leo IV made him a consul. He looked after the Church in his lands, and his friendship with Pope Marinus I was so strong it resulted in the English School in Rome being exempted all taxes. Alfred summoned leading clergy and theologians to his court in order to learn from them, and even had a learned Welsh monk-bishop chronicle his life. Faith was so important to him that in settling the protracted negotiations over the Danish occupied half of England, he oversaw King Guthrum's conversion to Christianity with Alfred as his appointed Godfather.

In addition to all his other achievements, Alfred was a practical scholar in his own right, whose works show a preoccupation with religion. He translated a number of Latin texts into Anglo-Saxon, including the first 50 psalms, Pope Gregory the Great's guidance on the office of priesthood, and even Saint Augustine's Soliloquies.

Given all this, it just seems, well, disrespectful—and historically dishonest—to give Alfred a genteel modern Anglican ceremony, however stirring.

Alfred cared deeply about his Roman Catholic faith. He thought about it a lot, sharing with his people what he saw as its rich storehouse of wisdom.

And we should respect that.

So, if the Winchester hip bone is Alfred's, let's build a fitting tomb in Westminster Roman Catholic Cathedral, and let his remains be reinterred there with a solemn rite in a language he'd understand (having learned Latin fluently in his 30s).

And, at the same time, let's see if we can cease coughing loudly at the mention of England's embarrassing Catholic past, deluding ourselves that the heroes of medieval England were all secretly proto-Protestants with a clandestine suspicion of Rome.

Perhaps, if the Winchester archaeologists really have found the last mortal remains of King Alfred the Great, we can start recognizing that Roman Catholicism was, for around a thousand years, the solid faith of our nation.

So, let's give Ælfred Kyning the full old English!

6

King Harold's England was multicultural and decidedly European

Elections to the European parliament regularly cause deep cultural navel gazing in Britain. As European elections loomed, this piece was written for the anniversary of the coronation of Harold Godwinson, the last Anglo-Saxon king of England. It focuses on the many different peoples that made up medieval England, reminding us that Britain has a long and involved history with continental Europe.

With crucial European elections approaching, this is a good time to think about Britain's historical ties with the people of Europe.

On this day in 1066, the 6th of January, one of England's most famous kings was crowned. Yet, within a year, the England he knew was smashed and gone for ever.

King Harold II was born in 1022 in *Ængla Land*: the land of the Angles. The language he learned at his mother's knee was *Ænglisc*. Today we'd call it Anglo-Saxon or Old English.

The ruling class buzzing around Harold's royal court were of Germanic descent—Angles, Saxons, Jutes, and Frisians. These groups had started migrating to England in the AD 400s during the dying days of Roman rule. Although the Germanic settlers had at first been invited in to protect against raiders, their presence eventually turned into a full-blown conquest, with the native Britons being pushed into the Welsh Marches, Devon, and Cornwall. It was the age of Celtic resistance—the age of Arthur.

The influx of Germanic tribes was the second wave of conquest the native Celts had suffered. Five hundred years earlier, the Italian-led

Roman military had, in several phases, subjugated the Britons. Although Roman rule was distant and lay on top of Celtic culture rather than obliterating it, the cosmopolitan nature of the Roman Empire drew merchants, soldiers, and citizens from far afield, many of whom settled permanently in England.

Yet Anglo-Saxon rule did not ensure peace, as had originally been hoped. Before long, the Vikings started successfully seizing large chunks of central, northern, and eastern Britain, embedding yet another culture into these islands, and bringing fluctuating ties with the powerful royal houses of Scandinavia.

So, as the 42-year-old Earl Harold of Wessex ascended the throne in 1066, his kingdom was culturally diverse and complex.

Despite the thrill and promise of his coronation—the first ever to be conducted in the brand-spanking-new Westminster Abbey, where the paint was barely dry—Harold's reign was a disaster for Anglo-Saxon England.

The Royal Family's official website describes Harold II as 'an outstanding commander', which he undoubtedly was. But the repeated assaults on his kingdom from the Vikings and Normans proved too much.

By mid-October that year he was dead (with or without an arrow in his eye, who knows), and Britain was rocked by another conquest as the crown fell into the hands of a foreign warlord—William 'the bastard' of Normandy. (He was touchy about being born out of wedlock, therefore non-Norman medieval chroniclers referred to it frequently.)

William and his nobles did not see themselves as conquerors. They maintained that St Edward the Confessor and Harold II had both promised William the throne. Whatever the truth, the nobles William brought with him had no desire to work with the existing people or structures. They ripped it all up, seizing virtually all the land, imposing a new system of military government, culture, and law.

Out of interest, given our nation's famous lack of skill with languages: in 1066 England became a trilingual country. The rulers communicated in Norman-French (eventually Anglo-Norman) and Latin. The English continued to read and write in Anglo-Saxon, which gradually morphed into the Middle English of Wycliffe, Langland and Chaucer. Vast numbers of French words crossed the divide, and became embedded into English. Yet, even today, there are some standout survivals of Anglo-Saxon, most notably the days of the week—still redolent of early Germanic paganism after so many centuries: Tiw's day (god of war and sky), Woden's day (the supreme deity, god of victory and the dead), Thunor's day (god of thunder), and Frigga's day (Woden's wife, goddess of love and the hearth).

So, as we contemplate where we stand vis-à-vis modern Europe in the twenty-first century, it is worth remembering that sewn into the fabric of modern Britain, into the heart of what we recognize as Britishness, there is the legacy of historic peoples who occupied the lands we now call Italy, Germany, Scandinavia, and France, and there are tangible contributions they each made to the unique cultural identity of these islands.

The economic and social case for Britain's participation in the European Union is about the future, not the past, and it must be judged in modern terms.

But any argument against Britain's participation based on the premise that Britain or its inhabitants are somehow uniquely set apart from the people of the European mainland is simply wrong.

Two millennia of European invasions have made Britain, genetically, culturally, and linguistically, one of the most European countries on the map.

7

The Battle of Hastings (1066) wasn't such a big deal

The Battle of Hastings is often romantically portrayed as the day that old England died. This piece was published on the anniversary of Hastings, and explains the phases of the battle, before putting it into the context of the wider northern wars of the period, showing that the Normans were not really alien to Anglo-Saxon culture.

As we wait for the next series of *Game of Thrones*, I cannot help but think I have seen it all before—dynastic families so intermarried that the members' only loyalty is to self; ambitions so uncompromising that war is the inevitable result; and carnage so total that the threat of defeat is existential. But whenever the story takes me to the throne room in the Red Keep at King's Landing, all I see is Westminster Abbey—because this is an old, old story.

We like to think that Anglo-Saxon England was brutally cut down in 1066—unexpectedly—in a battle lasting just one day. To reinforce our assumptions, we still revel in Victorian and Hollywood melodrama stereotypes of dastardly Normans persecuting flaxen Saxons in box-sets of *Ivanhoe* or Tolkein's thinly disguised versions set in Middle Earth.

The reality, of course, is far more complex.

For a start, in 1066 England was not ruled exclusive by Anglo-Saxons, and the Normans were not an alien race. Leading Anglo-Saxon and Norman families were already deeply intermarried. For instance, that famous eleventh-century Anglo-Saxon king Saint Edward the Confessor was mixed race. His father, Æthelred II 'the Unready' (*unraed*, no counsel or unwise) was as Anglo-Saxon as they come. But his mother, Emma, was a powerful Norman noblewoman—daughter of Duke Richard II of Normandy.

Edward's connections to Normandy ran deep throughout his life. Although born in the Oxfordshire village of Islip, the unrelenting Viking threat meant he was taken for safety to Normandy in 1013, and again from 1016–41. So when he ascended the English throne aged 37/40, he had spent the last 25 years of his life in Normandy. Understandably, as soon as he got the chance, he set about appointing Normans to many of the senior positions in English government and the Church. So, decades before Hastings, there were already a lot of Normans over here.

It was an age when kings and dukes were primarily warlords. Their worth was measured in land and spilled blood. It was therefore inevitable that as the governments and noble houses of the Anglo-Saxons and Normans became ever more intertwined, the Normans would come for the throne of England sooner or later.

The road to Hastings began ordinarily enough. A man lay dying. As it happened, it was Edward the Confessor. But what marked the event out as singular was that he had failed in one of his key royal responsibilities—he was leaving the world childless. To no one's surprise, as the end approached, he nominated as heir his brother-in-law, the 46-year-old Earl Harold Godwinson of Wessex.

Harold was the kingdom's richest noble, and a great military commander who had subjugated Wales in 1063. The Witenagemot promptly proclaimed him king, and Archbishop Stigand of Canterbury crowned him at Edward's gleaming new Westminster Abbey the following day, the 6th of January 1066, the same day Edward was buried there.

But the dead king's ineffectual leadership had passed Harold a major headache, as one of Edward's favourite political strategies had been to promise all sorts of people he would make them his heir. Given his strong attachment to Normandy, it is no surprise that he had, most likely in 1051, promised the throne to Duke William of Normandy, a distant cousin. In fact, Norman sources go further, saying that in 1064 Edward had even sent Harold to Normandy to confirm the arrangement. At the same time, in front of William and on a box of relics, Harold apparently swore a sacred oath to uphold William's claim to the English throne.

The headache did not end with William. There were other claimants, too. King Harald III 'Hardraada' (the ruthless) of Norway had a claim to the throne via an earlier agreement between Harthacnut (king of England and Denmark) and Magnus I (king of Norway and Denmark). Over in Hungary, Edgar the Ætheling had a claim as grandson of King Edmund II 'Ironside'. And in exile in Flanders and Normandy, Tostig Godwinson, Harold's rebellious brother, was nursing a venomous grievance against the Anglo-Saxon establishment.

So, with the sacred coronation oil still wet on Harold's head, a lot of steel began to be sharpened across the water, from Normandy to Norway.

Harold identified the most immediate threat as Duke William of Normandy.

William, like his predecessors, was of Viking stock, tracing his direct male line back to Rollo the Viking, who had moved south from Scandinavia into France around AD 900, where he and his people were recognized as *Nortmanni* or northmen, eventually giving rise to the name Norman. They converted to Christianity, began speaking French, gave up boats and learned the ways of Frankish cavalry combat, but remained fundamentally fired up by their traditional lives of warfare and looting.

William did not have an easy childhood. His father was true-blue Norman nobility, Duke Robert I 'the Devil' of Normandy. But his mother, Herleva, was a concubine and tanner's daughter—hence the taunts of bastardy that William received throughout his life, about which he remained highly sensitive. For instance, when the defenders of a castle at Alençon hung animal hides out to taunt him, he captured the fortification and showed his appreciation by cutting off all their hands and feet.

When he unexpectedly became duke at the age of seven, Normandy immediately descended into anarchy and warfare, as all levels of the nobility (including his family) tried to exploit his youth—murdering three of his guardians and even his tutor. Somehow he survived the free-for-all, and the experience hardened him into a survivor. Once knighted aged 15, he immediately set about pacifying and restoring order to his duchy, seizing back possessions that had been taken from him, and imposing justice on the lawless opportunists who had destabilized his inheritance.

It was a remorseless apprenticeship in blood and power that turned him into one of the most accomplished warriors and rulers of the age. He earned his authority by the sword, and these early experiences profoundly shaped his character. He was always open to innovation, while his strategies in war and government were consistently pragmatic—ruthlessly exploiting any weaknesses, but withdrawing when the odds were against him. Away from the battlefield, he reformed the Church in his lands, and supported it with the piety expected from someone in his position, appointing his maternal half-brother, Odo (who later fought alongside him at Hastings), as bishop of Bayeux.

By the time Harold Godwinson was crowned at Westminster Abbey in 1066, William was 38 years old, had spent his entire life fighting, and was very, very experienced at taking what he believed was rightfully his.

William prepared the ground before Hastings thoroughly, even going so far as to seek the approval of the pope, who blessed battle banners for William to carry, demonstrating the Holy See's displeasure with Harold for his alleged perjury, and also generally with the state of the English Church under the excommunicated Archbishop Stigand, who claimed to be both bishop of Winchester and Archbishop of Canterbury at the same time.

Winners write history, and the Battle of Hastings (or, more precisely, the Battle of Senlac) was no exception. The main accounts we have are the *Song of the Battle of Hastings* (1066), the chronicle of the Norman monk William of Jumièges (1070), and the chronicle of William of Poitiers, who was a former soldier and William the Conqueror's personal chaplain (1071). Then, from some time in the 1070s or 1080s, there is the extraordinary and unique Bayeux Tapestry, probably commissioned by William's brother, Bishop Odo of Bayeux (then also regent of England and earl of Kent), woven to his order in England. There are also a few lesser descriptions, including some Anglo-Saxon accounts, notably in versions of *The Anglo-Saxon Chronicle*. But all these records are biased, and none has the detail needed to reconstruct events minute by minute. There is therefore a lot about 1066 that remains contested and unknown.

On the 27th of September, after bad weather forced an eight-week delay, William crossed the Channel in around 600 transports with perhaps as many as 7,000 infantry and cavalry. He faced no opposition at sea or on landing at Pevensey, so was free to move east towards Hastings.

Harold was busy elsewhere. It had been a long summer, with threats to his crown coming from all angles.

In May, Tostig Godwinson (King Harold's exiled brother) raided the east coast, but was beaten off by Earl Edwin of Mercia. Harold had been guarding the south coast against an anticipated attack by William, but by the end of the summer he had run out of supplies and had to let his militia go back to their fields for the harvest. Then, in mid-September, King Harald Hardraada of Norway landed an army near York, which was quickly reinforced by Tostig and his men. Together, on the 20th of September, they comprehensively defeated the northern earls at the battle of Fulford.

To head off this very serious threat. Harold raised men again and rushed to the east of York, where he annihilated Hardraada and Tostig's armies on the 25th of September at the battle of Stamford Bridge, leaving both invading leaders dead on the battlefield.

The distance between Hastings and Yorkshire meant that Harold did not hear of William's arrival until the 2nd of October. A battle on the south coast was the last thing he or his tired army needed. Nevertheless, he headed south. After 11 days—and having stopped to raise local militias and collect some fresh but inexperienced troops in London—he drew near to Hastings on the 13th of October, where his army of around 7,000 pitched camp on the ridge of Senlac Hill, south of Wealden Forest, around 10 miles north-west of Hastings.

The stage was set.

As the sun rose on the 14th of October, William moved out to meet Harold. He had his archers in front, his infantry behind, and three divisions of cavalry bringing up the rear. The men were a mix of Norman, Breton, Flemish, and French, with a significant number of mercenaries and adventurers.

Harold's army was simpler, just infantry, Anglo-Saxon style, who rode to battle but fought on foot. The majority came from the *fyrd* (locally raised militia), but at the centre of the force were the *housecarls*, the king's professional, personal troops, among the toughest infantry of the period anywhere in Europe.

Some medieval accounts say that Taillefer, a Norman *jongleur*, rode out first, juggling a sword and whipping the men up with a spirited recitation of the *Chanson de Roland*. He slew an Anglo-Saxon who ran out to silence him, before running into the enemy ranks and being cut down.

Attacking from the south, William's archers scored initial success against the Anglo-Saxons on the top of the hill, but at the cost of many dead from javelins and slingshot. He then unleashed his mounted cavalry up the slope, but they fled after being savaged by Anglo-Saxon double-handed battle-axes and being spooked by a rumour that William was dead.

William took off his helmet to show he was still alive, regrouped the knights, and set up a rhythm of alternating volleys of arrows and cavalry charges. The Anglo-Saxon shield wall held firm on top of the hill, but William fooled them with two feigned retreats, luring groups of Anglo-Saxons down off the ridge in pursuit, only to be rounded on and massacred.

The grind and gore of close quarters battle wore on throughout the day. Three horses were cut down from under William, but he drove on until eventually the Anglo-Saxons began tiring of their defence against mounted cavalry. As the shadows lengthened, two of Harold's brothers fell, and—in the late afternoon—Harold was killed. His men fought on for a while, but as dusk came they broke and scattered.

It was over. As the Shropshire monk Orderic Vitalis recorded:

The mangled bodies that had been the flower of the English nobility and youth covered the ground as far as the eye could see. (The Ecclesiastical History)

William wasted no time. He swung his army north-west to London, and the remaining Anglo-Saxon leaders submitted to him at Berkhamstead. He was crowned king of England in Westminster Abbey on Christmas Day 1066. As an indication of divisions to come, when the crowd in the abbey cheered him in English and French, the guards outside were unnerved by the foreign shouts and thought there was treachery afoot, so set fire to surrounding buildings. The coronation descended into chaos as people ran out of the abbey to go looting, while William, the bishops, clergy, and monks finished the ceremony.

To quash the ensuing revolts, William rapidly built castles across the land (most famously the Tower of London), which he used as bases from which to crush opposition. The most dangerous revolt came from Northumbria in 1069–70, but William's troops smashed it, before decimating vast tracts of northern England in the almost genocidal 'Harrowing of the North', principally designed to waste the land to stop further Viking incursions (like the earlier Danelaw) or support for them.

The king stopped at nothing to hunt his enemies. He cut down many people and destroyed homes and land. Nowhere else had he shown such cruelty. This made a real change. To his shame, William made no effort to control his fury, punishing the innocent with the guilty. He ordered that crops and herds, tools and food be burned to ashes. More than 100,000 people perished of starvation. I have often praised William in this book, but I can say nothing good about this brutal slaughter. God will punish him. (The Ecclesiatical History)

Small-scale resistance persisted in isolated pockets—most famously orchestrated by Hereward the Wake from his base on the Isle of Ely in the Fens—but before long the rebellions fell quiet.

One of the enduring mysteries of the Battle of Hastings is what really happened to Harold. The famous image from the Bayeux

Tapestry has him felled with an arrow in his eye, but none of the six broadly contemporary chronicles mention this, and the tapestry was made probably 10 or 20 years later. It is most likely that the tapestry weavers included it as a symbolic death—a visual code identifying Harold's perjury, for which blinding was a common punishment, just like Zedekiah in the Bible. Tradition says Harold was buried at Bosham church or Waltham Abbey, and in the wake of the discovery of Richard III's body, a camera crew is currently following archaeological attempts to find Harold at Waltham Abbey.

In the aftermath of the victory, Pope Alexander II imposed heavy penances on William and the Norman army for the sheer numbers they killed at Hastings. William therefore ordered the construction of an abbey, where monks could pray for the souls of the dead. It was the first religious foundation to be built by the Normans in England, and was as much a symbol of Norman might as an act of penance for the bloodshed. Despite the difficulties of building on a hill and establishing a monastery nowhere near any water, William insisted it be raised on the battlefield, with the high altar over the spot where Harold fell. The abbey thrived, and gave life to the nearby town of Battle, playing an especially important role managing local defences and feeding and clothing refugees during the Hundred Years War. Abbot Hamo is perhaps its most famous superior, remembered for leading local troops to victory against the French during the battle of Winchelsea in 1337. Battle Abbey remained one of England's most notable monasteries until Thomas Cromwell dissolved it in 1538, at which point William the Conqueror's cloak, which had been kept there, also disappeared from history.

So, was the Battle of Hastings one of the key turning points in English history? Did William's gamble and good luck change the fortunes of England forever? The schoolchild's essential guide to English history certainly thinks so:

> When William the Conqueror landed he lay down on the beach and swallowed two mouthfuls of sand. This was his first conquering action and was in the South; later he ravaged the North as well. The

> *Norman Conquest was a Good Thing, as from this time onwards England stopped being conquered and thus was able to become top nation. (Sellar and Yeatman, 1066 And All That, 1930)*

Generations of historians have pointed to the immense rupture in English life that followed the conquest. The Anglo-Saxon nobility was replaced wholesale, while Norman nobles assumed absolute control of the country's levers of power—the throne, government, and the law. All land was appropriated by the crown then parcelled out as fiefs to around 180 Norman nobles, who held the land in return for knight service, revolutionizing patterns of landholding and military infrastructure. The Church was reformed by the removal of Anglo-Saxon bishops and abbots, and Norman replacements were parachuted in. Centuries-old links with the royal houses of Scandinavia were definitively broken, and relations with France became much closer. The language of power changed, and written English largely ceased to exist, as Norman-French (later Anglo-Norman) and Latin took over for almost all purposes.

On the other hand, many things did not really change for the vast mass of ordinary people. They continued to speak Anglo-Saxon, a language which has evolved directly into our modern English of today. It acquired many Norman-French words after the conquest, but the fundamental mechanics of the language suffered almost no structural impact, remaining resolutely Germanic. Even when French vocabulary was assimilated, the new words often came as additions not replacements. So today we have pig/swine and pork, cow and beef, sheep and mutton, murder and homicide, ghost and phantom, freedom and liberty, harbour and port, and so on. It was a process of linguistic enrichment rather than destruction.

If you want to know what the *Ænglisc* sounded like that Harold and his men shouted to each other on top of Senlac Hill, then these opening lines of *Beowulf* give you as good an idea as any:

> *Hwæt! wē Gār-Dena in gear-dagum þēod-cyninga þrym gefrūnon, hū ðā æþelingas ellen fremedon.*

So. The Spear-Danes in days gone by and the kings who ruled them had courage and greatness. We have heard of those princes' heroic campaigns. (transl. Seamus Heaney)

Many other important Anglo-Saxon innovations were also retained. The fabric of central and local government was largely unaffected, and the apparatus of the Anglo-Saxon legal system—including its jewel, trial by jury—was kept, preserving the country's ancient legal heritage, keeping it distinct from the Romanized processes on the continent.

In reality, as invasions go, the country had seen worse. Far more devastating was the displacement 600 years earlier of the indigenous Britons, when the Anglo-Saxons (or Angles, Saxons, Jutes, and Frisians to be precise) invaded and imposed their alien Scandinavian-Germanic ways onto the islands' Celtic peoples, driving them from the centre into the Welsh Marches, Devon, and Cornwall. In that invasion the Anglo-Saxons came in large numbers to settle—which the Normans never did.

Ultimately, all of these people, Anglo-Saxons and Normans, were Nordic/Viking-type warrior people, whose endless wars ravaged northern Europe throughout the Early Middle Ages—sowing the seeds for conflicts in every subsequent century up until 1945.

In the grand scheme of these endless battles for land and wealth, the Battle of Hastings was more of a local *fracas* than an epochal shift. Nevertheless, the consequences for these islands have shaped our history ever since, tying us to dynastic English possessions in France right up to the loss of Calais in 1558, bringing to an end what Edward the Confessor had started 500 years earlier.

8

The cult of Magna Carta is historical nonsense:
Oliver Cromwell called it 'Magna Farta'

Magna Carta has a unique and iconic status around the world, where it is widely seen as the founding charter of democracy. This piece was written for the anniversary of its birth at Runnymede to demonstrate that it is a misunderstood document which has been mythologized beyond recognition.

Magna Carta has an iconic status. To many, it is the foundation stone of English liberty—the guarantor of the freedoms we cherish, and the solemn legal basis for our centuries-old way of life.

It is unique in many ways, and widely appreciated as such. When an 'original' 1297 Magna Carta was sold by Sotheby's in New York in 2007, it went under the hammer for $21.3 million, a record price for a single sheet of vellum.

Appreciation of Magna Carta stretches beyond the British Isles. In the United States, its hallowed phrases are cherished as a political inheritance from England that underpins the United States Constitution, as well as the charters of Massachusetts, Maryland, Connecticut, Rhode Island, Carolina, and Georgia (all published between 1629 and 1732). Franklin D Roosevelt summed up a widely-held American view in his inaugural address of 1941, 'The democratic aspiration is no mere recent phase in recent history ... it was written in Magna Carta'.

Although England has no written constitution, most people assume that if we did, Magna Carta would be it. Its status is so unimpeachable that last century's best-loved maverick judge, Lord Denning (Master of the Rolls, 1962–82), rhapsodized that it was 'the foundation of the freedom of the individual against the arbitrary authority of the despot'. And only this week, Prime Minister David Cameron noted that in it 'King John had to accept his subjects were citizens—for the first time giving them rights, protections and security'. He went on to encourage all schools to teach it when inculcating British (sic) values, as well as exhorting towns to commemorate it, and events to celebrate it.

But sadly, this widespread worship of Magna Carta as one of the planks of an English person's rights has no basis in law or history. In fact, almost everything commonly attributed to Magna Carta is wrong.

For a start, the document waved about at Runnymead on the 15th of June 1215 was not called Magna Carta, and King John did not sign it.

Despite widespread beliefs about the charter's contents, it actually contained very little of significance. The Articles of the Barons (as it was known) did not guarantee freedom to all true-born English people, subject the king to Parliament, enshrine the notion of trial by jury, guarantee freedom of speech, embed the concept of no taxation without representation, or anything else along these lines. It was a largely dull document that dealt with dozens of administrative matters (inheritance laws, feudal obligations, church, land and forestry rights, fish weirs, prisoners, and so on). It also had a number of clauses we would not want to highlight today, like 'No one will be taken or imprisoned upon the appeal of a woman for the death of anyone except her husband' and punitive clauses against Jewish bankers.

Another fact not widely recognized is that the grateful recipients of the rights granted in the Articles of the Barons were not the long-suffering English people, but the aristocracy: John's Anglo-Norman (i.e., French, but living over here) barons, who were largely responsible for most of the oppressing going on in the country. The Articles of the Barons was, basically, an agreement between King John and his uppity aristocratic military henchmen. For example, one of the barons was none other than our good friend King John's Sheriff of Nottingham, one of English folklore's greatest villains.

So, the crowds at Runnymead were not grateful English serfs. The Articles of the Barons had nothing to say about them, and they remained the abused majority.

If that was not surprising enough given Magna Carta's mythical status, it is perhaps even more odd that, as it turned out, the Runnymead agreement was only honoured by the barons and King John for a total of nine weeks, before being ignored and consigned to the midden heap.

So why do philosophers, politicians, judges and litigants across the English-speaking world, idolize Magna Carta as the fount of freedom?

Well, as usual, it's down to people not being a hundred per cent clear about the facts. Magna Carta would have been lost in relative obscurity, and known only to people who like to know such things, were it not for parliamentarians in the 1600s fighting to find an answer to the absolutism of the Stuart monarchy. They eventually located their prize in Magna Carta, which they exhumed from dusty legal digests, holding it aloft as a time-honoured cornerstone of the English constitution.

The only trouble was, they ignored all the little details that got in the way of their story, and simplified it into something that would suit their purposes. For example, they squidged over four entirely separate versions of it into their one historic 'Magna Carta'.

The document's real history, unsurprisingly, was far more complex. And interesting.

Royal charters setting out good kingly practice were well over a century old. The practice had started with the Norman king, Henry I (1100–35), fourth son of William the Conqueror. When Henry seized the throne, he published a 'coronation charter' in which he assured everyone he would observe the good laws and customs of King Edward the Confessor. Which of course he then singularly failed to do.

Henry published the charter because the country was still going through the upheaval of meshing together Anglo-Saxon and Norman law, so the declaration was designed to reassure his subjects that he was going to play by the rules. He had not invented the idea. Over half a century before him, Edward the Confessor himself had sworn at his coronation to uphold the laws of King Cnut.

When Henry I died in 1135 and Stephen of Blois (a city south of Paris) usurped the throne, Stephen carried on the tradition and issued his own coronation charter. His purpose was, predictably, to reassure his new subjects that even though he knew very little about England, he would govern properly and responsibly. Of course, once the ink was dry, civil war and anarchy raged, and England burned for 20 years under him.

When Stephen in turn died and the throne passed to Henry II in 1154, England became an even more tense place. Henry II was from Anjou, a region bordering Normandy and in fierce competition with it. So with Henry's accession, the Anglo-Norman barons of England suddenly found themselves subject to the rule of their arch-rivals. In line with tradition, Henry II also duly issued a coronation charter.

Predictably (this is the twelfth century), Henry II, and then his two sons, Richard I and John, all proved themselves cruel and venal. Their family, the Plantagenets, became a byword for murder and sacrilege—think Henry and Thomas Becket, or John's suspected murder of the 12-year-old Arthur (his rival for the throne that he was supposed to be looking after). Henry II had been no angel, but John excelled at cruelty and the sexual predation of his nobles' wives and daughters. It was hardly a secret that his courtiers loathed him intensely.

And all the while, the Plantagenets taxed England as hard as they could. They siphoned off money at an unprecedented level, and although Henry's legal reforms may be seen as having laid the basis for our modern legal system, the reason he did it was to industrialize the collection of fines, which were set at increasingly ruinous levels.

Although Henry was bad, John was worse. He lost the majority of the country's lands in France, and squeezed every penny out of the Church and his barons that they had managed to recover after his older brother, Richard, had bled them dry in order to fund his grandstanding on crusade. As a result, John was reviled by all. The monk Matthew Paris, writing at St Albans Abbey, summed up the feelings of many, 'Black as is Hell, John's presence there makes it blacker still'.

By early 1215, John's barons were in full revolt against him. The final straw came on the 17th of May, when they seized London. Facing the loss of his capital and his precious treasury, John capitulated, and agreed to meet with leading churchmen and his barons at Windsor to stave off a full civil war.

There were several speedy rounds of negotiations, with Archbishop Stephen Langton of Canterbury shuttling between both camps. The result was a final meeting at Runnymead on the 15th of June. The document John sealed that day is lost. But in the following months his Royal Chancery sent out around 40 charters, one to each county, to be read aloud in the county courts. The document was still not yet Magna Carta, but simply known as the Charter of Liberties. Four of these 1215 charters survive: at Salisbury cathedral, Lincoln cathedral, and two in the British Library.

Of the 40 documents John dispatched in 1215, there was, of course, no one single 'original' from which the others were 'copied'. Each was an identical original (called an engrossment), complete with John's great seal.

The form of the Charter of Liberties was closely modelled on Henry I's coronation charter. But John's document had a very different purpose. England was on the verge of a full-scale revolt. The negotiations leading to Runnymead were a last ditch attempt to stave off an outright civil war—the second in a century. The document John sealed was not a gesture of his royal grace and munificence—it was a desperate peace treaty.

In the event, the Runnymead charter failed completely in its aim. Its many solemn promises (replacement of named royal advisers, fate of specific hostages, repatriation of foreign fighters, and so on) were left unhonoured. The charter was completely dead by September 1215, not three months after it had first been sealed. Both sides had unequivocally repudiated it. The barons then renounced their oaths of homage to John and declared all-out war on him. Meanwhile, Pope Innocent III released John from his obligations under the charter on the basis that they were shameful, demeaning, and legally invalid because they had been exacted by force. The pope then excommunicated the rebels for good measure.

As the country was sucked into civil war again and the French occupied London, the Runnymead charter was forgotten—it was a failed accord, a botched attempt at finding middle ground. Yesterday's news.

However, an unexpected turn of events would, extraordinarily, soon resurrect it. John died in October of the following year, and his nine-year-old son, Henry III, found himself wearing the crown. To prove that he would be a good king, his regents had him issue a coronation charter in 1216 at Bristol. Henry could not very well take as his precedent the skimpy coronation charters given by Henry I, Stephen, and Henry II, so he modelled his new one on John's Runnymead charter. But whereas John's concessions had been forced from him under pain of war, Henry III's was back to being a noble act of royal grace and good will.

During Henry III's long reign (1216–72), his charter was reissued or reaffirmed many times—notably in 1216, 1217, 1225, 1237, 1246, and 1265. The 1217 version is significant, because the sections relating to English forests were removed and issued separately as the Charter of the Forests. To give a name to what was left, from around 1218 onwards it began to be called the Great Charter (*Magna Carta* in Latin, 'great' referring to its length, not its content).

The last two times Magna Carta was issued were under Edward I, in 1297 and 1300. Many of these post-1225 reissues were not because of current political tensions or the emergence of a muscular democracy, but rather to ensure that every county had access to a copy. The reason they ceased being issued after 1300 is that from 1301 the king no longer communicated through the county courts, but instead charters were read in Parliament.

So, far from being one, hallowed document, Magna Carta was in fact issued on multiple occasions by three separate kings, leaving us today with 17 physical copies.

As anyone would expect, in the process of being reissued many times, Magna Carta was updated and amended, resulting in at least four distinct versions. The biggest change came when Henry III issued it for the first time in 1216, as he removed the clauses that impinged most heavily on his royal power. For example, one of the most shameful provisions John agreed to was the establishment of a panel of 25 barons who would scrutinize his decisions. If they disagreed with his actions, they had the right, ultimately, to declare war on him. Unsurprisingly, with the threat of civil war receding, Henry III felt no need to have his powers curbed in the same way, so simply undid the provisions and jettisoned those parts of the settlement he did not like. This was no mere tinkering. By 1225, a mere 10 years after Runnymede, Magna Carta had lost a third of its words, and all of its teeth.

Not only was the charter butchered in the 1200s, but from 1828, what remained was dismembered so comprehensively that only three of its original clauses remain law today. This junking of all but a few of its sentences tells us something uncomfortable about what monarchs and Parliament truly think of Magna Carta.

It should perhaps come as no surprise that the articles of Magna Carta that do remain on today's statute book are all so vague and undefined that they are largely legally meaningless, and would take an unusual set of circumstances to be remotely useful in any modern litigation.

The three survivors (of the 1297 Magna Carta) are a sorry sight:

1. The English Church should be free from royal interference.
2. The customs and liberties of the city of London and other cities, boroughs, towns and ports are to be respected.
3. There is to be no imprisonment of a freeman without trial at the hands of his peers and there is to be no sale of justice.

As a bulwark of the English constitution, it does not add up to much.

Church freedom is clearly an anachronism. The days are long gone when churchmen like Thomas Becket fought to free their institution from royal interference. In reality, the clause makes no sense in a post-Reformation world, where the monarch is the head of the English Church. Unless we give the clause a strained new meaning, it is utterly obsolete, as is the provision regarding the freedoms and customs of cities.

The only relevant clause is the ban on imprisonment without judgment by one's peers. It is something we would all applaud, but even here it is not quite what it seems. It was not new. It only applied to 'freemen' (so not the vast multitude of serfs bonded to their masters). And it was carefully qualified with the ability to junk it and apply instead the hopelessly vague 'law of the land'—nicely leaving open the possibility for good old-fashioned direct state interference. In any event, this provision has certainly never been observed: not before Magna Carta, at its time, or since. If this clause meant anything today, we would not have people languishing in prison on remand for months awaiting trial at which many are acquitted, nor would the special powers brought in post 9/11 be constitutional.

So where does that leave Magna Carta?

The act of writing something down or making it a law does not mean it is observed. To the contrary. Under dictatorships or tyrannies, laws frequently act as a propaganda shield to be enacted then ignored. For instance, Stalin's Constitution of 1936 contained specific detailed provisions guaranteeing numerous human rights. Certainly, the record of English monarchs for centuries after Magna Carta shows no absence of summary executions ordered on a whim—as true of Henry VIII, Mary Tudor, and Elizabeth I as of the Henrys, John, or Edward. Other strong but non-royal English rulers have also been happy to flout it. When it was shown to Oliver Cromwell, he dismissed it as 'Magna Farta'. The record shows that, for most absolute rulers of England, Magna Carta was—like Parliament itself—useful window dressing, but rarely something they took seriously.

The real question surrounding our fetishization of Magna Carta is: why, if it is so sacrosanct, have we hacked it down to three largely meaningless clauses? If it really is 'the foundation of all our laws and liberties' (*Our Island Story*, cited by David Cameron), why have we largely scrapped it?

The reality is that Magna Carta was never intended as a key constitutional document—it was quite explicitly a peace treaty cobbled together at a time when the country was being sucked into civil war. No more. No less. But, like Alfred, Arthur, Robin Hood, Lady Godiva, and so much of our medieval past, it has been taken up and mythologized beyond recognition.

9

The Magna Carta barons were guilty of treason

This piece was written to accompany a mock court case held in Westminster's atmospheric medieval hall with actors on trial before real judges. The accused were the barons who forced King John to agree to Magna Carta, and the question was whether they were guilty of treason. This piece explores the wider issues the barons' supporters tend to gloss over, like the barons giving the crown of England to the king of France.

Tonight, in Parliament's historic Westminster Hall, legal luminaries from around the English-speaking world will gather to hear a mock trial of the Magna Carta barons.

The charge the ancient nobles face could not be more serious.

Treason.

It may not be the word we first think of when considering Magna Carta, but it is an inspired slant on this year's octocentenary celebrations of 1215.

Most people's sympathies will, I imagine, lie with the barons. Their defence team will no doubt go to great lengths to milk this public sympathy. We will be asked to consider the priceless gift the barons left posterity—the cornerstone of parliamentary democracy, revered across the English-speaking world. The oratory will be powerful stuff, allowing the defence case to close, one suspects, with a teary-eyed rendition of 'Rule Britannia!', and possibly even 'Jerusalem' if all goes very well.

On the other side of the Hall, the prosecution will have more of an uphill battle. However, they should be bolstered by knowing that the facts are on their side. Their job will be to take apart the barons' patriotic story forensically, exposing the tawdry ambitious saga for what it really was.

The prosecution will begin with the facts, which are mercifully fairly simple.

In 1214, John lost the battle of Bouvines (just outside Lille airport), and with it a vast swathe of English land in France. It was a catastrophe for the English crown—a second Battle of Hastings.

Back home, John's barons were incandescent. They had been bled white to fund the ill-starred campaign, and in the end it had all come to nothing—no victory, no plunder, no continued power in France. They went into open revolt, renouncing their feudal obligations to serve in John's army or pay his taxes.

It was brinkmanship with the highest stakes. Less than a century earlier, England had been in the throes of 'the Anarchy'—a harrowing civil war.

At this stage, the prosecution will do well to point out that by no means of all John's barons joined the rebellion. Many held back. England was having a tough time. This was not the moment to strike at the king. The rebels were largely based in the north of the country, but they soon brought the fight south, eventually seizing London.

As the country collapsed into mayhem, Archbishop Stephen Langton of Canterbury pitched in, shuttling between both sides to broker a truce.

The result of his efforts came on the 15th of June 1215, when all parties met at Runnymead. The resulting peace treaty took the form of a spidery document called the Articles of the Barons. Over the following few months, John's chancery sealed 40 copies of the treaty and sent them out to the counties, although no one is quite sure if what he sent was the same as the original Runnymead document.

To Archbishop Langton's frustration, it was not to be. The peace did not last. Within nine weeks, both king and barons had stuffed Langton's document into the shredder and were on a war footing. Perhaps it had never been more than a stalling tactic for anyone. In any event, neither side ever did what they agreed in the document.

The country descended into another civil war.

Moving forward, the rest is well known. For the next 85 years, a succession of English kings periodically republished the Articles of the Barons, first changing its name to the Charter of Liberties, then splitting it into two: the Charter of the Forests and the Great Charter. What was left of it eventually entered the statute book in 1297.

During the process of multiple republications, the Articles suffered heavy surgery. Within a year of John's death, the only clause with any constitutional clout was quickly ditched. It had subjected all John's decisions to a council of 25 barons, who could declare war on him if they did not like his ideas. Without this clause, Magna Carta was toothless. It became a piece of Plantagenet royal window dressing, a proclamation of good intentions, which could then be systematically ignored.

The prosecution will be working away at the barons' motives. They will dutifully point out that the privileges in Magna Carta relate only to the wealthy aristocracy of England, not the ordinary English person. It was never a charter for the good people of these isles, just extorted privileges for the nobility.

If the judges seem sympathetic to the defence's claims of 'democratic significance', the prosecution will need to gently demonstrate how history has falsified what Magna Carta actually says. Not many people read it these days, but instead rely on word of mouth. Dangerous.

They can show that Magna Carta in fact contains no clauses guaranteeing every citizen trial by jury. Nor does it have anything to say about no taxation without representation. These are fictions. It was not a great day for women, either, as it loudly declares that a woman's evidence in a murder trial is not to be believed unless it relates to her own husband. It is also not very supportive of Jewish moneylenders, who are deprived of their assets in various ways.

If the judges are feeling mischievous tonight, they might ask the defence why, if Magna Carta is so important, Parliament has repealed all but three of its 63 clauses? That does not sound like a document we venerate as a cornerstone of our democracy.

So, there is not a lot in the Articles of the Barons for the average English person, and the barons' motives begin to look less altruistic, and more concerned with looking after themselves.

Perhaps the nail in the coffin of the barons' story of democratic heroism, though, is the moment when they offered the crown of England to the future King Louis VIII of France. The young dauphin grabbed it hungrily, landed in Thanet, marched on London, and was proclaimed king at St Paul's cathedral.

Louis went on to subdue half of England until, with spectacular timing, John played his trump card—by dying. John's right hand man promptly declared John's nine-year-old son, Henry, king. Seeing a chance to get in with a new English king, the barons did a volte-face, told Louis to sling his hook back to France, and flocked to their new best friend, the young Henry.

By this stage of the evening, some members of the audience will be starting to squirm a little in their seats. This, after all, is not how it was taught at school.

The sordid tale of calling in Louis of France should lead the prosecution nicely into explaining that the barons did not even establish some great new constitutional principle by hogtying a tyrannical ruler. The reality was that kings in the period ruled by consent. John's problem was that he lost that consent. The affirmations in the Articles of the Barons that John would listen to the barons was merely restating age-old tradition.

In fact, Magna Carta was, in large part, a reheated version of the old coronation charters issued by John's predecessors. It only became an instrument in the people-vs-king democracy debate when the English lawyer Sir Edward Coke dug it out in the early 1600s and claimed— entirely falsely, but it suited his anti-Stuart view —that it was an ancient constitutional document curtailing the power of kings. Over in the USA, lawyers drafting state constitutions were listening and receptive, and so the modern myth of Magna Carta was born.

Witnesses always spice up trials. Sadly, neither the prosecution nor the defence will be able to call on much star-quality independent testimony. Except one. Pope Innocent III.

Innocent would be a strong prosecution witness, even though he and John were not what you would call good friends. Innocent (a highly accomplished lawyer) had only just lifted a four-year sentence of excommunication on John for a typical medieval church-state power struggle. Nevertheless, when Innocent heard of the agreement at Runnymead, he was outraged, declaring that John was released from his sacred oaths under it as the treaty had been extorted by force and was therefore invalid. For good measure, he excommunicated the barons for their part in the scandal.

When the nominated judge comes to sum up tonight, he will doubtless explain the elements of the offence of treason. It was, in 1215, a common law offence, which did not become the subject of a statute until 1351, when it defined treason as killing the king, queen or heir; violating the queen, the king's eldest daughter, or his eldest son's wife; waging war on the king; adhering to the kings enemies; and killing various senior officials.

So, how will the judges decide? (Amusingly ironic that there will be no jury, *n'est-ce pas?*)

Assuming they stick to the law as opposed to following 'Jerusalem' with 'I Vow to Thee my Country', it looks rather bleak for the barons. They broke their feudal oaths of allegiance to John. They raised arms against their king. And they invited a Frenchman into London to take the throne.

If that is not treason, then I do not know what is.

I imagine a flunkey has already been delegated to hunt out three black caps.

Just in case.

10

Save the Statute of Marlborough (1267): our oldest law

Every now and then Parliament gets rid of old laws that pointlessly clutter up the statute books. The current round of trimming will spare only two clauses of the hallowed Statute of Marlborough, which is Parliament's oldest law. This piece looks at a number of ancient, outdated laws, and suggests why we should keep them.

If you peer deep into the statute book, you will see that it is still an offence to enter Parliament wearing armour. Even more amazing, it has been a crime since 1313.

I mention this because the moment has again come for Parliament to clear some of the redundant legislative noise off its books. This is a time-honoured process, and one that is becoming increasingly complex thanks to the sheer volume of modern legislation.

A cursory wander through a suitable library will reveal that the statutes passed during the reigns of our medieval monarchs are neatly grouped together in a handful of surprisingly slim volumes. Back then, good rule was not measured by the legislative yard. But shuttle forward to today, and libraries need several shelves for every year of Parliament's output. To give some perspective, Magna Carta is traditionally divided into a mere 63 clauses, whereas the Blair government legislated on such an industrial scale that its oeuvre in criminal matters alone amounted to over 3,000 new offences, or around one a day for their nine years in office. (That said, we have to thank the Thatcher government for that most weighty modern offence of 'handling salmon in suspicious circumstances'.)

As the next wave of repeals goes through, few people will miss a vast swathe of impenetrable tax laws from the nineteenth and twentieth centuries. Likewise the 1997 act allowing for referenda on a Scottish parliament and Welsh assembly are now surplus to requirements. But the 1865 act to help the Assam tea company in British India is an interesting reminder of the brute economics at the heart of empire, while an obscure provision on landlord and tenant law is perhaps the jewel of them all.

It is part of the Statute of Marlborough, our oldest piece of surviving parliamentary legislation. It dates to 1267, to a parliament held by King Henry III in the Wiltshire town, and is notable for lots of reasons, including the fact it pre-dates Magna Carta, which did not become parliamentary law until 1297.

By far the Statute of Marlborough's most important provision forbids revenge against debtors without the involvement of the courts. Yet of its original 29 sections, only four lone provisions remain unrepealed. The Law Commission is now proposing to cull two of these four, as they relate to the concept of 'distress', a landlord's remedy which has not survived the new regime brought in by the rather unmemorably titled Tribunals, Courts and Enforcement Act 2015.

As we prepare to ditch half the mortal remains of our oldest statute, it is worth looking at what else has been quietly repealed over the years.

The most notable, surely, is Magna Carta itself, which once had a whole host of things to say. Despite a widespread belief that Magna Carta is somehow a sacrosanct pillar of this country's laws, in fact only three of its provisions have survived waves of zealous repeals: freedom of the English Church from royal interference; respect for the customs and liberties of the City of London and other cities; and no sale of justice or imprisonment of a free man without trial by his peers.

In all honesty, even though this year is the octocentenary of the 1215 Charter of Liberties (Magna Carta's predecessor), what is left of Magna Carta is not really a great deal of legal use to anyone today. King Henry VIII drove a juggernaut through the requirement that the monarch stay out of the affairs of the Church when he made himself head of it. The freedom and customs of cities are now largely ceremonial. And the right to trial by jury has been hacked away incessantly by the mission creep of magistrates and plummeting legal aid budgets.

It is entirely logical and orderly to repeal obsolete acts and broken cross-references. But in doing so we risk losing some glorious oddities, whose value sometimes lies precisely in the fact they have survived so long, innocuously, beyond any meaningful relevance. Is it therefore truly necessary to repeal so many historic statutes? If the provisions in them have been superseded, or if their realistic legal impact is zero, then what is wrong with leaving them on the books, adding gravitas and continuity to the foundations of Parliament and our uniquely historic law?

For instance, the death penalty was temporarily abolished in 1965, then permanently in 1969. But a handful of historic capital offences clung on in dusty corners of the legislative locker, until individually repealed. They included death for arson in the Queen's docks (abolished 1971), espionage (abolished 1981), piracy with violence (abolished 1998), treason, including violating the princess of Wales, the king's wife, or the king's eldest daughter (abolished 1998), and a number of military offences (abolished 1998). The reality is that these sanctions were never used after 1965, and likely never would have been, although HMP Wandsworth did rather dutifully keep a working gallows until 1994. So did these laws really need to go? Some of their provisions were spectacularly ancient and historic. For instance, the statutory death penalty for treason goes back to Edward III's Treason Act of 1351 (parts of which are still in force).

The survival of the few outdated and meaningless provisions of Magna Carta 1297 and the charming but pointless 1313 ban on wearing armour in Parliament prove that we may keep certain statutes for their historic value and inherent cultural interest rather than their modern functional relevance. So as we wave a sad goodbye to half the four remaining clauses of the Statute of Marlborough 1267, let's hope they leave the remainder, and in two centuries' time Parliament can celebrate its oldest act's one thousandth anniversary.

11

Medieval cathedrals are bursting with colour again

Controversial restoration work underway at Chartres cathedral in France is provoking outrage at its use of bright coloured paint on the saintly old grey stones. This piece explains that the restorers are entirely right: medieval churches and cathedrals were boldly and intensely coloured buildings, decorated with paint, stained glass, and rainbow light.

As cathedrals swell with once-a-year congregations for carols and midnight Mass tonight, many on the pews—even regulars—will not fully appreciate the real story of the buildings in which they sit.

To have an opinion on medieval interior decoration you should first recall the English priest Robert Grosseteste. One of his many ideas was an early 'big bang' creation theory based on expanding light ('God said, let there be light'), colour, and luminescence. It is for good reason that he is ranked among the fathers of science, and he should be compulsory reading for all who visit Chartres cathedral today.

Take the architect, Martin Filler, who recently dropped into Chartres to enjoy its sepulchral gloom. He left swiftly, outraged by what he decried as 'scandalous', 'a desecration', akin to 'adding arms to the Venus de Milo'. Unknown to him, exciting restoration work had been afoot since 2009. So instead of the familiar vanishing penumbra of soaring oil-and-soot-blackened walls pierced by jewels of stained glass, he found the sanctuary washed in light ochre, and adorned with intricately delineated gold, red, green, and black bosses on the ceiling's now bone-white ribs. It was all too much for him.

I, on the other hand, can hardly keep still with the excitement. Medieval buildings were carnivals of colour and light. Wonderfully, the French government and the European Union have allocated £12 million to allow us once more to experience what a medieval cathedral offered the first people who entered it. But those like Mr Filler who like their cathedrals served up with a Protestant austerity are outraged. Colour? In a cathedral?

Actually: yes, please. This is a truly visionary initiative.

Our medieval cathedrals are astounding buildings, built by hand with no electricity or combustion engines, yet they huddle in city centres as museums for tourists. They no longer serve at the vibrant heart of the country's religious life. So why not try something different and educational?

Chartres is engaged in a game-changing makeover. It is not putting in smoothie-bars, bouncy castles, or mediocre modern art. Instead, it is honouring Grosseteste with its own big bang, giving us a visceral sense of what the cathedral looked like on the day of its consecration.

The medieval world adored light and colour. It had no bright plastics, cheery clothes, or colour printing. But the one place a person could go for a visual punch in the solar plexus was the local cathedral, which was painted, inside and often out: walls, ceilings, statues, and especially the serried ranks of figures on the great west fronts. Once inside, the stories they told in their frescoes and windows were the *biblia idiotarum* (the books of the unlettered), where the illiterate majority could see stories etched pictorially into the building's fabric. They were a cross between libraries and cinemas.

The team working on Chartres is not a group of eccentric hobbyists or a bunch of minority academics who have hit the funding jackpot. The French (post-revolution, *bien sûr*) take their unparalleled architectural heritage seriously. Twenty years ago, they found the fifteenth-century paint, and beneath that the original thirteenth-century paint, proving that the entire cathedral had been brightly coloured, a temple of light, filled with dancing tunnels of rainbows from the colossal stained-glass windows. Its builders had wanted to bring a slice of heaven down to a squalid earth, and there was no more inspiring way to do it than with vivid colour. Let's not forget that blue, made up of ground lapis lazuli, only came from Afghanistan, and was more valuable than gold.

They had classical precedents to lean on. We may be used to the Parthenon in Athens as a sand-coloured monument. But to the Greeks of the fifth century BC, it was a riot of colour, vividly painted with pigments that have faded only with time. Mr Filler should bear that in mind and head up to Paris and join the queues for the Saint-Chapelle. Do the unending lines of visitors there want to see another grey gothic church? No. They are waiting to experience the explosion of midnight blue and gold built by Saint Louis to house his crusade treasures. It is a soul-stealing jewel box of thirteenth-century Limoges enamel in stone and glass.

For Mr Filler, the crepuscular gloom of a gothic building is a matter of aesthetics. But to a medieval person, vision was more complex. What was seen by the eye entered the body and (on the basis of Aristotelian and Galenic theory) was absorbed into the animal spirits in the brain. Benefits or damage to health were only a glance away. Gazing at flowers strengthened the body. Bright colours and gemstones energized and healed. Lewd images corrupted, turning the mind into a sewer of filth. So the very lightness, airiness, and colour of Chartres was as much about physical health as spiritual inspiration.

When Mr Filler thunders that it is 'foolhardy' to try to recreate the medieval world because we now have electric lights, he is missing the fact the restored Chartres is giving us back medieval philosophy and spirituality, awe and inspiration, a world long mislabelled as the 'Dark Ages', but which lies at the heart of our modern identity. And to appreciate this intimate cultural reconnection with our past, it really does not matter whether you leave the lights on or off.

12

Richard the Lionheart and Saladin: chivalry and atrocities

Richard the Lionheart is one of England's most famous kings. But in recent years people have increasingly questioned whether he was the chivalric hero we think of, or whether his arch foe, Saladin, was nobler? This piece was written on the anniversary of Richard's death, and examines each of their lives and legacies.

As the young Pierre Basile gazed down from the windy battlements of Châlus-Chabrol castle, he could barely believe his eyes. It was the 25th of March 1199, and there, within crossbow range, was the infamous warlord who had killed his father and two brothers. And he was not even wearing his chainmail.

Pierre did what any self-respecting twelfth-century boy from the Limousin would have done. He took the shot, and hit one of the most famous warriors of all time.

When the festering shoulder wound began to turn gangrenous, the 42-year-old soldier pardoned young Pierre, and gave him a bag of money. Then, on the 6th of April 1199, a full 11 days after having been shot, the celebrated duke of Aquitaine and Normandy, count of Anjou and king of England, died of the wound.

Eight hundred and fifteen years later, Richard the Lionheart remains a shining national hero, with a unique place in popular culture—a name every schoolchild repeats with conviction when asked for a great medieval English king. Richard inspires a misty reverence, and somehow, like Arthur, personifies a certain historic Englishness. An indomitable equestrian bronze statue of him even prances outside the Palace of Westminster, patrolling with a drawn sword—daring anyone to challenge the good government of this country.

His implicit embodiment of justice is so ingrained into our collective conscience that folk-heroes such as Robin Hood demonstrate their moral credentials by unswerving loyalty to him. And, since the 1930s, Hollywood has been unable to resist the temptation to insert a cameo appearance from an armoured and mounted Richard whenever a semi-divine presence is required.

In all this, Richard is perhaps best known for a lethal rivalry, in both life and death, that has become a metaphor for the age.

His struggle was with a man who lies over 2,000 miles east of Westminster, in Damascus. Although the oriental warrior is buried in a simple wooden sarcophagus, an elegant marble one beside it tells an equally powerful story. It was presented in 1898 by Kaiser Wilhelm II as a mark of respect, from one great ruler to another—from the emperor of Germany and king of Prussia to Yusuf ibn Ayyub, better known as Saladin.

Despite history's obsession with Richard as an ardent cross-toting crusader, he actually only fought for just over a year in the Holy Land, compared to 25 years of ceaseless warmongering in Europe. Nevertheless, popular sentiment has elevated his year of crusade into an epic and defining point of the High Middle Ages—a distillation of the seething currents coursing through the age of chivalry.

Richard and Saladin's respective qualities have been an endless source of fascination over the centuries, and the pendulum has swung many times. Both men have been variously hailed as the truest incarnations of chivalry, or denounced as bloodthirsty butchers.

In Richard's case, for all the adulation he has traditionally received from the English, historians in the last two centuries have been less kind. For instance, Bishop William Stubbs (1825–1901) was Regius Professor of History at Oxford. He towered head and shoulders above all other British historians of his age. Yet, his assessment of Richard would not have pleased those Victorians who erected the triumphant equestrian statue in Westminster's Old Palace Yard. Stubbs judged that Richard was:

A bad son, a bad husband, a selfish ruler, and a vicious man.

Perhaps most shocking, he went on to conclude:

He was no Englishman.

Stubbs was, in fact, not alone, or even of his time. Most historians, then and since, have not found much need to revise his unfavourable opinion.

We can start with the notion Richard was no Englishman. Although there is an implied criticism of his moral compass, the main point is that Richard despised England. It sounds blasphemous, but for all our centuries-old affection for him, the simple truth is that Richard could not abide this country.

As an adult, he visited England only twice, and on each occasion for as short a period as humanly possible. The first was in 1189, when he came for four months to be crowned (an event he could hardly avoid) and also to oversee a fire sale of everything that was not nailed down. He famously remarked that he would have sold London if he could have found a buyer.

Once back in France with his shiny English crown, he took no ongoing interest whatsoever in the running of his new kingdom. He was an absentee landlord, only concerned with the rents England yielded to fund his personal wars of dynastic consolidation and self-aggrandizement.

His second visit was in 1194, after he had finished crusading, and England had helped raise the eye-watering 100,000 marks ransom for his release from imperial captivity. When two months of dutiful plodding around England were up, Richard promptly took the first boat he could find back to the battlefields of France. England was, he said, cold and always raining, and it plainly held nothing for him—which is hardly surprising, as he was a thoroughbred Frenchman.

His mother, Aliénor (Eleanor) of Aquitaine, was one of medieval Europe's most powerful, memorable, and extraordinary figures.

Yet although queen-consort of England, she was most definitely southern French.

His father, King Henry II of England, was likewise from across the water. He had Norman-Angevin blood, and controlled vast swathes of *L'Hexagone*, from the Channel to the Pyrenees. For Richard, who was never destined to ascend the English throne, everything north of the White Cliffs was secondary. His heritage and inheritance were in France, and this was perfectly reflected in the fact his two languages were Occitan and French (*langue d'oc* and *langue d'oïl*). There is no evidence he ever showed any interest in English. In all likelihood, he would have had no idea what the reverential epithet 'Lionheart' meant.

Even in death, after he had held England's crown for ten years, his kingdom was not important enough to warrant any of his remains. The royal abbey of Fontevraud got his body, Châlus kept his intestines, and his heart (embalmed with frankincense, myrtle, mint, poplar, bellflower, and lime, according to recent chemical analysis) was dispatched to Rouen.

The simple reality is that Richard was duke, count, or lord of a breathtaking array of fiefs all over France. But what he (and his poisonous brothers) all really wanted was a crown—a VIP pass into a far more exclusive club. England eventually offered Richard that opportunity, and he took it, along with the country's wealth. It was a means to an end, and that was the extent of his interest.

So was Bishop Stubbs right to say he was no Englishman? Many would find it difficult to disagree.

The statement he was a 'bad son' is also hard to deny. Richard was his mother's favourite, and he was dutiful to her. But he did not show anything like the same loyalty to his father, Henry II.

Henry took the job of nursing a war-torn and fractured England back to health very seriously. Twenty years before his accession, Stephen of Blois had usurped the throne and unleashed a vicious civil war that left England burning for two decades. The Victorians called it the Anarchy, while the medieval Peterborough Chronicle famously said it was a time when '*Christ slep, and his halechen*' (Christ and his saints slept).

Henry II healed the country's wounds with dedication and skill. Yet Richard and his brothers Henry, Geoffrey, and John undermined and distracted him by spending years of their adult lives allying with Henry's enemies and sending armies against him (at times with orders to kill him) in order to seize their inheritances early.

All their ingratitude, plotting, and treachery eventually wearied Henry into an early grave. Gerald of Wales notes that Henry's deathbed lament was that of all his children, it was the legitimate ones who were the real bastards.

So despite being good to his mother, Richard's relationship with his father left a lot to be desired.

His record as a husband was likewise not spectacular. And here we tread on controversial territory, so let's let the chronicles do the talking. This is how Roger of Howden (a close confidant of Henry II and Richard) describes Richard's friendship with King Philip Augustus of France in 1187:

> *Every day they ate from one table and one bowl, and by night the bed did not separate them. The king of France loved him as his own soul, and they loved each other so much that the king of England (i.e., Henry II, Richard's father) was absolutely astonished at the passionate love between them.*

A minority of historians believe this passage records no more than a ritual symbolic show of political harmony between the two great royal lords. The majority of historians has never heard of the princely 'bed-and-bowl rite', and assumes Roger meant exactly what he wrote.

In any case, four years later, a political union was struck between Richard and Berengaria of Navarre, and the couple married in Cyprus en route to the Crusades. However, for whatever reason, Berengaria did not hang around for more than a few months, and soon headed back to France.

But that is not the end of it. In 1195, Roger of Howden tells us that a hermit cautioned Richard to desist from certain same-sex acts, which he identifies clearly, and I do not need to. Despite the warning, Roger says Richard did not heed the words until a serious illness caused him to take his wife back again, although the marriage remained distant and childless to the end.

So, no one would give Richard the award for husband of the year, either. (As a side note, Berengaria is England's only queen never to have visited England while reigning.)

All that said, Richard did impress people with a range of virtues that were widely and deeply admired.

In a violent age, his battle skills, both as combatant and strategist, were truly exceptional. As, on occasion, was his devotion to his men. Like when he went after a foraging party that had stumbled into serious trouble. 'I sent those men there', he said. 'If they die without me, may I never again be called a king.'

He was also a skilled orator. When prisoner of the Holy Roman Emperor, he awed everyone with his eloquent defence against the charge of having paid the Ismaili Assassins in the Holy Land to murder his rival, Conrad of Montferrat. (He was, in all likelihood, guilty of the charge.)

He knew some Latin, and Muslim sources say he had a keen interest in Arabic culture. He was not a musician, but he loved music and wrote songs and poetry in Occitan and French. An Islamic chronicler summed him up as a man of wisdom, experience, courage, and energy.

The difficulty is that these attributes are permanently besmirched by accounts of his increasing cruelty.

The most famous example occurred near Acre in the Holy Land. Richard and Saladin had been negotiating for months. Richard was to give Saladin back several thousand prisoners. In return Saladin was to pay a ransom and yield up the True Cross, which he had captured in 1187 at the Horns of Hattin. When Saladin stalled the discussions one time too many, Richard flew into a rage. He had 3,000 captured Muslim prisoners (including large numbers of women and children) taken to the nearby hill of Ayyadieh. There, in full view of Saladin and his army, they were beheaded and disembowelled. Even in an age of atrocities, this was an act of exceptional and shocking barbarity.

So Richard was, undoubtedly, a different and more complicated character than the chivalrous and noble 'Lionheart' of legend.

Leaving Richard for a moment, Saladin's story is equally as fascinating. And surprising.

Joseph son of Job (Yusuf ibn Ayyub) was a Kurd from Tikrit, in northern Iraq. His family served Zengi of Aleppo and Mosul and his son, Nur ad-Din, whom they followed south. After a range of intrigues, Saladin found himself, aged 32, in charge of Egypt. Little by little, he expanded his influence, until by 1187 he held a vast swathe of the Neat East.

With the land surrounding the Crusader States now unified for the first time, Saladin set about expelling the Crusaders. Despite some stunning victories, he ultimately failed to oust the European settlers, and died a pauper in 1193, the year after Richard left the Holy Land.

Across the Middle East, Saladin is today a cultural hero. Not only for his popular *jihad*, but also for his chivalry, honour, decency, and generosity.

Bizarrely, a good deal of his modern reputation in the Muslim world is down to the Western memory of him. He was, it seems, largely forgotten in the East, eclipsed by Baybars, who finally and definitively expelled the Crusaders in 1291. But Crusader chroniclers and European writers strongly admired Saladin's qualities, and they kept his story alive.

For instance, the twelfth-century crusading archbishop, William of Tyre, wrote that Saladin had:

> ... *a keen and vigorous mind, valiant in war and generous beyond measure.*

The thirteenth century bestseller, the *Ordene de Chevalerie*, made him a popular hero throughout Europe. Dante honoured him by putting him in Limbo, along with the noble heroes of Greece and Rome. Boccaccio flattered him in the *Decameron*. And finally, as part of the Victorian romanticization of the East, Sir Walter Scott depicted him in *The*

Talisman (1825) as the perfect incarnation of knightly values. Given all this adulation, it was no wonder that Kaiser Wilhelm II made a special pilgrimage to his tomb.

Saladin's chivalry is not really in doubt. Two well-known examples speak powerfully.

The first was at the battle of Jaffa, when Richard the Lionheart's horse fell under him. Saladin immediately sent a groom through the dust of battle to present Richard with a pair of fresh horses, along with the splendid message that a king as great as Richard should not fight on foot.

Months later, when Saladin heard that Richard was ill, burning up with a fever, Saladin sent him a gift of peaches and sherbet cooled with the snow from Mount Hermon. (Maybe he just wanted his spies to reconnoitre Richard's camp, but either way it shows charm and grace.)

Both of these incidents occurred after the massacre at Ayyadieh, which tells us something about how quickly such brutality was forgotten.

The event that is often seen as the high point of Saladin's chivalry was his capture of Jerusalem in 1187. But, in fact, here is where the picture starts to crack. Everyone knows how the Crusaders turned Jerusalem into a charnel house when they first took the city in 1099. By contrast, Saladin's fans stress his clemency when he recaptured the city 88 years later.

However, it is more complicated. The standard practice for Christians and Muslims was that inhabitants of cities or castles which surrendered were spared, but those that put up opposition were slaughtered. (The cost of keeping them fed, apart from anything else, was often prohibitive.)

It was therefore always Saladin's plan to execute the captured inhabitants of Jerusalem. However, he eventually decided on using them to raise money instead. The scheme he devised was that inhabitants should buy their safe passage out: ten dinars per man, five per woman, and two per child.

Needless to say, not everyone could pay. Sixteen thousand, to be exact. Although Saladin did not kill them, he did not free them, either.

According to his close confidant Imad ad-Din, the women and girls were all taken forcibly by his soldiers for their carnal pleasure, and then, together with the men and children, enslaved.

This is where we get closer to understanding these two men, because neither of their popular reputations gives the full medieval picture.

For instance, although the Crusaders are widely labelled as religious fanatics (which many undoubtedly were), Muslim chroniclers freely record that Saladin also beheaded Christians who refused to convert to Islam.

And in terms of general mayhem, we know European knights regularly razed the countryside (Richard certainly did, in France and Cyprus), and it should come as no surprise that Saladin did, too. A Muslim chronicler tells us of an occasion when Saladin was unopposed by Crusaders, and was:

… free to besiege and pillage, burn and ravage the whole region, which he did.

Both sides committed atrocities. Saladin executed hundreds of Crusaders after the battle of Hattin. And after Richard murdered the 3,000 prisoners at Ayyadieh. Saladin retaliated by slaughtering all the Christian men, women, and children he held.

When all is said and done, history has paired Richard and Saladin together because, even allowing for their vastly different cultures, there were strong similarities in personality and outlook. Despite Saladin's seniority by 20 years, they were warriors of an age.

For instance, both understood the nature of acquiring and protecting power, and neither was a stranger to political assassinations. We have already seen that Richard was implicated in the murder of Conrad of Montferrat. There was a similar incident in Saladin's past, too. When he started his ascent to power in Fatimid Egypt, he executed Shawar, his only real competition to Nur ad-Din's lands.

That said, Saladin was more refined than Richard. He came from a culture in which manners, decorum, humility, and respect were essential attributes of a civilized person—long before European knights developed any meaningful semblance of chivalric values.

On the other hand, Richard was probably the better military strategist. The score sheet for their battles in the Third Crusade was three out of three to Richard. However, Richard failed to fight Saladin for Jerusalem—the whole purpose of his Crusade—and he returned to Europe ostensibly a failure, pulled away from his prize by the more pressing need to defend his interests from intriguers back home.

Chivalry is, ultimately, in the eye of the beholder. Both Western and Eastern commentators hyped up Saladin and Richard's *courtoisie*, but neither of them was particularly enlightened by modern standards. Richard was even fond of the idea that he was a monster. The chronicler Gerald of Wales records that Richard liked to say he was descended from Melusine (a diabolical European fairy), and that his whole family 'came from the Devil, and would return to the Devil'.

Despite the burnished legends on both sides, the story had no happy endings. Richard failed at his Crusade, and then failed to secure his legacy in France. Arguably, he also failed as king of England. Over in the Near East, Saladin failed to dislodge the Crusaders, and on a personal level his Ayyubid dynasty soon fractured.

Even poor Pierre Basile, despite receiving forgiveness from Richard for having shot him with a crossbow bolt, was soon captured by Mercadier, Richard's longstanding right hand man, who skinned him alive and hanged him.

The truth is that whatever the legends say of Richard, Saladin, and the late 1100s, fully-fledged medieval chivalry was still many years away.

13

Saladin and the fateful battle of Hattin (1187): lessons for the modern Middle East

On 4 July 1187, Saladin smashed the Crusader army and seized back Jerusalem after nearly 90 years of Christian rule. It was a defeat the Crusaders never fully recovered from. This piece was written to mark the battle of Hattin's anniversary as a reminder how quickly and often land changes hands in the Middle East.

The Levant, the region running inland from the eastern seaboard of the Mediterranean, has been fought over for millennia. Its vital trade and military roads linking Anatolia to north Africa and Arabia have been guarded and coveted since time immemorial. Control is everything, as Moses found out to his cost when he wanted to move north up the ancient King's Highway out of the Sinai and into Edom (modern day southern Israel):

> 'Now let us pass through your land. We will not pass through field or vineyard, or drink water from any well; we will go along the King's Highway, not turning aside to the right hand or to the left until we have passed through your territory.' But Edom said to him, 'You shall not pass through, or we will come out with the sword against you.' The Israelites said to him, 'We will stay on the highway; and if we drink of your water, we and our livestock, then we will pay for it. It is only a small matter; just let us pass through on foot.' But he said, 'You shall not pass through.' And Edom came out against them with a large force, heavily armed. Thus Edom refused to give Israel passage through their territory; so Israel turned away from them. (Numbers 20:17–21)

Countless cultures have fought for dominance in the region—Canaanite, Philistine, Hebrew, Assyrian, Babylonian, Persian, Greek, Roman, Byzantine, Rashidun, Umayyad, Abbasid, Fatimid, Seljuk, crusader, Ayyubid, Khwarazmian, Mamluk, Ottoman, British, French, Jewish, the list goes on. Most of the conquests have been bloody. All have caused regional upheavals. Some have spread even further, sending international shockwaves east and west.

This week marks two major anniversaries of crusader history, both of which had a profound impact on the whole of Europe. On the 4th of July 1187, Saladin crushed the crusaders at the battle of the Horns of Hattin—one of the most important military encounters of the medieval world. Ninety years later, on the 1st of July 1277, Sultan al-Malik Baybars died. Although less well known in the West than Saladin, Baybars was a far more brutal and effective warlord. It was his devastating campaigns that finally ripped the heart out of the crusades, propelling the whole project into its darkening, twilight years.

When the crusaders had first conquered Jerusalem in 1099, waves of elation crashed across Latin Christendom. Jerusalem was the *umbilicus mundi*, the centre of Europe's conception of the world as depicted in medieval maps like Hereford's glorious *Mappa Mundi*. God clearly favoured the Christian settlers, and had given their armies Jerusalem to prove it.

The crusades were not the first time Jerusalem was under Christian rule. The Holy Land had been Christian in the days of the Byzantine Empire (*c.* AD 325–637). Emperor Constantine the Great and Empress Helena had Christianized the city, renaming it 'Jerusalem' and wiping out the pagan remains of Aelia Capitolina built by Hadrian in AD 130 on the rubble of Jerusalem. At the heart of his new Jerusalem, Constantine built the Church of the Holy Sepulchre, and made it the pre-eminent Christian pilgrimage destination. However, since the Rashidun Caliphate under Umar the Great had conquered the Near East in AD 637, Jerusalem had been under Islamic rule.

Hand in hand with the crusaders' initial elation in 1099 came the practical problem of controlling vast swathes of conquered territory far from home in their new land of '*Outremer*', the place 'beyond the sea'. The result was countless famous battles in which the pendulum swung one way then the other during the 192 years of crusader presence in the Levant. Although many of the engagements are still famous—like Jacob's Ford and the Field of Blood—the Horns of Hattin stands head and shoulders above them as one of the turning points of world history.

Today, as the politically unrelated and separate conflicts in Syria and Iraq coalesce and evolve into an all-consuming regional power struggle, it is worth looking at the battle of the Horns of Hattin as a reminder of the region's merciless ability to keep redrawing its borders and reinventing itself in blood.

First, put Ridley Scott's epic 2005 film, *Kingdom of Heaven*, out of mind. It excels in evoking the existential crisis of the crusader kingdom at the tail end of the reign of the leper king, Baldwin IV. And it is a seductive and visually sumptuous world, where faith, honour, ideals, and love vie alongside ambition, bloodlust, venality, and the ugly side of unchecked militarism. But it is not a faithful account of the events leading up to the cataclysmic battle of Hattin and Balian of Ibelin's doomed defence of Jerusalem. For a start, the real Balian was 44 years old at Hattin, did not know one end of an anvil from the other, was married to a member of the Byzantine royal family, and was born and lived his whole life as a powerful, wealthy noble in the crusader states.

The true story of Hattin is nevertheless every bit as soaked in romance and ambition as Scott's *Kingdom of Heaven*.

Some years earlier, Lucia of Botrun, a beautiful and wealthy Levantine heiress, was ignominiously placed onto a huge set of scales and publicly weighed. A merchant from Pisa piled up the pan on the other side with gold bezants until he had measured out her weight in gold, which he then gave to her overlord as payment for her hand in marriage. In the wings, a headstrong Flemish crusader, Gerard de Ridefort, vowed revenge. He had previously asked Lucia's overlord, Count Raymond III of Tripoli (of Toulouse) for her hand, but his request was refused. Despite the fact Raymond was one of the kingdom's wisest and coolest heads, Gerard immediately left Raymond's service, nursing a grievance that would lead to the downfall of a kingdom.

After recovering from a serious illness, or perhaps sensing faster promotion as a professional crusader, Gerard soon took the dramatic step of professing solemn monastic vows as a Knight Templar, devoting himself to a celibate community life of praying and fighting. His exceptional abilities were quickly recognized, and he rose swiftly through the Order's ranks to become their tenth Grand Master. This unique position gave him privileged access to Christendom's royalty—especially in Jerusalem—an influence he used, among other things, to oppose and thwart Raymond whenever he could.

In 1185, on the death of the leper King Baldwin IV, his seven-year-old nephew took the throne under the regency of Raymond. But when the young king died within a year, the crown passed to his mother and step-father: Sibylla of Jerusalem and Guy of Lusignan. The kingdom promptly tore itself into two poisonously opposed factions—those like Gerard de Ridefort and the Templars who supported Queen Sibylla and King Guy, and those like Count Raymond who backed Isabella, Sibylla's half-sister.

With the kingdom hopelessly divided, the scene was set for a catastrophe. It just needed someone to light the touch paper.

King Guy counted among his camp a maverick one-man army: Raynald of Châtillon, 'the Elephant of Christ'. Raynald had been in the crusader states since the second crusade, and had spent 15 years in a Muslim jail before leading the crusader forces to a spectacular victory against Saladin at the fêted battle of Montgisard, Saladin's most crushing defeat. Raynald was therefore a seasoned operator in the region, and had been rewarded with the lordship of *Oultrejourdain* (the lands beyond the River Jordan). However, he is usually most often remembered for his cruelty, endless piracy and plundering, unwillingness to obey kings, and repeated breaking of delicate truces to the annoyance of all sides.

In 1187, when Raynald again broke a truce and attacked yet another Muslim caravan travelling the King's Highway near his Red

Sea outpost at Kerak, Saladin could stand by no longer. He declared the truce to be a sham, and led an invasion army across the Jordan. Raynald's lawlessness had finally provoked the largest united Muslim force the crusaders had ever seen.

The end began quickly. On the 1st of May 1187, at the Springs of Cresson near Nazareth, a small group of around 140 Templars and Hospitallers found themselves confronting a 7.000-strong detachment of the Muslim army under al-Afdal, Saladin's son. The master of the Hospitallers and several senior Templars counselled retreat, but Gerard de Ridefort accused them of cowardice and ordered an attack. The result was a charnel house. Gerard de Ridefort and two other Templars were the only known survivors.

Back in Jerusalem. King Guy and the royal court knew that a full-scale onslaught from Saladin's 30,000 men was now imminent. All they could do was wait to see where it would come.

Saladin made the first move. He advanced to Tiberias on the west shore of the Sea of Galilee. The castle belonged to Count Raymond III of Tripoli, who was away with the royal court, leaving it garrisoned by Eschiva, his wife.

On the 2nd of July, King Guy held a war council to decide on a response. And it was here, at this critical moment in the history of the crusader kingdom, that the memory of Lucia of Botrun on the gold scales filled the room. Count Raymond calmly advised King Guy that Saladin was setting a trap, trying to get the crusaders to leave the safety and water of Sepphoris. He was, Raymond explained, hoping to lure the crusaders onto arid open ground where the Muslims' numerical advantage could be best used. But whatever Raymond said was always wrong in the eyes of Gerard de Ridefort and Raynald of Châtillon, who shouted him down, accusing him of cowardice. They argued long into the night that King Guy should immediately lead the crusaders to march on Tiberias. In undoubtedly the worst decision of his life, Guy allowed himself to be persuaded by Gerard and Raynald, and ordered the army to ready itself. He was a politician not a soldier, and his lack of experience was about to cost the crusaders dearly.

The following day, the 3rd of July, the pride of the crusading army thundered out of the springs of Sepphoris heading east for Tiberias and the Sea of Galilee. From the moment they left, the outcome was sealed. Saladin had to do very little. The summer heat was unbearable, and the mail-clad crusaders lacked water. To make them even thirstier, Saladin lit brushwood fires around them, engulfing the advancing columns in clouds of billowing smoke. Panicked, choking, and dehydrated, the crusader army broke apart, allowing Saladin to encircle them. The crusaders were finally corralled on the two hills known as the Horns of Hattin, just six miles short of Tiberias, where the massacre began.

King Guy, Gerard de Ridefort, and Raynald of Châtillon were all taken prisoner. The crusaders' most sacred relic, the True Cross discovered by the Empress Helena in the AD 320s, was also captured, taken in triumph to Damascus, and never seen again.

As depicted in *Kingdom of Heaven*, Saladin invited King Guy and Raynald of Châtillon into his tent, where he offered a groggy Guy a cup of iced water to slake his thirst. When Guy then passed the cup to Raynald, Saladin responded that he had not personally offered refreshment to Raynald, and was therefore not bound by any rules of hospitality towards him. He asked Raynald why he had broken so many oaths over the years. Raynald replied that kings had always acted thus, and he had done no more. Saladin then personally beheaded Raynald, before dragging his decapitated body over to a terrified Guy. 'Kings do not kill kings', he reassured Guy, but explained that Raynald was an oath-breaker whose repeated 'maleficence and perfidy' had warranted immediate death.

Guy and the other captured nobles were all eventually ransomed, apart from the 230 Knights Templar and Knights Hospitaller whom Saladin judged too militarily dangerous to be allowed freedom. He ordered them beheaded on the spot:

> *With him was a whole band of scholars and sufis and a certain number of devout men and ascetics, each begged to be allowed to kill one of them, and drew his sword and rolled back his sleeve. Saladin,*

his face joyful, was sitting on his dais, the unbelievers showed black despair. (Imad ad-Din, On the Conquest of the Holy City)

With their army decimated, the crusaders could only watch as one by one their cities then fell. Queen Sibylla and Patriarch Heraclius mounted a last-ditch defence of Jerusalem, before roping in Balian of Ibelin, who had dropped by to collect his family. Balian's involvement was in strict defiance of an oath of non-belligerence he had given Saladin in order to be allowed to travel to Jerusalem, but he wrote to Saladin to explain his predicament, and Saladin seemed happy for Balian to try to organize Jerusalem's defences. In any event, they both knew Jerusalem could not withstand a siege. Balian had only a handful of knights, so spontaneously knighted the city's squires to help in the effort. But it was largely symbolic. On the 2nd of October, Balian went to Saladin's tent. Saladin confirmed that he had sworn to kill all Jerusalem's men and to enslave the women and children. In response, Balian threatened to execute the 5,000 Muslim prisoners in Jerusalem, kill the crusaders' families and livestock, destroy all treasures, and raze the al-Aqsa mosque and Dome of the Rock to the ground before he and the men marched out to meet their glorious deaths at Saladin's hands. Unnerved, Saladin suggested a peaceful surrender, which Balian accepted. Saladin then granted safe passage to all inhabitants who could pay their way, and sold the remaining men, women, and children into slavery.

The reaction across Christendom was utter disbelief. It was unthinkable that Jerusalem was no longer a Christian city. Four generations of Western children had grown up knowing that Jerusalem was part of Christendom. The grief at losing it tore deep into the soul of the West. On hearing the news, Pope Urban III died of shock. Within two years, Europe's leading warrior, Richard the Lionheart, was personally in Outremer to set things right. But the tide had turned, and he failed ever to set eyes on Jerusalem.

Although the crusader states would limp on for another 105 years from their new headquarters at Tyre and then at Acre, medieval Christendom never again owned Jerusalem outright, and life became immeasurably harsher for the remaining crusaders and settlers—notably as a result of the campaigns of Sultan al-Malik Baybars, who died on the 1st of July 1277, providing the other major Levantine anniversary this week.

Unlike any of the crusaders' previous opponents, Baybars was a military machine. On some levels, Saladin was not an especially talented general—over the course of 17 years of campaigning against the crusaders, he was regularly not successful on the battlefield. Baybars, on the other hand, was a highly effective general. He rose to power by murdering two Sultans of Egypt (including the last Ayyubid of Saladin's dynasty), before finally taking personal control as Sultan, leading a hardened army of Mamluks from Egypt and Syria. He was a warlord who had built Egypt's military caste of slave soldiers (*mamluk* means slave) into a juggernaut that dominated without opposition, steamrollering both the crusaders and the Mongols invading from the east. To put that into perspective, the Mongols had recently blitzkrieged their way from China to Poland, slaughtering entire populations. No terror like it had ever been seen. In many cities, there was no one left to clear away the mountains of rotting bodies. When Baybars and his Mamluks defeated them in AD 1260 at Ain Jalut (in the Jezreel Valley, Galilee), it was the first time the massed Mongol forces had ever been convincingly beaten. It is little wonder that the Islamic world has always told stories of Baybars, whereas Saladin fell into relative obscurity until resuscitated by Western interest.

Saladin may have broken the crusaders' hearts, but it was Baybars who effectively snuffed out the crusade movement. As the news from Syria and Iraq in the last few weeks now makes clear, the complexion of the Levant region is changing again. The vacuum in Iraq and the disintegration of society in Syria have created new groups, alliances, and interests. We do well to remember that the region is one where nothing has ever stood still for long.

14

Forget the *Da Vinci Code*: this is the real mystery of the Knights Templar

Popular interest in the enigmatic Knights Templar has been growing since the early 1980s, and any decent conspiracy theory now has to involve them. Almost all are nonsense. But there is one very real mystery remaining. This piece examines the current fascination with the Templars, and also reveals a little Templar chapel in the south of France that still keeps its secrets after 800 years.

Not so long ago, casually throwing the Knights Templar into polite conversation was a litmus test of mental health. One of Umberto Eco's characters in *Foucault's Pendulum* summed it up perfectly. He declared that you could recognize a lunatic 'by the liberties he takes with common sense, by his flashes of inspiration, and by the fact that sooner or later he brings up the Templars'.

But all good things come to an end. The enigmatic medieval monk-knights are no longer a fringe interest for obsessives. They are now squarely mainstream. And as the 18th of March 2014 draws closer, Templarmania is going to be ratcheted up several more notches.

Everyone loves an anniversary, and this is going to be a big one. It will be exactly 700 years since the legendary Jacques de Molay, last Grand Master of the Templars, was strapped to a stake in Paris and bonfired alive. For centuries after de Molay's execution in 1314, everyone wanted to sweep the ashes of the whole dreadful affair under the carpet. The official line was that the Templars, the former darlings of Christendom, had fallen from grace. Power had gone to their heads, and they had degenerated into something unspeakable (for a medieval order of monks, at any rate): spitting and urinating on crucifixes, worshiping idols, and finding sexual release with each other.

King Philip IV 'the Fair' of France had personally overseen seven years of inquiry into the order's suspicious practices. Based on the information it unearthed, he was convinced that he had exposed something rotten in society. The world, he was sure, would be better off without their sort—so he moved to have the Order stamped out. In the end, faced with Philip's sustained pious outrage, the yellow-bellied pope of the day (a stooge who owed everything to Philip) had little alternative except to close the Templars down on the basis their reputation was irreparably shot. Philip then spent the next few years getting his hands on the Templars' vast wealth, which he justified as compensation for having financed the enquiry to expose their dreadful sins.

For the following centuries, no one really spoke of the Templars. They were an embarrassment, and the less said about them the better. It was as if they had never been.

An attempt to rehabilitate them came first from a Scottish Freemason in the early 1700s, but his views did not spread wider than the royal Jacobite court where he presented them. A century later, the Order's traditional reputation as depraved deviants re-emerged, but this time as the arch-villains in books—most famously in Walter Scott's *Ivanhoe*. But fast-forward to 2013, and for some reason the Templars are everywhere. Promotional stands in bookshops buckle under the weight of credulity-busting Templar plots. Bug-eyed computer gamers, cloaked in the Templars' iconic white robes and blood red crosses, slash and parry through historical adventures of derring-do. Cruise-ships of sightseers descend on original Templar buildings. And in central London, you can now even unwind with a pint in The Knights Templar pub.

Yet the increasing popularity of the Templars is something of a mystery, because it is hard to see how or why the modern world identifies with the Order at all. The Templars were medieval monk-knights, the crack troops of the Crusades—so effective and feared on the battlefield that Saladin once famously executed all captured Templars for fear of ever having to face them again. As a sideline to fund their wars, the knights experimented with international finance. They proved so talented at it that they were soon richer than Europe's leading kings, whom they dutifully bankrolled.

They were, by anybody's standards, then or now, a startling bunch: one only the medieval world could have conceived of. It is difficult to imagine what a modern equivalent would be. Perhaps a massive international army of chaste militant Christian zealots who also happened to own most of the world's investment banks? It is hard to see how such a modern group would be remotely popular with the public. So what do people see in the Templars?

Darker interests focus on the Templars as the rallying point of a network of violent European white supremacism—a lodestar of racial hatred around which extremism can gravitate. The appeal of the Templars to extremists is probably inevitable. The Templars were founded during the Crusades, which can hardly be described as a time of religious and cultural tolerance. But the Templars are always full of surprises, and the historical record shows that even in that climate, the Templars' sworn mission was in fact to protect pilgrims and the vulnerable. Nowhere in the over 600 provisions of their medieval Rule does it ever refer to anything approaching a mandate for ideological murder of people holding a different faith.

The extremists' vision of the Templars as a kind of proto-SS ethnic extermination squad is simply ahistorical. The evidence does not bear it out. For instance, take Usamah ibn Munqidh, an adventurous twelfth-century Syrian nobleman, diplomat, and poet. He recorded that when he used to visit Jerusalem, the Templars, who were his friends, would let him into their headquarters in the Temple of Solomon (the al-Aqsa mosque), where they would clear a space for him to pray. On one occasion, a nameless European knight repeatedly seized him, and spun him so he was facing East, ordering him to pray as a Christian. The Templars quickly intervened and ejected the knight, before explaining apologetically to Usamah that the knight was fresh off the boat from Europe and new to the ways of the Orient.

Accounts like this have spawned a growing camp of people who look to the Templars' spiritual side, and see in the Order a fascinating enigma. The idea that the Templars had an alternate spirituality, perhaps even a slightly mystical one, is, interestingly, not a New Age invention. People were saying it before the Templars were closed down. The poet-knight Wolfram von Eschenbach, writing sometime between 1200 and 1225, gave the German people their first Holy Grail epic: *Parzival*. In it, he described how the Grail was kept at the castle of Munsalvaesche, guarded by a company of chaste knights called Templeise. This is the earliest association between the Templars and the magical supernatural, and predates *The Holy Blood and the Holy Grail* crowd by at least seven-and-a-half centuries.

The other ancient association of the Templars with the supernatural is perhaps better known, but sadly more garbled. It was reported by medieval chroniclers that as the flames of the funeral pyre began to lick at Jacques de Molay, he prophesied that within a year the king and pope (who had together effectively destroyed the Templars and condemned him to a heretic's death) would meet him before God's celestial tribunal, where they would be judged for their corruption. Although both men died within the year, the story of Jacques de Molay's 'curse' seems to have been embellished from his actual words, which may have been a simpler threat that God would avenge his unjust death.

Nevertheless, versions of this legend are widespread, and have long added to the Templars' mystique. Although all King Philip's public statements on the Templars were steeped in a viscous piety and an endlessly-repeated desire to act as the Church's protector, the reality was the magnetic opposite. His 'inquiry' was, in fact, a brutal persecution, which involved seven years of barbarous incarcerations, horrific tortures, and multiple burnings at the stake. Philip was not remotely motivated by religion, despite his sanctimonious flannel. His coffers were filled with nothing but dust and air, and he urgently needed eye-watering sums of money to fuel his appetite for European wars. At the same time, pope-baiting was high on his list of hobbies, and he clearly felt that destroying the Vatican's invincible army would be a distinct milestone in his effort to position France as the dominant power in Europe.

Unsurprisingly, it was fashionable for many years to see the Templars as the wholly innocent victims of Philip's squalid politics. Philip was indeed shameless in the way he hurled as many charges at the Templars as he thought were necessary to whip up public outrage and disgust. He was an experienced master at the all-important game of spin, having garnered support against the previous pope using the identical charges of heresy and homosexuality. It had worked magnificently on that occasion—his men even kidnapped the elderly pope, and when the old cleric died of shock, Philip insisted on a posthumous trial to prove the trumped-up charges against the dead pope. So there is no doubt that Philip was a gifted bully—a spectacularly unscrupulous manipulator with no concern at how much blood needed spilling for him to get his way.

However, there are always twists in the tail when it comes to the Templars, and it seems Philip may have found a tiny ember of genuine Templar heresy, which he deftly fanned into a fire big enough to consume the Order.

A detailed reading of the complicated sequence of confessions and retractions made by both the rank-and-file knights and the leaders of the Order leaves little doubt that the Templars were up to something. King Philip's allegations of them worshipping a head that could make trees flower and the land germinate were plainly fabricated, and no evidence of anything remotely related was ever unearthed. Likewise, his accusations of institutionalized homosexuality proved to be invented. But many knights, including Jacques de Molay and some of his most senior lieutenants, did openly admit, at times with no torture, that new members of the Order were pulled aside in private after their monastic reception ceremonies and asked to deny Christ and spit on a crucifix. None of the knights could give an explanation why this was done. They said it had simply always been a tradition, and that the new brother usually complied *ore sed non corde*, with the mouth but not the heart.

After so many centuries, we can only guess at the bizarre ritual's significance. It may originally have been a character test to get some idea of how the new recruit might react if captured and subjected to religious pressure. But no one can say for sure. Nevertheless, it does clearly demonstrate that the Templars were subversive when they wanted. In fact, the clearest evidence that the Templars were not all they seemed is largely unknown, even among Templar experts. But it is potentially extraordinarily important. It takes the form of an original Templar building, still standing, nestled in a quiet corner of green countryside. Inside, it contains an enigma that may yet cause experts to revisit the entire question of the Templars' religious beliefs.

It is not Rosslyn Chapel in Scotland, which has no Templar connections at all, having been built a century and a half after the Order was suppressed. Instead, it is a small mid-twelfth-century chapel in the village of Montsaunès, set in the foothills of the French Pyrenees, on one of the principal medieval highways leading from France into Spain. It was in a critical location. The fight to wrest Spain back from Islam was in full flow, and Montsaunès was on a strategic defensive line. Surviving medieval charters prove beyond doubt that the chapel was unquestionably built by the Templars, then occupied and maintained by the Order for 150 years. It was the heart of one the Order's great European commanderies (fortified monasteries), although nothing else of it survives.

The reason for its importance to the question of Templar spirituality is immediately apparent the moment you enter the ancient building. The whole interior is painted, as most medieval churches and cathedrals were. But the Templars' chosen decorations for this particular chapel were not saints, bible scenes, and the usual range of religious imagery. The surviving frescoes are a bizarre collection of stars and wheels, rolling around the walls and ceiling in some mysterious, unfathomable pattern. Interspersed among them are also grids and chequer-boards, painted with equal precision—but also with no apparent sense or meaning. There is nothing remotely Christian about it. The overall effect is calendrical and astrological, with a whiff of the Qabbalistic. It is like some strange hermetic temple, whose meaning is obscured to all except initiates.

The conclusion of the few experts in medieval art who have looked at the frescoes is that they are unlike anything else they have ever seen. They are 'unknown esoteric decoration'. Anyone studying the startling paintings quickly realizes that they transcend the small French commune where they remain unnoticed, 850 years on. They demand answers. What did they mean to the Knights Templar? Why did they paint them so meticulously? And what prompted them to put them in their chapel, the building at the heart of their spiritual life, which they entered to pray in nine times a day?

We simply do not know the answers. But the chapel at Montsaunès is proof, in its own enigmatic way that the religious life of the Templars was not as straightforward as we have perhaps come to believe. As Umberto Eco's lunatics, and a growing swathe of more ordinary people, prepare to mark the anniversary of Jacques de Molay's death, there will be discussions about individual freedom and the abuse of power, about political show trials and miscarriages of justice, and about Europe's transition from theocracy to autocracy. But there will also be time to think again about what knowledge went up in flames with Jacques de Molay, and to the grave with the other knights.

The little-known chapel at Montsaunès reminds us that there is much we still do not know about the Templars, who increasingly baffle us the more we discover about them.

15

A stain on history: the burning of Jacques de Molay, Grand Master of the Knights Templar

Many people know that the Knights Templar were abolished amid accusations of heresy, idolatry, murder, fornication, and homosexuality. But few people are aware quite how ruthless and devious the king of France was in falsely pinning these 'crimes' onto the crusading knights. This piece was written for the anniversary of Jacques de Molay's execution, which brought the sordid affair to a close.

The fall of Acre in 1291 was one of the defining battles of the medieval world. As the Mamluks smashed down the city's walls, Christendom's 195-year experiment with crusading crashed into the sea along with the vast blocks of defensive masonry.

When the overwhelming forces of Sultan al-Ashraf Khalil massed around the city, most dignitaries fled by sea, leaving only the Templars and a crowd of terrified civilians. The Templars' Grand Master fell fighting, so a senior Templar, Peter de Severy, went to the sultan to surrender on condition the civilians were given safe passage to Cyprus. The sultan agreed, but when the Templars opened the city's gates, the attackers began committing atrocities against the women and children. The Templars immediately slammed the gates shut and loaded the panic-stricken civilians onto their remaining ships. Then, with their last transports gone, they turned to face the enemy. The sultan called for de Severy to come to his camp again so he could apologize. When de Severy arrived, there was no apology. Instead, the sultan had him beheaded in full sight of the Templars on Acre's walls.

The Templars defended Acre for as long as they could. But the result was never in question. The city fell, and the Holy Land would not come under Christian rule again until Britain and her imperial allies took it in 1917. The fall of medieval crusader Acre was a seismic moment in European history. As late as 1853, the Royal Navy commemorated it with a ship—the HMS St Jean d'Acre.

There were barely any survivors. But a man named Jacques de Molay was almost certainly one. Before long, the Templars elected him their Grand Master.

To the local Latin Christians, the Templars were heroes. But when the knights returned to Europe, they suffered the fate of many of history's soldiers.

Two millennia earlier, when Odysseus finally reached Ithaca after a decade fighting at Troy and another battling his way home, he barely recognized the society he found. And, more tragically, few recognized him through his beggar's clothes (save for his faithful Argos, who only had the strength to wag his tail before dying).

American soldiers returning from Vietnam faced a similarly disconnected homecoming. And so did Jacques de Molay and the last crusaders. Europe had moved on, and the battles they had bled for no longer seemed valued by most of the people or rulers in whose name they had fought.

Today's 700-year anniversary of the burning of Jacques de Molay, last Grand Master of the Knights Templar, marks one of history's most vivid and poignant stories of the discarded soldier.

For two centuries, the Templars waged the bloody wars for Christian Jerusalem that Europe's people demanded. But when the defeated crusaders came home, early 1300s Europe was preparing for Dante, Giotto, Marco Polo, Petrarch, Boccaccio, de Machaut, Chaucer, and a world of new discoveries. There was no room for knights bent on recapturing an oriental desert 3,000 miles away.

On Thursday the 12th of October 1307, de Molay was an honoured pall bearer in Paris at the royal funeral of the titular Empress of Constantinople, sister-in-law of King Philip IV of France. But the following dawn—Friday the 13th of October—King Philip's men kicked in the doors of the Templars' commanderies all over France, and arrested all but a handful who evaded capture. (It is still popularly believed that these arrests are why Friday the 13th is unlucky.)

Philip charged the Templars with offences designed to scandalize and horrify the public: denying Christ, spitting on the crucifix, idol worship, blasphemy, and obscenity. He struggled to believe it himself, he said, but his priority was to protect the fabric of Christendom. It was:

> *A bitter thing, a lamentable thing, a thing which is horrible to contemplate, terrible to hear of, a detestable crime, an execrable evil, an abominable work, a detestable disgrace, a thing almost inhuman, an offence to the divine majesty, a universal scandal. (Philip IV, arrest order)*

Naturally, Philip had invented most of the charges, along with his phony remorse, as he needed to get people heated up in order to drown out the papacy's inevitable outrage at such a blatant and unprovoked attack on the Church.

Nevertheless, Philip was feeling confident. He had played the game well. Pope Clement V could huff and puff, but Philip had wangled the papal throne for the untalented Clement two years earlier, so the rules of cronyism applied. None of this was lost on Dante, who railed against Clement's toadying to Philip, his lust for power, nepotism, and simony. He accused Clement of being a lawless shepherd, of turning his office into a *cloaca del sangue e de la puzza* (sewer of blood and stink), and he specifically saved a place for him in *Malebolge*, the eighth circle of Hell.

When Clement heard of the arrests, he was furious at the full-frontal attack on his sovereignty. But he had no room for manoeuvre. So, rather than confront Philip (as Gregory VII or Boniface VIII would have), he opted to salve his wounded pride by trying to take charge of the matter.

As October ran into November, the French Templars were tortured mercilessly. Virtually all (including de Molay) confessed to Philip's charges. Vindicated and flushed with self-righteousness, Philip wrote to the kings of Europe, inviting them to follow his most pious example.

Over in England, King Edward II was in no mood to play Philip's cynical game. He knew and liked Jacques de Molay, and the Templars had served England and its kings with distinction. Instead, Edward went onto the attack, writing to Europe's kings to rubbish Philip's claims.

Meanwhile, in his attempt to steer events, Clement issued the bull *Pastoralis praeeminentiae* ordering Europe's kings to arrest all Templars in the name of the pope.

In England, Edward felt he ought to comply, but had no real appetite for it. He gave the Order two weeks' notice of the arrests, before rounding up a few Templars and relocating them to comfortable lodgings, while leaving the remainder in their commanderies.

Back in France, Clement dispatched cardinals to interview de Molay and a key lieutenant. To King Philip's horror, now the two knights were talking to the pope's men and not royal goons, they promptly withdrew their confessions and confirmed the Order was innocent of Philip's charges.

Emboldened, Clement suspended the enquiries. Incensed, Philip threatened Clement with violence, and insisted he reopen the enquiries. Clement eventually acquiesced, and announced that final judgement would be given in October 1310 at Vienne.

However, Philip was too experienced to attack on a single front alone. To keep the pressure on, Philip forced Clement to move the whole papal court to Avignon. This was the infamous 'Babylonian Captivity' (1309–77), in which seven French popes ruled from Avignon in an environment so luridly described by Petrarch.

To leave Clement in no doubt who was boss, Philip also forced him to open a posthumous trial into Pope Boniface VIII, who had died from shock a few years earlier after Philip's men had violently kidnapped him. Philip's lawyers even drafted the usual trumped-up charges: heresy, idolatry, homicide, simony, fornication, and sodomy.

In London, Edward was still not taking the charges seriously. The Inquisition had never set foot in England, but on Pope Clement's insistence, two French inquisitors arrived in September 1309 and began examining the Templars in London, York, and Lincoln. No confessions were forthcoming, as even though the inquisitors eventually forced Edward to allow them to use torture, they could find no skilled or willing torturers.

In a request with a familiar and sinister post-9/11 ring, they asked to transfer the English Templars to the County of Ponthieu in Picardy, which was an English crown possession but subject to French law. There, they explained, they would be on English land, but free to apply as much torture as they needed. Edward refused.

Back in France, Clement wanted to talk to de Molay, who was now at the French royal castle at Chinon. However, de Molay was too weakened by the prolonged torture to travel, so Clement sent three cardinals to interview him. It was here, in the Loire valley, that the cardinals drew up the so-called 'Chinon parchment', which provoked such excitement when discovered in the Vatican's Secret Archives in 2001. (The archives are not actually secret. *Secretum* means 'private' in the sense of belonging to the pope rather than any specific Vatican department.) However, despite the hype, the parchment's content has always been known from other documents.

It records that five of the most senior Templars, including de Molay, with no torture, of their own free will, all openly and voluntarily confessed.

However, what really matters is exactly *what* they admitted. Sadly for the conspiracy theorists, it is not much. They said that new Templar recruits were pulled aside after their ceremonies. Geoffroi de Gonneville gave a description:

> *His receptor, after bestowing the mantle of the Knights Templar upon the newly received member, showed him a cross depicted in some book and said that he should denounce the one whose image was depicted on that cross. When the newly received did not want to do so, the receptor told him multiple times that he should. And since he completely refused to do it, the receptor, seeing his resistance, said to him: 'Will you swear to me that if asked by any of the brothers you would say that you had made this denouncement, provided that I*

allow you not to make it?' And the newly received answered 'yes'.
He also said that the receptor told him that he should spit on the
aforementioned cross. When he did not wish to do so, the receptor
placed his own hand over the depiction of the cross and said, 'At
least spit on my hand!' And since the initiate feared that the receptor
would remove his hand and some of the spit would get on the cross,
he did not want to spit on the hand, but instead chose to spit near the
cross. (Chinon parchment, 1308)

This bizarre tradition may have been part of some long-forgotten
character test or psychological preparation for capture. Geoffroi de
Gonneville had two suggestions of his own. He had heard the denial
was in imitation of St Peter. Or that a former Grand Master had been
captured by the enemy, and a condition of his release was that he
introduce this ritual—as a humiliation, and a foretaste of what awaited
any captured Templar.

Whatever the extraordinary tradition's origin and function, de
Molay and the others confessed to it and begged forgiveness from
the cardinals, who granted them absolution and reconciled them to
the Church.

We will never know what truly happened at Chinon. Maybe the
senior Templars made up these small admissions in order to gain
absolution? Or maybe they knew that professing innocence would
lead to their execution as relapsed heretics? Alternatively, perhaps
the cardinals made it up, either to implicate the Templars or to
prevent them from relapsing? Who knows. The following year de
Molay insisted that he had not confessed to anything serious at
Chinon. And, most oddly, one of the others confessed to seeing the
famous idol (usually known as Baphomet) at Montpellier, which
almost certainly takes the parchment into the realm of fantasy. The
only question is: whose?

Towards the end of the year, something very significant began to
happen. Slowly, the Templars started to fight back. One by one, they
withdrew their blood-soiled admissions. By May, some 600 Templars

had withdrawn their confessions. Sensing no end in sight, Clement postponed final judgement at Vienne by a year.

In Paris, King Philip immediately saw that the tide was turning against him, and that he needed to do something decisive. He therefore summoned the bishop of Sens and forced him to re-examine the Templars in his diocese. When 54 Templars insisted on their innocence, the bishop dutifully denounced them as relapsed heretics.

As Philip had known all along, a heretic who confessed was welcomed as a lost sheep, given penance, and reconciled to the Church. But if the penitent then slipped back into the heresy, he had rejected all grace, spurned salvation, and was a direct threat to Christian society.

On the 12th of May 1310, as Philip knew he would, the bishop of Sens burned the 54 Templars alive. This appalling cruelty gave Philip the shot in the arm he needed. The remaining Templar resistance petered out.

The sorry tale was drawing to a close. In October 1311, the long-awaited Council of Vienne opened to give final judgement. The evidence did not amount to much. The only Templars who had comprehensively confessed to Philip's 127 charges were the ones tortured in his dungeons or those in territories loyal to him. There were virtually no confessions from abroad.

True to form, Philip showed up to threaten Clement with physical violence unless he shut down the Templars. There were protests from the other church delegates, who felt the Templars had not been given an opportunity to defend themselves. They also pointed to the suspicious similarity of the charges with those Philip had recently brought against the dead Pope Boniface VIII. None of this helped Clement, who threatened anyone who spoke further with excommunication.

Finally clear to impose Philip's will, in March 1312, with Philip and his son flanking him, Clement issued the bull *Vox in excelso*. Citing the irreparable damage done to the Templars' reputation, he pronounced judgement with a formula that completely sidestepped the question of innocence or guilt:

> We suppress, with the approval of the sacred council, the order
> of Templars, and its rule, habit and name, by an inviolable and

perpetual decree, and we entirely forbid that anyone from now on enter the order, or receive or wear its habit, or presume to behave as a Templar. (Clement V, Vox in excelso)

It was over. All that remained was to tie up the loose ends. Templars who had confessed crimes were sentenced to imprisonment. Those who had remained silent were sent to other religious Orders.

To draw down the final curtain, on the 18th of March 1314 the four most senior living Templars were hauled to Paris. On a rostrum erected on the parvis before the great cathedral of Notre-Dame, they were publicly condemned to perpetual imprisonment. Hugues de Pairaud and Geoffroi de Gonneville accepted the sentences in silence. But Jacques de Molay and Geoffroi de Charney stunned the crowd by talking over the cardinals and professing their innocence and that of the Temple.

The electrifying news was rushed across the city to King Philip at the Louvre. Desperate to crush this dangerous new defiance, he abandoned all legal procedures and ordered the two old Templars to be burned without delay.

So as dusk fell and the canons of Notre-Dame lit the candles and incense for the *lucernare* before Vespers, the provost of Paris's men torched two nearby pyres and sent de Molay and de Pairaud up in smoke alongside the canons' prayers.

A royal chaplain eyewitness described de Molay's last words (in verse):

'God knows who is in the wrong and has sinned. Misfortune will soon befall those who have wrongly condemned us; God will avenge our deaths. Make no mistake, all who are against us will suffer because of us. I beseech you to turn my face towards the Virgin Mary, of whom our Lord Christ was born.' His request was granted, and so gently was he taken by death that everyone marvelled. (Geoffroi de Paris, Chronicle)

Rumours began to circulate that, at the end, de Molay had also shouted out, summoning Philip and Clement to meet him within a year and a day before God, where they would be judged for their crimes.

De Molay and de Pairaud quickly came to be seen as martyrs. In the cold dawn light, Parisians foraged in the pyres' ashes for relics. Medieval writers took up the popular outrage. Dante accused King Philip of undermining Christendom. A Tuscan chronicler even declared that the abolition of the Templars was one of the leading causes of the Black Death.

It had taken Philip seven years, but he finally had what he wanted—the Templars' vast treasury he had coveted for so long, and a demonstration that he could destroy one of the Church's most powerful organizations. But, as it turned out, he did not live to enjoy either victory.

Clement and Philip were both dead within the year. The 'curse' of Jacques de Molay had been fulfilled.

De Molay's death was more than just the brutal execution of a 72-year-old soldier. It was the culmination of a cynical, politically-orchestrated miscarriage of justice masterminded by a ruthless king and facilitated by a craven pope—both of whom owed de Molay and the Templars far better.

If de Molay had ever learned the skills of high politics, he may have saved his Order. But he was a simple monk and soldier who trusted in authority and the chain of command—believing up to the end that the pope would come through for them. He relied on the notion, as soldiers do, that on coming home from fighting the battles he had been ordered into, his masters would recognize and respect his contributions.

Today should perhaps stand as a national day to remember former members of the armed forces. Not a memorial for the fallen, but for the living—those who are all too often written off as having fought yesterday's conflicts. It is easy for observers to look back over history and exercise twenty-twenty hindsight, judging which conflicts were just and worthwhile and which were not. But perhaps on 'De Molay Day' we can recognize that many in the armed forces do not have the luxury of this choice. And there should be an appropriate time to remember that.

16

The Turin Shroud is one of the greatest medieval artworks ever created

The Turin Shroud is the most famous and controversial holy object in Christianity. This piece was written to coincide with one of its rare exhibitions to the public, and it analyses all the known evidence about what the Shroud is, and how it was made.

Last week something rather unusual happened in the quiet Italian city of Turin.

Inside the fifteenth-century cathedral, an ancient, stained, and burned piece of medieval linen was removed from its airtight, bulletproof case and put on display. The exhibition will last 67 days.

Last time the intensely controversial textile was brought out, in 2010, over 2.5 million people poured into the cathedral to see it. Or, more precisely, to see the images on the ivory-coloured fabric, which seem to depict faint life-size brown impressions of the front and back of a man.

The details of the sepia images are rather indistinct, and it was only in 1898, when a lawyer named Secondo Pia photographed the cloth, that the world was able to see the man's horrific injuries, which showed up extraordinarily clearly on Pia's photographic negatives.

The Catholic Church has made no miraculous claims for the object. Pope John Paul II called it 'a mirror of the Gospel', while Popes Benedict XVI and Francis have described it as 'an icon'.

So, from a historical and scientific perspective: what is the shroud— and what isn't it?

The history of the long sheet falls into two categories: what is known, and what people have speculated.

Our first definite knowledge of the shroud is an event in around AD 1355, when it was put on show in the tiny French village of Lirey, in Champagne. Its owners were the local knight, Geoffrey de Charney, and his wife, Jeanne de Vergy.

Despite the insistence of the conspiracy brigade, there is no known connection between this Geoffrey de Charney (or his son of the same name) and the famous Knight Templar called Geoffrey de Charney, who was preceptor of Normandy and was burned alongside Grand Master Jacques de Molay as a relapsed heretic in 1314, three quarters of a century earlier.

At the time of the 1355 exhibition, Henry de Poitiers, bishop of Troyes, conducted an inquiry into the cloth, concluding that it was a 'fraud' which had been 'cunningly painted, the truth being attested by the artist who had painted it, to wit, that it was a work of human skill and not miraculously wrought or bestowed'.

Nothing more is known of this episcopal enquiry, but in 1389 one of Henry's direct successors, Bishop Peter d'Arcis, wrote to Antipope Clement VII in Avignon to tell him of Bishop Henry's enquiry, and to complain that the linen was being displayed again. It seems that Peter did not succeed in getting the exhibition closed down, as Clement replied that he was happy for the cloth to be shown as 'an image or representation' of the true shroud.

After around 60 years of being moved about, in 1453 Geoffrey's granddaughter, Margaret, finally passed the shroud to the ducal house of Savoy, who took it to their capital at Chambéry in the Alps.

Nothing much happened for almost 80 years, until disaster struck on the night of the 4th of December 1532, when a fire broke out in the chapel where it was kept behind the high altar in a silver casket housed in a niche sealed with a metal grille. The keyholder could not be found, so a blacksmith and two friars broke open the grille, but part of the casket had already liquefied, and drops of molten silver had fallen onto the shroud, burning holes straight through it, which a team of Poor Clare nuns then repaired with the patching that can still be seen.

The remaining history is uneventful. The linen was eventually moved to Turin, where it has stayed ever since. Then, on the 18th of March 1983, Umberto II of Savoy died, and in his will, quite unexpectedly, passed the shroud out of his family, gifting it to the pope and his successors.

These, broadly, are the known facts.

Everything before 1355 is speculation. For instance, people have put forward claims that the shroud was once known as the 'Image of Edessa' (sometimes called the 'Mandylion') before it was moved to Constantinople, where it was seen in 1204 by the crusader Robert de Clari at the church of My Lady St Mary of Blachernae, before being secretly brought back to Europe by the Templar, Geoffrey de Charney.

There is, in fact, not a shred of evidence for any of this, and history contradicts most of it. For instance, the Templars did not take part in the 1204 siege of Constantinople, and Geoffrey de Charney the Templar lived a hundred years later.

More outlandish writers have claimed the cloth as the death shroud of the last Templar Grand Master, James de Molay, or even that it was made by Leonardo da Vinci. However, nothing approaching evidence has ever been adduced for any of these sensationalist theories. For example, de Molay was burned to death not crucified, and da Vinci was not born until 1452, a hundred years after the shroud was first exhibited in Lirey.

All in all, the historical evidence clearly points to a provable provenance starting in the mid-1300s.

So much for the historical data. In more recent times, scientists have also been able to add their opinions.

They are agreed what the object is: a linen sheet approximately 14'3" long and 3'7" wide, depicting the front and back images of a man who is around 5'7" tall.

The most obvious question science can answer is how old the material is.

After much toing and froing, the shroud was finally carbon dated in 1988 under the supervision of the British Museum. Laboratories in

Oxford, Tucson, and Zurich were each sent a 40-gram section the size of a postage stamp, along with three control samples. The laboratories worked entirely independently of each other, and when the results were in, they all concurred, providing 95 per cent confidence in a date range of AD 1260–1390.

For most people, this carbon-14 science finally established objective and definitive proof the linen can confidently be dated to the High Middle Ages.

However, a number of dissenting voices have since emerged. They have not suggested the science was faulty, but rather that all three samples tested were cut from the same area on the border of the cloth, which may be unrepresentative of the whole. For instance, they propose that the border may have been extensively repaired following the fire in 1532, or that the area may have bacterial contamination because it is where the shroud has most commonly been handled. However, overall, there have been no serious or convincing challenges to the carbon dating, and none have demonstrated in a laboratory that they are more than speculative theories.

Zooming in, scientists have also looked in detail at the physical characteristics of the image on the cloth.

In 1976, two American scientists fed a photograph of the shroud into a computer capable of generating isometric projections (brightness maps) to turn two-dimensional images into something approximating three-dimensional ones. When an ordinary photograph of a face was fed into the computer, the algorithm produced a garbled isometric projection because photographs lack sufficient information of depth and distance. However, to the operators' surprise, the photograph of the shroud's head produced the recognizable profile of a human face.

The two men were sufficiently intrigued to pull together a team of around 40 American scientists who named themselves the Shroud of Turin Research Project, or STURP. It included experts from NASA's Jet Propulsion Laboratory, the US Air Force Weapons Laboratories, the Los Alamos National (nuclear) Laboratories, the US Air Force Academy, IBM, Lockheed, the Brooks Institute of Photography, and other organizations with skills ranging from medicine to oceanographic computer imaging.

They applied for permission to examine the linen, and in 1978 were granted five days access to the shroud to conduct experiments on it.

The team worked around the clock, subjecting the cloth to black-and white, colour, ultraviolet and infrared photography, fluorescence, microscope magnification, spectrophotometry, thermography, UV-visible reflectance, X-ray fluorescence, and a battery of other tests. STURP published its findings in 1981, concluding that the image depicts, in accurate detail, a man tortured and crucified in the way the gospels describe.

There are multiple bloody puncture wounds in a ring around the head consistent with a crown of thorns. The man's back, buttocks, and calves are covered with over 100 small dumbbell-shaped lacerations consistent with whipping or scourging with a Roman *flagrum*. And the man's right side has a puncture wound consistent with an injury from a Roman spear tip.

In addition, there are, of course, the telltale marks of crucifixion.

Surprisingly, the image seems to show that the man depicted was crucified through the wrists, which flatly contradicts nearly two thousand years of religious art. In this, osteoarchaeology does not help much in understanding the wider picture, as victims of Roman crucifixions were usually left to rot on the cross, or taken down and either fed to wild animals or thrown onto the communal rubbish tip. Consequently, there are almost no skeletons of Roman crucifixion victims for scientists to use as comparisons. However, in 1968, archaeologists found parts of 'Yehohanan', who was crucified by the Romans in first-century Palestine, and the revealing feature of his remains was that the heavy iron crucifixion nail was not driven through Yehohanan's foot, but directly through his heel bone. While this may seem surprising, there is a growing modern body of opinion that the Romans crucified victims through a number of places on the body, with nails or rope, and on a variety of stakes, crosses, and even trees.

Regarding the physical (as opposed to visual) properties of the image, the STURP team found themselves baffled. They concluded that the image is only microns thick on the outer surface of the linen, and does not penetrate the textile's fibres the way paint, pigment, stain, or dye does. They reported that the image was more like a slight discolouration of the very top surface of the linen's fibres, as if by 'oxidation, dehydration and conjugation of the polysaccharide structure of the microfibrils of the linen itself'. They also concluded that what appear to be blood flows emanating from the many wounds are genuine blood containing haemoglobin and serum albumin.

For many people, STURP's conclusions constitute hard scientific evidence that a man crucified in the way described in the gospels had somehow been involved in the creation of the image on the linen.

However, as with the carbon dating, there were dissenting voices.

Critics pointed to various religious affiliations of some STURP members, claiming that their beliefs biased their findings. If this is true, then we are not left with much reliable science about the shroud, as there has been no other major investigation of it since.

There was also open scientific dissent at the time. For instance, Walter McCrone, a chemist and microscope expert, was initially associated with STURP, but broke away when he and STURP reached different conclusions. Specifically, his microscope analysis revealed the presence of red ochre and vermilion tempera, which he maintained demonstrated that the shroud was the work of an artist. However, McCrone's work has in turn come in for criticism as the paint residue was distributed over the whole cloth—including the blank parts—but everywhere in quantities too minute to be related to the actual image. His opponents maintain that what McCrone found was residue from the cloth having been in contact with painted objects such as storage boxes, or even other painted replica shrouds which were rubbed on it as a blessing.

Among all this assertion and negation, the most significant fact about the image—and one that, uniquely, is not disputed by anyone—is that the combination of all the image's elements have proved very hard to replicate. Scientists and artists have worked overtime to recreate the image, and have shown no lack of imagination, using corpses, herbs, spices, paint, metal, cameras, projectors, radiation, explosive releases of energy, the list is endless. Yet, bafflingly, none has yet been deemed a satisfactory success.

This particular area of sindonology (shroud studies) is perhaps the most fertile at present, with new theories coming regularly. For instance, in late 2011, a team of Italian scientists concluded that the image may have been made using ultraviolet lasers or radiation, while in 2014 a different team of Italian scientists announced that the Jerusalem earthquake of AD 33, estimated at 8.2 on the Richter scale, may have released neutron particles capable of creating an X-ray image and throwing off the results of any subsequent carbon dating.

So, to sum up the scientific evidence: the 1981 STURP team concluded that the image is of a man who was whipped and crucified, that the cloth has real blood on it, and that the technique used to create the image remains unknown. Seven years later, the carbon dating tests gave a confident result of AD 1260–1390.

Leaving the science for a moment and moving to wider historical questions, it is interesting to note that the gospels of Luke and John specify Christ was crucified through the hands, which is inconsistent with the shroud. Furthermore, although the synoptic gospels refer to 'a linen cloth', John states Christ was wrapped in 'linen strips' and a separate head cloth, which is not consistent with a complete image on one single sheet of linen. None of them mention any of the linen bearing an image, and nor is there any cult of such a cloth in the early Church.

Putting that in a historical context, eminent Romans like the Emperor Constantine and Empress Helena were avid archaeologists with a strong interest in tracking down sacred objects associated with Christ's life. Their passion for relics was shared by monarchs for most of the medieval period, for whom anything touched by Christ was a grade-one relic to be displayed with the best that money could buy, like Louis IX of France's exquisite Sainte Chapelle in Paris, built exclusively to house the crown of thorns.

However, no Roman, Byzantine, or medieval monarch seems to have been aware of the shroud, and the difficulty with claiming it dates from the first century AD is that there is no credible evidence for where it was during the 1,320 years following the crucifixion. Moreover, even once it surfaced in France around 1355, it made very little stir, with no interest from the French royal family or the pope, strongly suggesting they did not believe it to be genuine.

All the credible evidence points to the shroud being a medieval object. Even just looking at it, the face has identifiably elongated medieval proportions, entirely consistent with the figures of Jesus, John the Baptist, or Old Testament prophets that stare down at us from medieval buildings.

The gruesome detail of the shroud does, in fact, fit perfectly into the late medieval mindset. If you wander around a Gothic cathedral, you will sooner or later come across the giant effigies of nobles and bishops that are no longer resplendent in their fine robes or badges of office, but instead depicted as emaciated skeletons, rotting in agony. This was, after all, the period of the first Black Death (1347–51), when a third of Europe died suddenly, and the task of burying entire families and villages became a grim reality. For entirely understandable reasons, art followed life in these 'cadaver tombs', then in *danse macabre* images of revelling skeletons, and finally even in harrowing religious crucifixion paintings depicting a suffering, emaciated, and bloodied Christ.

The detailed knowledge of the human body available to modern scientists may be relatively recent, but brilliant, inquisitive, ambitious human minds have always been with us—in the ancient and medieval worlds as much as today. There is no reason to exclude the possibility of an artist experimenting with cadavers in order to understand the physiology of death and post mortem blood flows from wounds. Ancient Greek sculptors were meticulous in their depiction of every vein and artery. In the 1400s, Leonardo da Vinci filled his sketchbooks with anatomical drawings of flayed body parts. Caravaggio reportedly used a drowned prostitute as his model for the 'Death of the Virgin' (1606). And Géricault studied dead bodies for his 'Raft of the Medusa' (1819). So why should anyone discount the idea that a talented medieval artist went to obsessive lengths to recreate the burial shroud of a crucified man?

And here is where we come face to face with our cultural arrogance, which assumes that because we cannot understand every detail of how the image on the shroud was created, then it could not have been made by people in the past, whom we assume—against all the evidence— were crude and barbarous.

The Turin Shroud does not have to date to the first century to be an object of fascination and inspiration. If it truly is the work of a medieval artist—which the historical, scientific, and visual evidence all suggest it is—then it is a genuine wonder that brings us into the presence of the genius of the medieval world, and gives us insight into an exceptional artistic mind that created one of the most graphic and emotional visualizations ever made of the dreadful injuries that Roman-style execution can inflict on a body.

17

Regicide and ambition: Richard III and the death of the 'princes' in the Tower

A skeleton identified as King Richard III was found under a car park in Leicester. This piece looks at what we know of how Richard III took the English throne, and the fate of the child king, Edward V, and his younger brother, imprisoned by Richard in the Tower of London.

Late Tudor England was a lethal environment for the politically unwary, with errors of judgment frequently resulting in a one-way trip to Tyburn. Fortunately, Shakespeare knew the rules of the game well. When he brought out Richard III, he was keenly aware that his arch villain was not some random monarch from a bygone age—Richard was the last Plantagenet king of England, whose throne Henry Tudor (Henry VII) had seized in battle at Bosworth Field a century earlier.

For obvious reasons, the Tudors were a little sensitive when it came to Richard. Their preferred line was that he was depravity incarnate, which ensured everyone could remain grateful to Henry Tudor for having prised him off the throne.

Naturally, there were plenty of Tudor writers willing to cooperate. Take the chronicler John Rous (c. 1420–92) who swiftly stopped praising Richard as a 'good Lord' when Henry VII was crowned, and instead recalled how Richard had taken two years to gestate before eventually being born with teeth, long hair to his shoulders, and a hunchback. Sir Thomas More, Raphael Holinshed, and others carried on in much the same vein. But it was Shakespeare who created the

Richard that would become burned into our collective memory—'the son of Hell', a monomaniac murderous psychotic who 'know'st no law of God nor man'.

However, among the many bloody deeds Shakespeare laid at Richard's door—some genuine, many not—the most notorious is undoubtedly the murder of the two young 'Princes in the Tower'. (Actually, 'princes' is a bit of an understatement. One of them was the reigning king of England.)

So, when the mitred clerics solemnly pray over Richard III's mangled skull and bones in Leicester on the 25th of March, will the nation be reinterring a much maligned and worthy king, or a monstrous tyrant guilty of infanticide and regicide?

The facts are straightforward.

King Edward IV—Richard's older brother—died unexpectedly at Windsor on the 9th of April 1483. Edward IV's eldest son was Edward Prince of Wales, and over a decade earlier the lords had pledged him their allegiance as the next lawful sovereign.

Unfortunately, when Edward IV died, his heir was only 12, which triggered the provision in Edward IV's will that Richard should govern as Lord Protector until the young prince reached his majority at 14. However, Edward IV's widow, Queen Elizabeth—from the increasingly powerful Woodville family—had other plans, and arranged for her son swiftly to be proclaimed as Edward V, with the coronation set for the 4th of May.

Richard viewed the move as tantamount to squeezing him out to ensure the young king was surrounded by Woodvilles. Richard was not having any of it. Although he openly swore allegiance to the new Edward V, he unexpectedly seized the King at Stony Stratford in early May, arrested some of his Woodville advisers as a warning shot to the Queen, and brought the boy under escort to London.

Richard swiftly settled Edward into the Tower of London—a royal palace as well as a prison—and moved the coronation back to the 22nd of June. He then openly assumed the role of Lord Protector, and started running the country in the name of King Edward V.

Then, on the 13th of June, he made more arrests and summarily executed the prominent courtier Lord Hastings, accusing him of plotting treason. The real reason is more likely to have been that Hastings was an ally of Queen Elizabeth and one of Edward V's strongest supporters.

Three days later, Richard's men persuaded Queen Elizabeth (who had taken sanctuary at Westminster Abbey) to hand over the young King's nine-year-old brother, Richard Duke of York, who was also given rooms at the Tower so that, Elizabeth was told, he could participate in his brother's coronation.

With the first and second in line to the throne now firmly under his sole control, Richard mounted his coup d'état, postponing Edward's coronation until the 9th of November, before putting it about that all Edward IV's 10 children from Queen Elizabeth were illegitimate because Edward IV had previously been engaged.

Having widely published these damaging allegations, on the 25th of June Richard executed the two leading Woodvilles he had arrested at Stony Stratford in early May, and on the 26th of June he climbed onto the King's Bench in Westminster and declared himself King Richard III. His formal coronation was held on the 6th of July.

It had all happened so fast that no one had time to mount any meaningful opposition.

Richard promptly embarked on a victory tour of his new realm, but towards the end of July he received news of a botched attempt to rescue the young brothers from the Tower. It was almost certainly an attempt by Edward V's supporters to reinstate him as king, but it was equally likely the incident that sealed the boys' gruesome fate, as no more was ever again seen or heard of either of them. They simply disappeared from history.

Contemporaries rapidly concluded that the pair were dead, as within three months opposition to Richard had coalesced around Henry Tudor, a freebooting outsider with a flimsy and tortuous claim to the throne (whose mother, alarmingly, bore him aged 13). This support for Henry would have made no sense if people believed Edward V was still alive.

Centuries later, on the 17th of July 1674, an elm box was discovered in the Tower, buried beneath 10 feet of rubbish under a staircase leading to the chapel of the White Tower. Inside it were two children's skeletons. Excitement mounted, as the location broadly corresponded with where Sir Thomas More had reported that, years earlier, Sir James Tyrell, a retainer of Richard's, had confessed that the murdered boys had first been buried.

The grisly find was made known to King Charles II, who ordered the bones reburied at Westminster Abbey in a tomb designed by Wren and inscribed to the memory of the 'unhappy' King Edward V and Richard Duke of York. The urn was opened in 1933 and the bones were confirmed to be those of children, but all more recent requests for scientific or DNA tests on them have been refused.

So, assuming the boys were murdered—which historians do, as does the virtually contemporary Crowland Chronicle of 1486—the key question remains unanswered after 532 years: was Richard behind the dreadful killings, or did the Tudors pin them on him for propaganda?

Cui bono? is still the starting point for murder investigators the world over, and the main beneficiary of the princes' permanent exit from the succession in 1483 was undoubtedly Richard. Not only did he have the strongest motive, but he also had the boys under his absolute control, along with a proven disregard for their entitlements and well-being. He also never made any attempt to explain publicly where they were, or what had happened to them while under his 'protection'.

Over the years, other culprits have been put forward. The most interesting is Sir James Tyrell, who was identified as the murderer by Polydore Vergil, Henry VII's historian. Later, Sir Thomas More went further, writing that shortly before Tyrell's execution in 1502, Tyrell confessed to murdering the children on Richard's orders. However, no evidence of Tyrell's supposed confession has ever been found—and More's account was written long after Tyrell's death, from a Tudor perspective, and with obvious embellishments.

Another suspect is Henry Stafford, Duke of Buckingham, who is blamed in a document of 1512 now in the College of Arms. The general assumption is that if it was him, he also was following Richard's orders.

A third potential culprit is Henry VII, who some more recent writers have suggested may have ordered the killings after he was crowned in 1485 in an attempt to extinguish all rival Plantagenet claims.

However, it is significant that none of these people faced accusations at the time, whereas there was a good deal of rumour floating about, at home and abroad, pointing at Richard.

For example, Richard was publicly denounced as the murderer at the Estates General in France as early as January 1484.

Moreover, in 1934 a book came to light written by the Italian Dominic Mancini. He had been in England at the time, noting down the gossip and conversations he overheard. He recorded that there was much talk of the princes having been done away with while under Richard's protection, and even before Richard officially usurped the throne. He also preserved the damning detail that John Argentine, the princes' physician in the Tower, said that at this time the young Edward V anticipated his impending murder daily with confession and penance.

As a final piece of evidence, Queen Elizabeth and her daughters only left the safety of sanctuary in Westminster Abbey after extracting an oath from Richard that he would not harm the girls—a clear indication that the queen feared violence from Richard against her children. In the end, she had a degree of revenge when she married her eldest daughter, Elizabeth of York, to King Henry VII less than five months after his men had slain Richard at Bosworth.

So, as the nation prepares to rebury Richard, the princes' killings remain unsolved, and speculation about the murderer's identity will no doubt enjoy a revival as the media focuses its attention on the colourful royal pomp and pageantry that will unfold next month in Leicester.

There are those who point to Richard's well-attested piety, and conclude that he simply would not have done it. Others say that if he was responsible, it was done out of a sense of duty, as he feared that the kingdom's dangerous instability would be exacerbated by an immature child king advised by the equally inexperienced Woodvilles.

Given modern scholarship, it is unarguable that Tudor writers—including Shakespeare—turned Richard into a political parody: a theatrical sociopath drunk on power and death. Much of it is blatant fabrication. He did not murder Henry VI (Edward IV did) or his son, Edward of Westminster. He was not involved in the execution of his own brother, George Duke of Clarence (although it probably was carried out by drowning him in a butt of Malmsey wine). He did not kill his wife's first husband, or end up poisoning her in order to marry again. But in the matter of the murdered Princes in the Tower, one cannot imagine there would be many lawyers lining up to argue Richard's defence on a no-win no-fee basis.

18

Reburying Richard III: is it the right body?

The skeleton of Richard III was reburied in a grand ceremony in Leicester Cathedral. Behind the scenes, many questioned whose body was actually being interred. This piece sets out the lingering doubts.

Away from the Leicester-York battle or the Anglican-Catholic liturgical debate, the biggest question about the reburial of Richard III—the most unutterable one—is whether we are even burying the right bones. The evidence, you may be surprised to learn, is very far from clear.

The way you normally hear it is that the skeleton has a bent spine, is related to the House of York, died violently, and was buried in Grey Friars, the lost church of Leicester. Therefore, it is Richard.

However, there are major—and I do mean major—problems with this.

Richard died in 1485, but the two carbon dating tests performed on his bones gave dates of 1430–60 and 1412–49. These were then adjusted with a 'statistical algorithm' because he ate a lot of fish, resulting in a new range of 1475–1530. Really, you might as well stick your finger in the air.

The DNA analysis has also been controversial. The skeleton's mitochondrial DNA shows descent from the same female line as Richard. But every mother passes the same mitochondrial DNA to her sons and daughters, and her daughters pass it to their sons and daughters, and so on. Over generations and centuries, that means a large group of people in different places with different surnames.

The other usable DNA from the bones is the Y-chromosome DNA, which passes from father to son. Unfortunately, the Leicester car park bones do not have Richard's expected male-line DNA. This means either the skeleton is not Richard, or that the Plantagenet line has, at an unknown date, been broken by illegitimacy. This male-line DNA is therefore worthless, as it does not prove one way or another whether the skeleton is Richard.

Then there is the fact his DNA codes are for blond hair and blue eyes, when we know Richard almost certainly had black hair and brown eyes. Although blond hair can darken to a degree during childhood, blue eyes do not mutate into brown ones.

So the carbon dating and genetic evidence is a bit of a mess. Professor Michael Hicks, a leading Richard III scholar, has challenged Leicester University's claim that we can be 99.999 per cent certain it is Richard. The most we can conclude, he points out, is that the bones belong to someone with the same female-line DNA group as Richard. No more.

Away from the science, there are other difficult questions. Nothing actually links the bones to the Battle of Bosworth Field. In fact, the skeleton's fish-adjusted date range covers the entire Wars of the Roses as well as a number of other conflicts. Richard was a war veteran—but the bones show no healed wounds.

Nor can we know who else may have been buried at Grey Friars. Some believe that even if Richard had been buried there, his body was most likely exhumed at the Dissolution and thrown into the nearby river.

So, as we prepare for a week of royal spectacle, the sort England always does stirringly well, it is worth pausing during the pageantry to wonder if it is indeed King Richard III being given such a glittering reburial, or whether his cold, battle-scarred Plantagenet bones still lie out there, somewhere, undiscovered and unrecognized.

THE RENAISSANCE AND REFORMATION

19

Medieval al-Andalus: tolerance and totalitarianism

For nearly 800 years, Muslims ruled Andalucia in Spain. Many people look upon the period as a model of tolerance between east and west. Others see it as a time of inequality, fear, and bloodshed. This piece examines the reality, putting the great advances in knowledge into the wider context of ongoing religious division.

On the 2nd of January 1492, a 40-year-old Italian sailor stood amid the fluttering banners outside the fabled walls of Granada, and watched as Muhammad XII handed the city's keys over to King Ferdinand and Queen Isabella of Spain.

On Muhammad's ignominious ride south, as he looked back from a mountain peak now known as *el ultimo suspiro del moro* (the moor's last sigh), he wept for the 781-year old Islamic state he had lost forever.

Al-Andalus was no Muslim outpost. The Spanish Islamic society had been a quintessential part of the European continent for almost 800 years. In an English context, it was there from the time of the Venerable Bede and King Alfred, all the way through to William the Conqueror, the great medieval kings, the universities and gothic cathedrals, the guilds and ships, printed books, and finally up to Tudor England.

Muslim forces had first landed in southern Spain in AD 711 when the Berber general Tariq ibn Ziyad led his armies north from Morocco. Western history may have largely forgotten him, but he survives in the place-name Gibraltar, from *Jebel Tariq* (Tariq's rock), the staging ground where he massed his invasion force.

Memories of the Islamic state of al-Andalus are a highly emotional topic, still remembered keenly, and with polarized sentiments. In Spain, on the 2nd of January, they celebrate 1492 and the definitive completion of the *Reconquista*. Across the water in Morocco, the people remember the same event by flying black flags of mourning, and descendants of the inhabitants of Granada who left with Muhammad XII bring out keys to the properties they were forced to abandon.

The legacy of al-Andalus is hard to judge objectively.

Islamic rule in the early 700s revolutionized Visigothic Spain, bringing with it unprecedented prosperity in agriculture and mining. Commerce with North Africa and the Levant boomed. Luxuries such as silk-worms were introduced, along with never-before-seen crops like apricots, almonds, rice, and sugarcane.

The new wealth it all generated allowed the creation of some of the most striking buildings of medieval Europe.

The Alhambra in Granada is widely recognized as one of the planet's most beautiful palaces—a collection of serene galleries, courtyards, fountains, and decorated rooms that are largely unrivalled for pure sensual aesthetics. And 80 miles to the north west, the forest of iconic red and white *voussoirs* of the mosque at Cordoba is among the world's most photographed religious architecture.

Grandeur was everywhere. The now-destroyed Madinat al-Zahra palace outside Cordoba was sumptuous beyond description. Abd al-Rahman III used to enjoy welcoming visitors to its great darkened throne room, where he would spin a vast bowl of mercury on a central pedestal, while small apertures were opened in the windows to allow choreographed sunbeams to hit the mercury. The result, it is said, was like watching lightning flashing around the dark hall.

But the legacy of Moorish Spain can be measured in more than bricks, tiles, and disco balls.

Seven hundred and eighty one years is a long time—more than three times longer, for example, than the United States of America has existed.

In those eight centuries, many words seeped into European languages from Arabic, with a strong showing in science, the military, and foods—admiral, alcohol, apricot, arsenal, calipers, candy, chemistry, coffee, guitar, jar, jumper, lemon, magazine, mummy, sequin, sofa, spinach, sugar, talisman, and zero. Not to mention the most Spanish of all exclamations: *Olé!*

But al-Andalus's largest and most lasting contribution to the world was undoubtedly in the sciences and logic.

The medieval Muslims mapped the sky, leaving our modern museums with hundreds of beautiful and intricately built astrolabes—many signed by their makers in recognition of their skill and status. They also wrote the language of the stars, naming hundreds of heavenly bodies—most famously Betelgeuse, (at least, famous to readers of *The Hitchhikers Guide to the Galaxy*).

The influence of al-Andalus on western European learning was seismic. And undoubtedly the most impact was felt in the gift of Aristotle.

The West had lost almost all copies of the works of the Greek philosopher, but the Arabs had not. The leading Muslim scholar of al-Andalus, Averroës (1126–98), pored over Aristotle's writing line by line, commenting on it in detail, and extracting its relevance for modern analytical thought. In no time, Christian scholars piled into the intellectual hothouse of southern Spain, eager to translate Aristotle into Latin.

Aristotle may sound largely irrelevant today. But to twelfth-century Europeans, he was the most exciting thing to hit their scriptorium desks for centuries. He described ways of thinking and reasoning that were radical and revolutionary. He was a mesmerizing drug that young scholars and theologians scrambled to take intravenously.

The 'discovery' of so many works of Aristotle shook Christendom. The cathedral schools and emerging universities of Europe fell madly in love with the pagan philosopher, bent on using his systematic tools of logic and philosophy to reinvent and reinvigourate theology, science, and all existing learning.

So far so good—al-Andalus was a funnel through which knowledge poured one way, adding untold richness to Europe's largely moribund intellectual life.

But what of the reality of day to day life in southern Spain?

For the last hundred years, there has been a tendency to see al-Andalus as an exotic casket filled with sugar-dusted Turkish Delight. Victorian-era writers and thinkers, most notably Washington Irving, rhapsodized it as a beacon of beauty, learning, and tolerance—a golden age of harmony and civilization.

Well. No. The reality was more prosaic.

It is true that the scholarship of al-Andalus was unprecedented, and contributed massively to the twelfth-century renaissance and the development of Europe. But in al-Andalus, it probably did not exist outside small circles.

Nor was it free of strife. The initial invasion in 711 had been violent, as successful invasions usually are. The conquered people, Christians and Jews, became second-class citizens. They were largely well treated, but not always. For instance, in the early 1000s, the anarchy of the *fitnah* caused untold suffering for the people across al-Andalus. In 1066, a large number of Jews of Granada were massacred. In 1126, great numbers of Christians were deported by force to Morocco as slaves. And so on. No one should be surprised. This is a similar picture to that of life anywhere in Christendom or the Near-East in the period. Al-Andalus was no more or no less tolerant than a hundred other places.

For most of the period 711–1492, the three faiths rubbed shoulders, but they did not really come to understand each other any better. Perhaps this is nowhere symbolized better than in the sixteenth-century renaissance cathedral crudely hacked into a space smashed right out of the middle of the unending mathematical forest of columns making up the original great mosque at Cordoba. When Emperor Charles V saw the carnage, he emotionally rebuked all concerned: 'You have built here what you, or anyone, could have built anywhere. To do so, you have destroyed what was unique in the world'.

The triumph of al-Andalus is that it was not some piece of the Islamic world tacked onto a fully formed and functioning Europe. The knowledge bubbling out of Islamic Spain in science, medicine, mathematics, and logic was a key driving force in shaping a Europe still emerging from the intellectual torpor of post-Roman tribal society.

Without the scholarship al-Andalus pumped across the Pyrenees, there would have been no renaissance, no alchemy, no science, no Isaac Newton, no Christopher Wren, no Royal Society.

But the tragedy of al-Andalus is that, when all is said and done, the three cultures largely failed to grow in understanding or appreciation of each other. None seemed interested in looking beyond its own internal concerns.

As the 40-year-old Italian sailor standing watching the handover of Granada in 1492 walked away and into history, I wonder what he was thinking.

His name was Christopher Columbus, and later the same year he set out west on his first voyage.

As the old world of al-Andalus died, and as he weighed anchor to catch the wind for the new world, I like to think that perhaps he hoped we would all do a little better next time.

20

Savonarola and Mary Queen of Scots: the bloody underside of the 'civilized' Renaissance

The Renaissance is often seen as bringing an end to centuries of barbarous medieval power struggles. But the truth is more complex. The Renaissance was still a brutal place. This piece explores two infamous and bloody Renaissance executions—the firebrand prophetic preacher Savonarola in Florence, and the tragic Mary Queen of Scots at Fotheringay Castle in England.

If you looked only at the luscious paintings by Fra Angelico and Botticelli, and if you listened only to the soaring ethereal voices of Palestrina and Byrd, you would think the Renaissance was a release of centuries of pent-up creativity. You would conclude, as was once fashionable, that when the Renaissance detonated in late 1300s Italy, it sprayed hope, colour, and sensuality into a monochrome and rigid medieval world grappling with a plague that had slain a third of Europe.

But you would be wrong for many reasons.

For starters, there was nothing monochrome about the medieval world. You need only look at the extraordinary renovations now under way at Chartres cathedral, where they are restoring the hulking grey walls and statues to their former brightly decorated brilliance, injecting a vibrancy that those who grew up with 1960s architecture can barely take in.

Equally as importantly, there was a lot the Renaissance, for all its splendour, left unchanged. It may have been a celebration of living rather than earthly preparation for an afterlife, but it did not immediately improve life for everyone. For example, as the oligarchs of the day splashed their immense wealth around, patronizing works and monuments to their eternal glory, the majority of the population remained bound to the unforgiving and harsh drudgery of subsistence level agricultural and artisanal life.

We sometimes have a slightly deluded view of the period, seeing it as the dawning of a civilized age of 'high culture', with an intense new focus on art, writing, and music—quite unlike anything that had gone before.

There is some truth in this idea, but two gory anniversaries this week remind us that the tone at the top remained largely unchanged. Away from the vibrant portraits of patrons and the glories of twelve-voice motets, the harsh narcissistic world of Renaissance rulers was as power obsessed, self-interested, paranoid and brutal as ever. And as we think of the widespread apathy surrounding the modern political process, we do well to remember how far we have come.

This week marks the anniversary of two spectacular examples of violent Renaissance powerlust: one in late 1400s Florence, the vibrant city at the epicentre of the Renaissance, where two men played out a struggle for the heart and soul of northern Italy—the other in late 1500s England, at the glittering court of Queen Elizabeth I, where two British women settled their political ambition with an axe.

Both of these anniversaries remind us of how violent politics always was, even in the 'civilized' Renaissance.

First to Italy, where the proto-Renaissance arguably started with Francesco di Pietro di Bernadone (1181/2–1226), better known as St Francis of Assisi. His visionary idea, which the centuries have proved to be timeless, was to urge people to find beauty, inspiration, and meaning simply by looking around at the marvels of nature. Admittedly he had a head start, as he was preaching in Umbria and Tuscany, yet what he was saying found willing listeners from ever further afield.

But the Black Death soon chopped off the burgeoning interest in Francis's refreshing approach, which was wholly at odds with the stern scholasticism of the cathedral schools. Painters such as Giotto captured it for a moment, but then it was gone, buried under millions of plague-ridden corpses. It would not resurface again until the 1400s—in Florence, where the city was surging to prominence under the Medici, its wealthy banker-merchant rulers. With their patronage of Brunelleschi, Donatello, Fra Angelico, Masaccio, Botticelli, Leonardo da Vinci, Michelangelo and countless others, art began to fill the city, infusing whole areas with luxury and the fruits of affluence.

But as Renaissance alchemists and scientists could tell you, for every action there is an equal and opposite reaction.

Enter Girolamo Savonarola.

Although born in Ferrara in 1452, he soon made his way to the heart of the beast—to Florence.

Savonarola was Old School in every way. He came from a wealthy family, had a liberal arts education, was about to embark on a medical career, but entered the religious life as a Dominican friar instead. At first he was not very good at it. But he soon found his calling—as an angry hellfire and brimstone preacher, buoyed up by terrifying prophetic visions.

From Florence's exquisitely chiselled pulpits, he railed at the decadence and sensuality everywhere around him. He lambasted the people for their hedonistic ways. He harangued them for their immorality. But most of all, he excoriated the churchmen. All society's ills, he urged, started and ended with them. And he was not afraid to say that the pope was the worst of them all.

To some degree, he had a point. Rodrigo Borgia wangled the pope's Triple Crown in 1492 as Alexander VI, and went on to do for the reputation of the Church what the 2003 Dodgy Dossier has done for the integrity of modern British politicians.

Despite Savonarola's intolerance of any human pleasures, swarms of Florentines flocked to his sermons.

When his popularity coincided with the temporary collapse of Medici rule in 1494, he rather implausibly became the city's de facto ruler, while continuing to treat his audiences to firebrand sermons, and even running armies of street children to enforce his extremist vision.

This leads us to the first of our anniversaries.

On the 7th of February 1497, Savonarola organized the now infamous *Falò della Vanità*—the Bonfire of the Vanities.

The idea was simple, and there had been numerous similar burnings before. But this one was on an unprecedented scale, and has gone down in history. The city's incomparable luxuries were dragged to the town square, where Savonarola torched them for the glory of God.

He targeted anything redolent of decadence or temptation to sin—sensual dresses, mirrors, make-up and cosmetics; un-Christian art, statues, and books; cards, dice, and gambling paraphernalia; and even musical scores and instruments. (It is likely that Botticelli, an unlikely supporter of Savonarola, threw a number of his canvasses onto the fire.)

Unsurprisingly, Savonarola's hatred of the Spanish Borgia pope soon came to Rome's attention, as did his new position as ruler of Florence, for which he was singularly ill equipped. When he failed to join the papacy and others in a Holy League against a French invasion from the North, he was unambiguously pitting himself against the papacy in ecclesiastical and now secular matters.

A lethal dance of power followed.

Alexander invited Savonarola to Rome to discuss his prophecies. Fearing a trap, Savonarola pleaded ill-health and shunned the invitation. A series of letters between the two then swiftly turned into a bare-knuckle fight. At one stage Alexander tried to give Savonarola a Cardinal's red hat, to which he replied, 'I want no hats, no mitres either. I want nothing but what God has given to his saints: death. A red hat, a hat of blood; that is what I want!'

Meanwhile, the stalwart Florentines had become bored of Savonarola's moralizing. He had pushed them further than they wanted to go, even imposing death sentences for crimes he deemed immoral. When a trial by fire to prove his sanctity ended in fiasco because his champion failed to show up, the townsfolk turned on him. With his position in the Church and city becoming increasingly untenable, the people seized him, and handed him over to his Florentine enemies.

In the time-honoured fashion, a kangaroo court was duly convened. Savonarola and his two most loyal fellow Dominican friars were first tried by civil judges, then by Church commissioners, although neither result was ever in doubt. As one of the judges noted before the trial, 'We shall have a fine bonfire tonight'.

The three priests were quickly convicted, sentenced, stripped, walked over spikes, then hanged and burned in the central Piazza della Signoria. The once-adoring Florentines danced around the pyre, and the city's children threw stones at the burning corpses.

It was Renaissance politics at its least subtle.

It is ironic that many Protestants have adopted Savonarola as an early dissenter: a pope-hater and proto-Protestant. He is even regularly depicted in images and statuary alongside Luther and Hus. But it is way wide of the mark. Savonarola would spin in his grave—if he had one—at the thought. In his own mind, he was a staunch and resolute defender of the Church, the office of the papacy, and all traditional teaching. He had no argument with the fabric of the Church or its doctrines. He just didn't like its current leaders.

The year of his death was 1498—the high point of the Italian Renaissance.

This week's second bloody anniversary is a British one, from the court of Queen Elizabeth I, where Shakespeare, Marlowe, Jonson, Tallis, Byrd, Hilliard, and a raft of others were helping Renaissance England transition from a medieval to an early modern society.

But despite all the glitter, the politics were just as brutal and old-fashioned as in Savonarola's Italy.

This second anniversary relates to Mary Stuart, who was born in Scotland's Linlithgow Palace in 1542. When her father died within the week, she ascended the throne immediately as Scotland's queen.

But her kingdom was fractious and unstable, riven by wars and religion. Allies were needed, and she was soon engaged to the dauphin of France. Aged five, leaving regents to rule for her, she set sail to be brought up at the French royal court.

As soon as she was 15, she was married to François at a sumptuous ceremony in Notre Dame cathedral. And within the year he inherited the throne, making her queen consort of France.

But she was never far from tragedy, and it struck again in less than two years, when her husband, the young king, died of a probable ear infection.

The 18-year-old who returned to Scotland (by sea, as Elizabeth would not give her passage through England) was clever and perceptive, charming and witty, spoke French as a first language, composed poetry in French and Latin, played numerous instruments, danced wonderfully, was an able horsewoman, and the favourite of most of the French court. She was also exceptionally tall—five feet eleven inches, redheaded, and universally acknowledged to be a striking beauty.

Returning to the poisonous politics of Scotland and England was arguably one of the two worst decisions she ever made.

Scotland was officially a Protestant country, and ruling it as a quasi-French Catholic required skill and diplomacy. She quickly showed that she had both in abundance. She kept her religion low key, and supported the country's Protestants, even putting down a Catholic revolt. Most people assumed she was the natural successor to the childless Elizabeth I of England.

But powerful women in the period always collected enemies. Although they could not fault her handling of the kingdom, they finally managed to pull her down over her love life.

Her choice of second husband, Lord Darnley was not popular with the powerful pro-English lobby in Scotland. And it enraged Elizabeth I, because Darnley had a good claim to be third in line to the English throne, directly after Mary. Relations between the two women began to sour, as Melville recorded, 'All ther sisterly famyliarite was cessit, and insted therof nathing bot jelousies, suspitions and hattrent'.

The marriage was, in fact, a disaster all round. Darnley turned out to be dim and a wastrel—no use to Mary at all in managing her vast responsibilities.

As plotting against her intensified, Darnley was targeted by agitators who implied his wife was having an affair with David Riccio, an Italian adviser. Darnley immediately led a gang which broke into a supper she was having with Riccio and others, and dragged him into the next room before stabbing him 56 times.

But within a year, Darnley was himself the victim of a violent death, strangled or suffocated after two gunpowder explosions had ripped through the house at Kirk'o'Field where he was staying.

Mary was adrift and depressed. She could see the scandal brewing. Imprudently, she married a man named Hepburn, Earl of Bothwell, within three months.

Suspicion naturally fell on the newlyweds, although it was in fact all part of a meticulously orchestrated smear campaign. Forged letters were manufactured to 'prove' Mary and Bothwell were lovers. Even though the forgeries were laughably crude, they did the necessary damage.

It is quite likely that Bothwell was, in fact, involved in Darnley's death. But he and Mary were not lovers. To the contrary. He wanted to marry Mary purely to boost his standing.

With Darnley dead, Bothwell seized Mary by force, and there is considerable suspicion he violated her. With no alternative, the couple were duly married, and entered upon a joyless domesticity.

This was all gold dust for Mary's enemies. The scandal allowed them to capture her and offer her a stark choice: abdication or death. Mary duly signed away the crown, and then made perhaps her second greatest mistake, fleeing south to seek support from Elizabeth I, her English cousin.

Elizabeth seems to have been deeply conflicted over what to do about having Mary in her kingdom. On the one hand, Mary was a close relative, her cousin, a queen in her own right, and only nine years her junior. The two therefore had a lot in common. But there was *realpolitik* to consider. Mary had support from England's Roman Catholics, and that made her a permanent danger to Elizabeth.

Mary earnestly sought (as she always had) Elizabeth's friendship. And Elizabeth at one stage remarked that she wished both she and Mary could have been two milkmaids with pails upon their arms, away from all the politics, somewhere they could be friends. But Elizabeth was advised by hawks who saw Mary as a constant threat—a problem that would ultimately disappear with her death.

Although Elizabeth had no problem executing those she believed were against her, she baulked at the idea of killing a queen. Instead, she chose to imprison Mary. Although it would not stave off all plots, Elizabeth could console herself that any spies would first have to get past the gaolers.

The position between the cousins was at a stalemate. Mary was charged with no crime. So her imprisonment was illegal. But caught between the hawks among her advisers and her own periodic inclination for mercy, Elizabeth resorted to inaction.

As a result, Mary's incarceration wore on interminably for 19 years.

Devoid of any responsibilities, Mary sank into a depression. With no one to advise her and no future to look forward to, she allowed herself to become involved in largely absurd and fantastist plots.

The end came when Walsingham, Elizabeth's spymaster, set up a plot through his double agents. It was aimed precisely at entrapping Mary, and it worked, giving him all the evidence he needed to charge her with capital treason.

With the jubilant courtiers circling, Elizabeth finally signed Mary's death warrant and gave it to Walsingham's men, who carried it out immediately without consulting Elizabeth any further.

And this is the second bloody Renaissance anniversary falling this week—Mary's beheading at Fotheringay Castle on the 8th of February 1587.

It was a tawdry affair. Mary was not permitted a priest of her religion, so said her own prayers quietly in Latin. She remained poised and calm. Among her last words, she forgave her executioner with all her heart because 'now, I hope, you shall make an end of all my troubles'.

The first blow with the axe missed her neck and took off part of her head. The next was not hard enough. But the third finally severed her neck. Her dog, bloodied by the gore, lay between her head and shoulders, refusing to be parted from her. According to an eye witness, 'her lips stirred up and down a quarter of an hour after her head was cut off'.

As a final insult, her request to be buried in Rheims was overruled, and she was given a Protestant funeral in Peterborough.

The silent battle was over. Elizabeth's inner circle had eliminated the threat.

So, for all the brilliance of Elizabeth's Renaissance court, it was still a place where coteries of powerful advisors were willing to shore up their positions by engineering the death of anyone posing a potential threat. Self-preservation was paramount. And anyone who stood in their way—even an intelligent, fallible, slightly tragic queen—still paid the age-old price.

As a sign of how far things have come, these two anniversaries come in the week Buckingham Palace has announced an official visit by the Queen and Duke of Edinburgh to Pope Francis. And this single event throws the brutishness behind British Renaissance politics into even sharper relief.

Modern European democracy has many flaws. It inherently overpromises and underdelivers. Too often it smiles while lying, manipulating, and spinning. And frequently it depresses everyone with its predictably futility. That much would be familiar to both Savonarola and Queen Mary.

But it has largely taken absolute power out of the hands of those who guard it through terror and violence. And that is a significant achievement that the philosophers of the Renaissance would have welcomed. And so should we.

21

Columbus, greed, slavery, and genocide: what really happened to the American Indians

Christopher Columbus is regularly portrayed as a dashing explorer who discovered America and gave birth to the modern world. The reality is a horror story of looting, slavery, cruelty, and one of the planet's worst genocides. This piece was published shortly before the annual celebration of Columbus Day.

Christopher Columbus never set foot in the land that would become the United States of America. In fact, he never even saw it.

His four voyages took him to the Caribbean, a small detour to Central America, and a hop to the north-east coast of Venezuela. He had no idea the continent of North America existed, or that he had even stumbled into a 'New World'. He thought he had found China, Japan, and the region of King Solomon's fabled gold mines.

What he had categorically not done was 'discover' anything, as somewhere between 50 to 100 million people already lived there quite happily, just as they had done for tens of thousands of years. On the other hand, what he did was to start a brutal slave trade in American Indians, and usher in four centuries of genocide that culled them to virtual extinction. Within a generation of Columbus landing, perhaps only 5–10 per cent of the entire American Indian population remained.

People can argue the semantics of what genocide means, and whether it is applicable in this context. But if it sounds fanciful, consider the UN's Genocide Convention, passed by the General Assembly in December 1948. Although President Harry S Truman handed it to the US Senate the following year, the US only finally ratified it in 1986, along with a 'Sovereignty Package' requiring US consent for any actions brought against the US. The key reason for the delay and conditional ratification was the senators' concern that the US could be pursued in connection with its treatment of the American Indians (and also African Americans).

It should come as no surprise that the term 'genocide' is highly controversial in the context of the American Indians. Nevertheless, this article will tell the story of the destruction of the indigenous peoples of the Americas—predominantly by the Spanish *conquistadores*, British Puritans, and finally the American settlers—and you can make up your own mind. To start, here are two definitions:

> **genocide**. *The deliberate killing of a large group of people, especially those of a particular nation or ethnic group. 1940s: from Greek genos 'race' + -cide (Oxford English Dictionary)*

and

> *Genocide means any of the following acts committed with intent to destroy, in whole or in part, a national, ethnical, racial or religious group: (a) killing; (b) causing serious bodily or mental harm; (c) deliberately inflicting conditions of life calculated to bring about physical destruction in whole or in part; (d) imposing measures intended to prevent births; (e) forcibly transferring children (Article 2, UN Genocide Convention, abbreviated)*

On the 3rd of August 1492, Columbus slipped out of Palos de la Frontera on board his flagship, the carrack *Santa María*. Along with him were two nippier caravels, the *Pinta* and the *Niña*. Exactly 10 weeks later, on the 12th of October, he landed on 'San Salvador'—a still unidentified island in the Bahamas. By late October he was in Cuba, and on the 6th of December he had landed on the island of Haiti, which he renamed *La Spañola* (Hispaniola).

He described the islands as 'very fertile to an excessive degree', 'beyond comparison', 'most beautiful', 'filled with trees of a thousand kinds and tall, and they seem to touch the sky'. In addition he found: 'nightingale and other little birds of a thousand kinds', 'honey', 'a great variety of fruits', 'many mines of metals', and 'rivers, many and great, the most of which bear gold'.

He also described the 'innumerable' native Indians who greeted him:

> *They have no iron or steel or weapons, nor are they capable of using them, although they are well-built people of handsome stature, because they are wondrous timid. ... They are so artless and free with all they possess, that no one would believe it without having seen it. Of anything they have, if you ask them for it, they never say no; rather they invite the person to share it, and show as much love as if they were giving their hearts; and whether the thing be of value or of small price.*

However, power and greed soon took over. On the first voyage, Columbus seized men, women, and children to take back to Spain and parade like circus animals. Most died on the voyage, and all were dead within six months.

This spurred him to be more ambitious on his second voyage, in which he selected 550 of the best specimens he could find, and allowed his men to take whoever else they wanted, which turned out to be another 600. The journey back to Europe was so debilitating for the captives that Columbus ended up throwing over 200 corpses overboard. There are no records of what happened to the 600 taken by his men.

Columbus's second voyage had been on an altogether different scale to the first. Ferdinand and Isabella of Spain had kitted him out with 17 ships and 1,200 men, principally soldiers, including a cavalry troop of lancers. When they arrived at Hispaniola, the natives came out to meet them with fish and fruit 'as if we had been their brothers'. In return, Columbus dispatched his troops to the island's interior and the nearby islands to plunder the gold mines.

Armed with the latest weaponry and armoured mastiffs trained to rip people apart, the Spanish tortured, maimed, raped, slaughtered, and burned the inhabitants in search of gold. Bartolomé de Las Casas, an eyewitness who eventually became a Dominican friar and fought for the Indians' rights, left a harrowing description:

> ... *whenever the Spaniards found them, they pitilessly slaughtered everyone like sheep in a corral. It was a general rule among Spaniards to be cruel; not just cruel, but extraordinarily cruel so that harsh and bitter treatment would prevent Indians from daring to think of themselves as human beings or having a minute to think at all. So they would cut an Indian's hands and leave them dangling by a shred of skin and they would send him on saying 'Go now, spread the news to your chiefs.' They would test their swords and their manly strength on captured Indians and place bets on the slicing off of heads or the cutting of bodies in half with one blow. They burned or hanged captured chiefs.*

It was an orgy of looting and butchery, faithfully recorded by eyewitnesses. The accounts are too graphic to quote, but they detail the widespread massacres, including of children, dashing out their brains, and even feeding them to the armoured attack dogs. This senseless savagery was described as 'pacification'.

Wherever Columbus's men landed, they seized the land outright. His letter back to Ferdinand and Isabella is crystal clear:

> ... *and of them all have I taken possession for Their Highnesses, by proclamation and with the royal standard displayed, and nobody objected.*

The physical taking of new territories was farcical. The Indians were summoned, often manacled, and a proclamation called the *requermiento* was read to them. They spoke over 2,000 languages, but Spanish was naturally not one of them, so the ceremony was meaningless to them. Nevertheless, it stated that if they did not acknowledge Ferdinand and Isabella as their just sovereigns, all men, women, and children would be enslaved, and their possessions taken by force. In fact, the proclamation was actually meaningless for everyone—Columbus was there to enslave them and loot their property whatever.

The early records of kind and generous natives were soon replaced by descriptions of them as backwards savages and wild animals, who could therefore be treated as such. (This process of dehumanization is seen throughout history when one people settles on the land of another.) As a direct result, native blood flowed freely, and within 21 years—and four voyages by Columbus—Hispaniola was a ghost-island. The tropical abundance had been destroyed, and all its inhabitants were dead.

The Indians had originally moved into the Americas across the Bering Straits from Asia perhaps around 40,000 BC (some say as early as 70,000 BC). They had crossed between the eastern tip of Russia (the Chukchi Peninsula) and the westerly part of Alaska (Cape Prince of Wales) using the 'Bering land bridge', a vast slab of land now submerged under the Bering Straits leaving only a few rocky mountain tops poking out of the icy waters. The new land the people moved into—the Americas—was immense, covering a quarter of the earth's land mass.

There, entirely cut off from the rest of the world's history—unaware of ancient Egypt, China, Greece, Rome, Europe, or the rise of Hinduism, Judaism, Buddhism, Christianity, and Islam—the American Indians simultaneously developed their own civilizations.

When the Spanish finally saw the cities of the New World, they found themselves gazing on the stuff of fantasy—like in Aztec Mexico, where they came across the great cities around the Lake of the Moon, with Tenochtitlán rising mystically out of the centre of the water. The *conquistador* Bernal Díaz del Castillo wrote:

> ... *when we saw so many cities and villages built in the water and other great towns on dry land ... we were amazed and said that it was like the enchantments they tell of ... . And some of our soldiers even asked whether the things that we saw were not a dream? ... I do not know how to describe it, seeing things as we did that had never been heard of or seen before, not even dreamed about.*

Another marvel was the exuberant artwork they found everywhere. The *conquistador* Hernan Cortés brought some of it home to Europe, where the great Albrecht Dürer's reaction was rapture. He said he had:

> ... *never seen in all my days what so rejoiced my heart, as these things. For I saw among them amazing artistic objects, and I marveled over the subtle ingenuity of the men in these distant lands. Indeed, I cannot say enough about the things that were brought before me.*

The culture of the Indians throughout the Americas varied enormously, as would be expected for such a vast area. But the Spanish were nevertheless amazed to discover that many of the tribes were peaceful, harmonious, and egalitarian, with little sense of greed, crime, or warfare. This was naturally not true of all, but the passivity, hospitality, and community demonstrated by tribe after tribe fills the eyewitness Spanish accounts, which also note their frequently calm and respectful manner of exercizing authority, and even unheard of social systems like the cultural, spiritual, and economic matriarchy within the Iroquois.

As the Spanish seized ever more land, Columbus implemented the *repartimiento* (or *encomienda*), which gave each of the conquerors a number of Indians to enslave, turning the natives' previously peaceful way of life into a nightmare of unending brutality and violence as they were forced to mine precious metals and work plantations in sub-human conditions.

This subjugation was repeated throughout the Caribbean, before the *conquistadores* turned to the mainland, and wreaked the same carnage on the Aztecs of Mexico, the Maya of Central America, the Incas of Peru and Chile, and the other Indians they found.

Unlike the Caribbean Indians, the Aztecs in Mexico were familiar with warfare, although they had formal rules. A declaration of intention to declare war was required, along with the opportunity for the other side to make reparations to avert the conflict. The attacker might also supply the defender with weapons and food, as there was no honour in defeating the unarmed or weak.

However, Hernan Cortés, the *conquistador* who led the advance into Mexico, had no intention of observing these formalities. Having been welcomed by Montezuma into the great city of Tenochtitlán (now ruins within Mexico City), Cortés set about starving and slaughtering its people, before eventually levelling the city, burning all books, and feeding its priests to his war dogs.

This same pattern of annihilation and conquest was repeated throughout Central and South America. Tens of millions of Indians were rounded up and used as slaves on the coca plantations, or as labour down the gold and silver mines, where they worked and slept without ever seeing the light of day, constantly exposed to highly toxic cinnabar, arsenic, and mercury. Life expectancy was brutally low. The *conquistadores* calculated that with such an abundant slave workforce, it was cheaper to let them die of starvation and exhaustion than waste time and money providing food or survivable conditions. One *conquistador* recalled, 'If twenty healthy Indians enter [a mine] on Monday, half may emerge crippled on Saturday'.

As the conquerors moved south, the strongest resistance came from the Maya, whose empire extended across southern Mexico, Guatemala, Belize, western Honduras, and northern El Salvador. But even they were ultimately no match for the fanatical invaders, and the same fate befell them as everyone else.

In shockingly few generations, European greed, savagery, and disease had exterminated all but a handful of the citizens of the millennia-old American Indian civilizations. On average, the tribes' populations were reduced to around 5 per cent of the size they had been before Columbus arrived.

So much for Central and South America. Further north, in what is now the USA, the Spanish, French, and British pillaged the Atlantic coast for slaves, raiding today's Florida, Georgia, and Carolina. Finally, in 1607, the British settled permanently, initially at Jamestown, Virginia, where one of the British troops wrote they had found:

...a lande that promises more than the Lande of promisse: In steed of mylke we fynde pearl. / & golde Inn steede of honye.

However, the question of how to deal with the Indians was never far away. For instance, William Berkeley, one of Virginia's early governors, came up with the idea of massacring all the men, then selling all the women and children into slavery to cover the costs of the exterminations.

A particularly shocking episode involving the British Puritan settlers was the Pequot War (Southern New England, 1634–8). Following several tit-for-tat skirmishes, the British resolved to respond with crushing force.

> *The Indians spying of us came running in multitudes along the water side, crying, what cheere, Englishmen, what cheere, what doe you come for: They not thinking we intended warre, went on cheerefully untill they come to Pequeat river.*

The British then went on a village burning spree, in response to which the Indians marched on Fort Saybrook. After a few opening gambits by either side, the Indians sent a message to ask the British commander if he felt they had all 'fought enough'. Lt Lion Gardiner avoided a direct answer, prompting the Indians to ask if the British meant to kill their women and children. Gardiner replied 'they should see that thereafter'. Under cover of night, the British then attacked the Indian encampment at the Mystic River. Shouting 'we must burn them', Capt. John Mason torched the site, and shot or cut down anyone who tried to escape. He left a description of the massacre:

> *And indeed such a dreadful Terror did the Almighty let fall upon their Spirits, that they would fly from us and run into the very Flames, where many of them perished. ... [And] God was above them, who laughed his Enemies and the Enemies of his People to Scorn, making them as a fiery Oven: Thus were the Stout Hearted*

spoiled, having slept their last Sleep ... . Thus did the Lord judge among the Heathen, filling the Place with dead Bodies!

As feared, the majority of the 600 to 700 slain were women and children. But as John Underhill, Mason's co-commander, noted:

... sometimes the Scripture declareth women and children must perish with their parents.

To finish the job, the river Pequot was renamed the Thames, and the town of Pequot was made New London—to ensure that the Pequot people would be wiped from the map and forgotten.

It was also under the British that one of the few recorded cases of intentional biological warfare occurred. In 1763, General (later Baron) Jeffrey Amherst, governor of Virginia and commander-in-chief of British forces in North America, sanctioned the purposeful spread of lethal disease. In a set of orders given to Col. Henry Bouquet at Fort Pitt, he commanded:

You will do well to try to inoculate the Indians [with smallpox] by means of blankets, as well as to try every other method, that can serve to extirpate this execrable race.

Despite the relentless hostility of most senior European settlers towards the Indians, some of the less powerful saw things differently. As we have seen, Columbus's companion, Bartolomé de Las Casas, ended his days fighting for the proper treatment of Indians. And under subsequent British and then American rule, we know that Indian culture was not universally abominated. No less a figure than the Founding Father Benjamin Franklin explained:

When an Indian child has been brought up among us, taught our language and habituated to our Customs, yet if he goes to see his relations and make one Indian Ramble with them, there is no perswading him ever to return. [But] when white persons of either sex have been taken prisoners young by the Indians, and lived a while among them, tho' ransomed by their Friends, and treated with all imaginable tenderness to prevail with them to stay among the English, yet in a Short time they become disgusted with our manner of life, and the care and pains that are necessary to support it, and take the first good Opportunity of escaping again into the Woods, from whence there is no reclaiming them.

Penalties for this type of racial disloyalty were harsh. In 1612, Thomas Dayle, Marshall of Virginia, captured some young English settlers who had run away to live with the Indians. His retribution was swift and brutal:

Some he apointed to be hanged Some burned Some to be broken upon wheles, others to be staked and some to be shott to deathe.

So far the focus of the story has been the settlers' violence. But the biggest killer of the American Indians was undoubtedly the arsenal of diseases brought by the Europeans. The role of disease in this context remains a hotly debated issue. However, it is wholly misleading to think—as many now do—that the Indian deaths caused by these invisible microbial killers were unforeseeable, accidental, inadvertent, or otherwise an unintended consequence of peaceful contact between the Europeans and the Indians. The volumes filled with eyewitness accounts of settler savagery leave no one in any doubt that the conquerors of the New World wanted land, and were pleased by all opportunities to take it. The British Puritans viewed the decimation of tribe after tribe from disease as being an integral part of God's active support for their new colonies. For instance, the governor of the Massachusetts Bay Colony noted after an epidemic of smallpox in 1634 that the British settlers had been largely unharmed, but:

... for the natives, they are near all dead of the smallpox, so as the Lord hath cleared our title to what we possess.

The human devastation wrought by the diseases carried by Columbus's men and everyone who followed was cataclysmic: a rolling cocktail of diphtheria, influenza, measles, mumps, typhus, scarlet fever, smallpox, syphilis—the list is endless. Not only did these pathogens cull whole native populations, but they kept on killing, even once individual outbreaks had abated, because there was no one left strong enough to bury the dead or gather food.

In 1793, once the American War of Independence had concluded with the Treaty of Paris, the 'Indian Question' became a domestic matter for the new American administration.

Alongside growth in the African slave trade, the slavery of Indians continued undiminished right up to the general abolition of slavery in 1865. For instance, in 1861, in Colusa County, California, Indian boys and girls of three and four years old were still being sold for small sums. Such child slaves were often kidnapped and sold by traders, secure in the knowledge that the parents could do nothing, as Indians could not give testimony in court against whites.

As the settlers pushed across the Plains and the West, tales of whooping, tomahawk-wielding, Indians slaughtering whites became ever more widespread. But it is noteworthy that, pre-colonization, many of the Indians in the area did not have violent cultures. Among some tribes, sneaking up on an enemy and touching him with a weapon, stick, or even a hand was traditionally deemed the highest form of bravery. However, in the face of continual attacks, the Indians learned to respond with violence.

As alien as it may seem now, by the late 1700s, many American leaders were openly advocating the destruction and extermination of the encampments and tribes. For instance, in 1779, a decade before he became first president of the US, General George Washington told the military commander attacking the Iroquois to:

> ... *lay waste all the settlements around ... that the country may not be merely overrun but destroyed*

and not to:

> *... listen to any overture of peace before the total ruin of their settlements is effected.*

He insisted upon the military need to fill the Indians with a:

> *... terror with which the severity of the chastisement they receive will inspire them.*

Other presidents were more explicit still. In 1807, President Thomas Jefferson told his Secretary of State for War to use 'the hatchet' and that:

> *... we will never lay it down till that tribe is exterminated or is driven beyond the Mississippi ... in war, they will kill some of us; we shall destroy all of them.*

It was a theme Jefferson was to return to several times, freely using words like 'exterminate' and 'extirpate'.

Several decades later, in 1829, Andrew Jackson was elected president, although few now remember he had sacked Indian villages of 'savage dogs', made bridle reins of their flayed skin, sent souvenirs of corpses to the ladies of Tennessee, and claimed, 'I have on all occasions preserved the scalps of my killed'.

At the same time as the state-orchestrated wars of annihilation, the Indian Removal Act of 1830 required the resettlement of entire populations of Indians to new territories west of the Mississippi. When the Indians of Georgia won a ruling from Chief Justice John Marshall saying, effectively, they could stay, President Jackson ignored the Supreme Court and had the Indians sent on a death march anyway— the Trail of Tears. One former Civil War soldier said he had seen a great deal of brutality in his life, but nothing on the scale of the cruelty of the Indian death marches. Later forced relocations of Indians, like the Navajo Long Walk and the Pomo Death March in California, followed the same pattern.

The language of extermination coming from the top was also mirrored at state level. For example, Governor Peter Burnett of California stated in 1851 that war would:

> ... *continue to be waged between the races until the Indian becomes extinct.*

And the following year his successor, Governor John McDougal, reiterated the sentiment, urging that the whites' war against the Indians:

> ... *must of necessity be one of extermination to many of the tribes.*

All the while, elements within the press supported the incitement to mass murder. L Frank Baum (most famous as the author of *The Wonderful Wizard of Oz*) was editor of the *Aberdeen Saturday Pioneer* in South Dakota. In it, he wrote:

> *The Whites, by law of conquest, by justice of civilization, are masters of the American continent, and the best safety of the frontier settlements will be secured by the total annihilation of the few remaining Indians. Why not annihilation? Their glory has fled, their spirit broken, their manhood effaced; better that they die than live the miserable wretches that they are. (20 December 1890)*

He returned to the same theme the following week:

> *The Pioneer has before declared that our only safety depends upon the total extirmination [sic] of the Indians. Having wronged them for centuries we had better, in order to protect our civilization, follow it up by one more wrong and wipe these untamed and untamable creatures from the face of the earth. (29 December 1890)*

These seem to have been fairly standard and established views among sections of the population. A generation earlier, in 1864, the Rev. William Crawford had written of the prevailing opinion in Colorado:

There is but one sentiment in regard to the final disposition which shall be made of the Indians: 'Let them be exterminated—men, women, and children together'.

And, sure enough, one of the worst atrocities of the 1800s soon followed— the infamous November 1864 massacre at Sand Creek, familiar to anyone who has seen the 1970 film *Soldier Blue*, groundbreaking for its graphic depictions of the slaughter.

The Cheyenne and Arapaho men of Sand Creek were away on a buffalo hunt, leaving around 600 women and children together with some 35 braves and 25 old men. When the American cavalry approached, the elderly chief, Black Kettle, emerged with his family. He waved a white flag and an American flag, and explained that the village had already voluntarily surrendered all its weapons to prove they were peaceful. All the while, he reassured his people not to be afraid. However, the Cavalry commander, the Rev. Col. John Milton Chivington, a devout Methodist pastor and elder, was an extremist in no mood for peace. 'I long to be wading in gore', he had announced a few days earlier:

Damn any man who sympathizes with Indians! ... I have come to kill Indians, and believe it is right and honorable to use any means under God's heaven to kill Indians. ... Kill and scalp all, big and little; nits make lice.

The stomach-turning notion that 'nits make lice' was one of his favourite justifications for the wholesale butchery of Indian children. Accordingly, at Sand Creek he sent in his 700 troops, who slaughtered the entire village, including a six-year-old girl waving a white flag. When they were done, they scalped the bodies, hacked off fingers and ears for jewellery, and sexually mutilated a number of the corpses.

Soldier Blue was released at the height of the Vietnam War, and attracted some criticism for its timing. But it was a tearaway international box office success, chiefly remembered for introducing an audience weaned on films of spectacular and heroic cowboy derring-do to a far more shocking and sobering view of how the West was won.

Perhaps equally as shocking is that Chivington was never disciplined for the atrocity, and President Theodore Roosevelt (1901–9) declared the Sand Creek massacre was:

> *... as righteous and beneficial a deed as ever took place on the frontier.*

He later went on to say:

> *I don't go so far as to think that the only good Indians are dead Indians, but I believe 9 out of 10 are, and I shouldn't like to inquire too closely into the case of the tenth.*

Five years later, on the 15th of January 1891, the Sioux chief, Kicking Bear, finally surrendered. The wars were effectively over. By 1900, a people which once represented a hundred percent of the population of the USA, was reduced to a third of one per cent.

So what does this all tell us, apart from, as Secretary of Defense Donald Rumsfeld put it, 'war is hell'. And so was four centuries of genocide against the American Indians. In 2000, the US government's Bureau of Indian Affairs apologized with the full support of the Clinton administration:

> *As the nation looked to the West for more land, this agency participated in the ethnic cleansing that befell the western tribes. ... it must be acknowledged that the deliberate spread of disease, the decimation of the mighty bison herds, the use of the poison alcohol to destroy mind and body, and the cowardly killing of women and children made for tragedy on a scale so ghastly that it cannot be dismissed as merely the inevitable consequence of the clash of competing ways of life. ... We accept this inheritance, this legacy of racism and inhumanity. (Kevin Gover, Bureau of Indian Affairs)*

Perhaps one thing it all suggests is that the US celebration of Christopher Columbus Day on the second Monday in October every year is outdated and increasingly unacceptable to a growing number of those who have understood the man's motivations and his legacy of slavery, violence, and destruction.

Today, fanatics across the Middle East continue to bomb, shoot, or hack their way through non-combatant populations of men, women, and children for no more reason than the race or religion they were born into, or the land they were born onto. As the American Indians so tragically discovered, the world has become good at turning a blind eye to the genocides it prefers not to see.

At the start of this piece I suggested that readers could form their own view whether the American Indians had been the victims of genocide. Perhaps the final words on this should go to *The New York Times*.

Henry Wadsworth Longfellow retired as Smith Professor of Modern Languages at Harvard in 1854. The following year, he published his epic poem about the Indian chief, *Hiawatha*. On the 28th of December 1855, page 2 of *The New York Times* carried a review of the poem, which described it as:

> ... *embalming pleasantly enough the monstrous traditions of an uninteresting and, one may almost say, a justly exterminated race.*

22

How the Tudor spin machine hid the brutal truth about the English Reformation

For centuries, people have believed that King Henry VIII's break with Rome was welcomed by the English, who had grown to hate an oppressive Catholic Church. Historians are now uncovering the startling fact that the English doggedly resisted the religious changes, forcing Henry VIII, Edward VI, and Elizabeth I to impose the new religion with mass nationwide torture and executions. This piece was written on the anniversary of Henry's divorce from Catherine of Aragon—the event which kick-started the English Reformation.

In 2003, Charles Clarke, Tony Blair's Secretary of State for Education and Skills, expressed strong views on the teaching of British history.

> *I don't mind there being some medievalists around for ornamental purposes, but there is no reason for the state to pay for them.*

In response, Michael Biddiss, professor of medieval history at Reading University, suggested that Mr Clarke's view may have been informed by Khrushchev's notion that historians are dangerous people, capable of upsetting everything.

In many ways, Khrushchev was correct. Historians can be a distinct threat—both those who create 'official' history, and those who work quietly to unpick it, filling in the irksome and unhelpful details.

Rulers in all ages have tried to control how history sees them, and have gone to great lengths to have events recorded the way they want. The process is as old as authority itself.

The result is that generations of people learn something at school, only to find out later that it was not so. For instance, children brought up in the communist countries of the twentieth century have little idea of the indiscriminately murderous mechanics at the heart of their founding revolutions. More recently, in the United States, anyone young enough not to have lived through the two recent Iraq wars might, if they only read political memoirs, actually believe that the wars were fought to root out al-Qaeda.

So what about England? Has our constitutional monarchy and ancient tradition of parliamentary democracy protected our history from political manipulation? Can we rely on what we are taught and told, or are there myths we, too, have swallowed hook, line, and sinker?

Where better to start than with that most quintessentially English of events—the break with Rome that signalled the birth of modern England?

For centuries, the English have been taught that the late medieval Church was superstitious, corrupt, exploitative, and alien. Above all, we were told that King Henry VIII and the people of England despised its popish flummery and primitive rites. England was fed up to the back teeth with the ignorant mumbo-jumbo magicians of the foreign Church, and up and down the country Tudor people preferred plain-speaking, rational men like Wycliffe, Luther, and Calvin. Henry VIII achieved what all sane English and Welsh people had long desired— an excuse to break away from an anachronistic subjugation to the ridiculous medieval strictures of the Church.

For many in England, the subject of whether or not this was true was not even up for debate. Even now, the historical English disdain for all things Catholic is often regarded as irrefutable and objective fact. Otherwise why would we have been taught it for four and a half centuries? And anyway, the English are quite clearly not an emotional race like some of our continental cousins. We like our churches bright and clean and practical and full of common sense. For this reason, we are brought up to believe that Catholicism is just fundamentally, well … un-English.

But the last 30 years have seen a revolution in Reformation research. Leading scholars have started looking behind the pronouncements of the religious revolution's leaders—Henry VIII, Thomas Cromwell, Thomas Cranmer, Hugh Latimer, Nicholas Ridley—and beyond the parliamentary pronouncements and the great sermons. Instead, they have begun focusing on the records left by ordinary English people. This 'bottom up' approach to history has undoubtedly been the most exciting development in historical research in the last 50 years. It has taken us away from what the rulers want us to know, and steered us closer towards what actually happened.

When this approach is applied to the Reformation, what emerges is a very different picture to the one we were taught in school.

It seems that in 1533, the year of Henry's break from Rome, traditional Catholicism was the religion of the vast majority of the country. And in most places it was absolutely thriving.

It had developed a particularly English flavour, with a focus on the involvement of ordinary people in parish churches, village greens, plays, and pageants—much of which seemed to involve a good deal of community parties, dancing, and drinking.

It is true that English religion in the early 1500s was not especially studious or erudite. The people did not spend hours a day in biblical studies, contemplation, and moralizing in the manner of the more intense European reformers. But England had a nationally cohesive spirituality that was alive and exuberant, with a distinctly community feel.

If you looked inside an English parish church on the eve of the Reformation, you would have seen a space filled with the lives and loves of the community. The saints would be draped in the parishioners' best clothes, jewellery, and beads, often given as bequests in wills. The nave would have numerous side altars, most funded by local guilds to provide daily masses for favoured saints and the deceased of the parish. If the church had the relics of a saint, the reliquary or tomb would be festooned with gold, silver, and wax models of everything from healed limbs to ships saved from calamities at sea—it would be a mini-history of the gratitude of the people. Flowers and candles would be everywhere, as would parishioners, who regularly attended weekday prayers and masses at the many guild and chantry altars. In an age of increasing literacy, significant numbers of the upper and artisanal classes read along in their own devotional books. Religious printing had become big business. It has been estimated that, on the eve of the Reformation, over 57,000 Books of Hours were in circulation in England.

All in all, parish churches were at the heart of a vibrant English parish life, where the living celebrated their good fortune and remembered the dead.

The first thing to go under the reformers' axe was the cult of saints. The ancient robed and flower-garlanded effigies were smashed up and carted off. Stone and alabaster were ground up. Wood was burned. In addition to the dramatic loss of these cherished protector figures, the parishes were also deprived of around 40 to 50 saints' 'holy days' (holidays) a year, when no servile work was allowed from noon the previous day. This was a dramatic change to the rhythms of life the country had known for centuries. The reformers were keenly aware this would boost economic activity, and welcomed the increase in output it would bring.

The next biggest change was the abolition of purgatory. The reformers ridiculed the cult of the dead ('purgatorye ys pissed owte' one memorably wrote). But these age-old rites of death and the afterlife provided a unique framework that late medieval English people embraced to cope with death. When the reformers ripped out grave stones and brasses inviting prayers for the departed, when they burned the local bede-rolls remembering the dead of the parish, and when they sledge-hammered the chantry altars where relatives were daily prayed for, they did something even more profound than the vandalism. They stole the dead from the daily lives of their communities, rendering the deceased suddenly invisible to those long used to honouring and remembering their departed relatives and friends. Whether or not intentional, this was an attack on people's memories.

The Early and High Middle Ages were a time when cathedrals and monasteries dominated religious life. But by the late 1400s and early

1500s, religion had been taken over by the people—most notably in the form of the religious guilds that had mushroomed in every parish. For instance, King's Lynn had over 70; Bodmin had more than 40.

These guilds funded festivals, parades, and pageants—and the parish records show that the celebrations were regularly and widely enjoyed. The guilds' most spectacular contribution to late medieval religious life lay in the great mystery play cycles they sponsored. These moral dramas were performed in English (not Latin), often around the feast of Corpus Christi. Despite being declared illegal and destroyed by the Reformation, enough copies survive for us to get an idea of their sheer scale: from Chester, Cornwall (in Cornish), Coventry, Digby, Towneley/Wakefield, and elsewhere. They were a focus of intense regional pride, and took entire communities to stage them. The York cycle alone comprised 48 plays.

Inside parish churches, uniquely English customs had also developed. There was the festival of boy bishops and misrule on St Nicholas's day; the setting up of an Easter sepulchre as a mini stage-set for re-enacting the Passion; and the dramatic 'creeping to the Cross' on Good Friday—a humble barelegged and barefoot procession on the knees to adore the cross, before swaddling it and laying it inside the Easter sepulchre. These rituals, as well as the many festivals in honour of local or patronal saints, were deeply embedded into communities, and people stubbornly persisted with them long after they had been outlawed.

Away from the life of the churches, increasing literacy meant more stories, poems, songs, and carols. A favourite theme was, unsurprisingly, the Virgin Mary, who was frequently portrayed as that most English flower, the rose:

> *Of this rose was Cryst y-bore,*
> *To save mankynde that was forlore;*
> *And us alle from synnes sore,*
> *Prophetarum carmine.*

This rose is so faire of hywe,
In maide Mary that is so trywe,
Y-borne was lorde of virtue,
Salvator sine crimine.

(Of a Rose Synge We, c. 1450)

Finally, the cult of relics was junked. It is true that provenance was rarely scientific, and the reformers were able to jeer at their favourite fakes. But the records suggest that this empirical approach, which counts the number of duplicated and inauthentic relics, misses the point. These objects brought people into the presence of the numinous, and joined the living with the dead. Many relics were even practical. For instance, articles of saints' clothing were given to expecting women to wear in the hope of a healthy delivery. Relics were therefore a part of day-to-day life, offering people a sense of protection and connection with the sacred.

Given the intensity of people's attachment to early sixteenth-century popular religion, the stark Tudor reforms were met with incomprehension, outrage, and sometimes passionate violence.

The men sent to smash up the churches knew this grassroots anger all too well. There are innumerable records of the hostility and violence they faced from distraught parishioners trying to protect churches and graves.

Once the bussed-in workmen had inevitably triumphed, and the heat of confrontation had worn off, people were left bereft:

On the feast of the Assumption 1537 Thomas Emans, a Worcester serving-man, entered the despoiled shrine of Our Lady of Worcester, recited a Paternoster and an Ave, kissed the feet of the image, from which jewels, coat, and shoes had been taken away, and declared bitterly for all to hear, 'Lady, art thou stripped now? I have seen the day that as clean men hath been stripped at a pair of gallows as were they that stripped thee.' He told the people that, though her ornaments were gone, 'the similitude of this is no worse to pray unto, having a recourse to her above, then it was before.' (from Eamon Duffy, The Stripping of the Altars)

There was, before long, coordinated dissent. In 1536, an uprising known as the Pilgrimage of Grace came south from northern England and occupied Leicester, demanding an end to the radical changes and personal revenge on Thomas Cromwell, whose mercenary looting of the abbeys had shocked people profoundly. Meanwhile, around 30,000 (including the Archbishop of York) took York, with similar demands for the reforms to stop. Predictably, it all ended in catastrophe. Some 250 protestors were executed, killing off any further mass protests. The Tudor monarchy was, after all, one of the most powerful in Europe.

The conclusion of this modern grassroots scholarship is that bulldozing the Catholic Church off the face of medieval England was not a 'bottom up' revolution in which Henry merely acquiesced to his people's wishes by throwing off a widely hated foreign domination. To the contrary, it looks increasingly like Henry and his circle imposed the Reformation 'top down', unleashing 100 years of deep anger and alienation that was only overcome by sustained politicking and ruthless force. Politics and economics have always fitted together snugly, and it was no different in Henry's day. By spreading some of the lands and wealth stolen from the monasteries, Henry was able to create a firm coterie of influential landholders who had a financial interest in seeing the reforms through.

While we are debunking, we should also look to another 'fact' we have been commonly taught, which is that England was moving towards Protestantism by Henry's time owing to the widespread popularity of Wycliffe and his Lollards. This movement, according to Protestant legend, embodied and expressed the true sentiment of English people. However, the evidence is overwhelmingly that this is a red herring, as research is revealing that Lollardy was never more than a small regional and dynastic movement in select parts of England. Moreover, it was almost dead by the mid-1400s—over a century before Henry's divorce. Although Lollardy had, in its day, been a genuine expression of dissent (like many others across Christendom for the last two thousand years), it was never a mainstream—let alone a majority—English religious movement.

That is not to say everyone loved the Church. By the time Cromwell was sharpening his pen to gut the monasteries more thoroughly than the Vikings ever had, there were known and identifiable pockets of English Protestants, especially in London, the South-East and East Anglia. But the records show they were a small minority of the population, and the tone of King Henry's *Defence of the Seven Sacraments* (more below) solidly reflected mainstream thought.

However, nothing ever stands still, and England in the early 1500s—just like everywhere else—had its modern humanist philosophers and theologians. But here there is sometimes a misunderstanding. Humanists were not atheists or anti-Church. They were merely interested in applying the philosophies and knowledge of the day, as thinkers had done in every century. The Netherlands produced Erasmus, who was great friends with England's leading humanist: the exceptionally talented St Thomas More, one of the first victims of the English Reformation, executed by Henry for not agreeing to the split with Rome.

So how did all this happen? Why did Henry VIII, in 1533, cut a wound so deep into his country that four and a half centuries later it has still not healed?

The story is a tragedy.

On the 23rd of May 1533, Thomas Cranmer, the Archbishop of Canterbury, sat in the lady chapel of Dunstable Priory to pronounce one of the most significant legal judgments in English history—infinitely more seismic than Magna Carta.

The underlying issues was that Henry VIII's marriage of 16 years had produced no boys. But his mistress, the Marquess of Pembroke, was pregnant, so time was ticking. The usual legal channels had failed to grant Henry a divorce, so the Archbishop of Canterbury stepped up to the mark.

In order to give Archbishop Cranmer the unprecedented legal authority to do what he was about to do, Henry's slippery hard man, Thomas Cromwell, drafted and rushed The Act in Restraint of Appeals 1532 through Parliament. Cromwell's Act suspended all the usual laws in this regard, and give Cranmer full authority to give judgment. (Interestingly, to do this, Cromwell claimed that Cranmer had full authority because England was an empire. At the same time, his spin machine was working overtime, pumping out fantastical ancient histories linking the English empire to Troy, therefore making it older than, and so independent from, Rome.)

Therefore, in the hope that the King's mistress was carrying a boy, Cranmer solemnly declared King Henry VIII divorced from Catherine of Aragon.

In the event, Henry's mistress, Anne Boleyn, gave birth to a girl (and would, with Cromwell's help, be beheaded within three years). But the deed was done. Cromwell had divorced Henry from Catherine, and England from Rome.

The whole affair was radical.

Since time immemorial, canon law had reserved appeals on marriage and divorce to the Archbishop of Canterbury's boss, the pope. English kings, like all monarchs in Latin Christendom, had always observed this ancient legal structure. Henry had happily used it himself, when he had needed a dispensation to marry Catherine of Aragon (his brother's widow) in the first place.

The reason Cromwell had pushed for a break with Rome was that everyone knew Henry had no legal basis for divorcing Catherine.

Henry's argument (which he worked out himself, and was proud of) insisted that the Bible forbade a man from marrying his brother's widow, and therefore his marriage to Catherine had all been a dreadful mistake and was, regrettably, invalid. However, all canon lawyers in England and Europe (apart from Henry's circle of advisers) knew it was a hopeless argument, as there was a well-recognized exception to this rule. In a 'levirate' marriage (*Deuteronomy* 25:5–10), a man was required to marry his brother's widow if she had no children, which was the case here, and why Henry had been permitted to marry Catherine and seal a vital bond between England and Spain.

Therefore, to no one's surprise, the pope said no to the divorce.

Until this point, Henry had been an ardent Catholic. When he first read Luther's works, he had been so outraged by Luther's attack on the Church that he wrote a book (in Latin) systematically taking Luther's arguments apart. He published it in 1521 with a dedication to the pope. In it, he referred to 'the pest of Martin Luther's heresy ... a deadly venom ... infecting all with its poison'. He continued:

> *But, O immortal God! what bitter language! What so hot and inflamed force of speaking can be invented, sufficient to declare the crimes of that most filthy villain [Luther], who has undertaken to cut in pieces the seamless coat of Christ, and to disturb the quiet state of the church of God!*

Henry made his personal position very clear:

> *Convinced that, in our ardour for the welfare of Christendom, in our zeal for the Catholic faith and our devotion to the Apostolic See, we had not yet done enough, we determined to show by our own writings our attitude towards Luther and our opinion of his vile books; to manifest more openly to all the world that we shall ever defend and uphold, not only by force of arms but by the resources of our intelligence and our services as a Christian, the Holy Roman Church. (King Henry VIII, Defence of the Seven Sacraments)*

In grateful recognition, the pope awarded Henry the personal title 'Defender of the Faith'. (Since the break with Rome, Parliament has, slightly strangely, conferred this title on all British monarchs.)

However, when the pope refused to allow Henry to divorce, Thomas Cromwell came up with a corker of a solution—break with Rome; turn the country Protestant; and, at the same time, solve the problem of the empty royal coffers by trousering all the wealth in the country's innumerable abbeys and parish churches.

Like King Philip IV of France two centuries earlier surveying the wealth of the Templars, the temptation for Henry was just too much to resist.

The only problem was that although Cromwell's plan suited Henry and his circle (who would all get very rich off the scheme), there was the small matter of the English people.

To change a country's religion lock, stock, and barrel was no easy task. In the end, it took Henry VIII, Edward VI, and Elizabeth I. The strategy was fairly predictable for a medieval monarchy, and again, it has striking similarities with how Philip IV took out the Templars. Cromwell's plan only needed three steps: outlaw everything to do with Catholicism; denigrate and malign it at every opportunity in official pronouncements and sermons; and execute anyone who objects.

One example of the type of propaganda deployed must stand for many. Turning a blind eye to the hundreds of English Catholics executed by Henry VIII, Elizabeth I's administration came up with the notion of convincing people that religious executions had been invented by Elizabeth's older sister, Mary I. Despite the fact that images were banned in churches, they ordered a copy of Foxe's *Book of Martyrs,* hot off the press with the ink still wet, placed in every collegiate church in the land, where all people could be appalled by its 150 gruesome woodcut illustrations showing the Protestant martyrs executed by Mary. What it failed to show, of course, were those Catholic victims that Henry had consigned to identical deaths before Mary's reign, and the hundreds that Elizabeth was now ruthlessly persecuting in exactly the same way. But, of course, that is the nature of propaganda. Elizabeth forbade the printing of any Catholic materials in her kingdom, leaving her full control of all books and pamphlets.

The Tudor violence meted out to enforce the break with Rome was extreme, designed to deter by shock. For instance, one of Henry's earliest victims was Sister Elizabeth Barton, a Benedictine nun. When she criticized Henry's desire to marry Anne Boleyn, he had her executed, and her head spiked on London Bridge—the first and only woman ever to have suffered this posthumous barbarity.

Henry and his inner circle of politicians and radical clerics put to death hundreds of dissenters, *pour encourager les autres.* None of these people were plotting to kill him or destabilize his rule. Their 'treason' was to oppose the destruction of their religion or the despoiling of their property. The brutal strangulation, emasculation, disembowelling, beheading, and quartering they endured as traitors was hideous, as was the total absence of any form of due process or justice.

Take the death of Richard Whiting, the elderly abbot of Glastonbury, England's greatest abbey. Thomas Cromwell's administrative diary entry about him reads starkly:

> *Item. The Abbot, of Glaston to be tryed at Glaston and also executyd there with his complycys.*

Whiting was, in fact, a member of the House of Lords, and entitled to be arraigned before Parliament if he was to be charged with any crime. But that was much too cumbersome for Cromwell, who just wanted the abbot out of the way in order to seize the abbey's wealth and line his own pockets with it. Whiting was therefore dragged on a hurdle to the summit of Glastonbury Tor, where he was subjected to the full horrors of a traitor's death. And he was not alone. Similar summary executions took place up and down the land to clear the way for Cromwell's commissioners, who boxed up every last cross and candlestick they could find, and shipped them back to London to be melted down and pumped into their personal accounts.

The evidence shows that it actually took the Tudors around 45 years to eradicate all memory of this country's Catholic past.

Henry started it all, from 1533–47. His reforms were harsh on the people, yet he rather hypocritically remained a practising Catholic himself. He had a newfound hostility towards the pope, born of his divorce debacle, but he continued to hear Mass regularly. Although he presided over the looting of the abbeys and a good deal of local church vandalism, he nevertheless exercised certain restraining influences over Thomas Cromwell, Archbishop Cranmer and the other zealots. Things therefore only really kicked off once Henry was dead and the reformers were able to take the nine-year-old King Edward VI on a radical six-year Calvinist journey (1547–53). This was the period of the harshest destruction of English religious art and culture, when even the smallest church in the kingdom was ransacked and all its valuables seized. For several generations, people said that they had suffered under Henry's reforms, but they dated the utter desecration of the English church to Edward's reign.

When Mary I briefly returned England to Catholicism from 1553–8, many churches and parishioners cautiously took out the few treasured saints' statues and missals they had recklessly managed to hide, and they set up their churches again, happy for normality to have returned.

But when Mary unexpectedly died and Elizabeth began the persecutions again, people started slowly to give up. By the end of Elizabeth's reign, no one remembered religious life before Henry. The memories were gone, and so was the will to fight the regime any more.

Amid the turmoil of the English Reformation—with its wanton destruction of communities, their imaginations, and centuries of their books and art—the one thing that stands out most is the sheer scale of the undertaking.

Under the influence of Calvin and Zwingli's puritan doctrines, Edward VI ordered his commissioners to:

> *Take away, utterly extinct and destroy all shrines, coverings of shrines, candlesticks, pictures, paintings and all other monuments of feigned miracles, pilgrimages, idolatry and superstition so that there remain no memory of the same in walls, glasses, windows or elsewhere within their churches or houses.*

And following Edward's reign, Elizabeth I repeated the command and finished what he had started. The result was the wholesale destruction of a millennium of irreplaceable English craftsmanship in windows, statues, frescoes, and paintings. The Tate recently estimated that over 90 per cent of all English art was trashed in the period, and scarcely a handful of books survived the burning of the great monastic and university libraries. Oxford's vast Bodleian, for instance, was left without a single book.

Anyone who doubts there was a political aspect to the destruction needs look no further than the shrine of St Thomas Becket in

Canterbury. It was England's most popular pilgrimage destination, and Becket's cult had international reach, with mosaics, icons, and relics of him venerated as far afield as Sicily and the Holy Land. Henry ordered his tomb pulverized, his bones scattered, and his name effaced from history. The reason for this special harshness is not hard to see. Becket's claim to fame was as a churchman who stood up to royal interference in the Church. Becket was therefore a natural rallying symbol for anyone thinking of challenging Henry's reforms. Becket represented the sanctity of dissent, and Henry could absolutely not have that.

In the process of all the destruction, it was not just traditional day-to-day spiritual life, the free medical and social care provided by the monasteries, and a country full of creative thought and art that were obliterated. The reformers hacked out and discarded an entire slice of England's history, alienating the English from an especially vibrant part of their own amazing past.

So Khrushchev was right—historians are dangerous. In the case of the Reformation, generations have perpetuated the artful story spun by the Tudor machine, with the result that we fail to acknowledge that medieval religion in this country was, for a thousand years, as English as tea, warm beer, Maypole dancing, and cricket. As has been said many times: within three generations, England went from being one of Europe's most Catholic countries to one of its most anti-Catholic.

The medieval world was quite capable of outrageous smears. One needs only think of the blood libel against the Jews. Yet it seems that we, too, are the victims of politicized and twisted history because we are still living with the radical agenda of a small group of Tudor reformers who seized upon a king's marital needs in order to effect a change they (not the country) desired, and at the same time treated themselves to undreamed of personal wealth.

The United Kingdom is the only European country to use the phrase the 'Dark Ages' for the medieval period, and in large measure it is because we have retrospectively made it dark. Henry VIII started it by denigrating and destroying the intellectual, artistic, and spiritual output of ten centuries, emptying out cathedrals and library shelves, leaving them barren and devoid of any human ingenuity or beauty. It is no wonder that, looking at the slim remnants of English medieval life, it appears dark to us. To compound matters, rather than recognize the Tudor sack of our culture, we have collectively stuck to their breathtakingly arrogant claim that England was a backward, gloom-filled wasteland until Henry brought the searing flame of enlightenment.

Our complicity in this myth is partly because the sectarian language of the Tudor court and its clerics' sermons has proved immensely durable and is now so deeply ingrained that we continue to be blinded to the vitality and unique Englishness of our pre-Reformation culture. Instead of celebrating our nation's vivid and exuberant history, we swallow Henry's spin and damn it all as nothing more than the output of an infested ragbag of 'corrupt abominations', 'papistical superstitions', and 'unsavery teaching'. The result is a gross distortion, and equates to the theft of our past. Happily, it is a wrong that historians are now, in increasing numbers, eloquently addressing.

Perhaps the final word should go to Robert Peckham, who died in Rome in 1569 during the reign of Elizabeth I:

> *Here lies Robert Peckham, Englishman and Catholic, who, after England's break with the Church, left England because he could not live in his country without the Faith, and, having come to Rome, died there because he could not live apart from his country.*

23

Thomas Cromwell was the Islamic State of his day

Hilary Mantel's Booker prize winning novel, *Wolf Hall*, hit the television screens as a BBC drama series. Everyone applauded its visual beauty and serenity. But the character of Thomas Cromwell was distorted beyond recognition, from a greedy vandal and murderer to a sensitive intellectual. This piece gives Cromwell back his historical personality.

On the 24th of July 2014, worshippers in Mosul were asked to leave one of the city's most historic and famous buildings—an ancient Nestorian-Assyrian church that had long ago been converted into the Mosque of the Prophet Younis (biblical Jonah). The Islamic State then rigged the entire building with explosives, and blew it into oblivion. Tragically, it was a Shia mosque—one of many that have suffered the same fate.

The UK's current primetime TV fantasy blockbuster du jour is *Wolf Hall*. Everyone loves a costume drama, but there is a world of difference between fictional history and historical fiction. One dramatizes real people and events. The other is an entirely made-up story set in the past. The current tendency is to blur the two, which *Wolf Hall* does spectacularly.

Thomas Cromwell, whose life it chronicles, comes across as a plucky, self-made Englishman, whose quiet reserve suggests inner strength and personal nobility. Back in the real world, Cromwell was a 'ruffian' (in his own words) turned sectarian extremist, whose religious vandalism bears striking comparison with the iconoclasm of Islamic State or the Afghani Taliban.

Thanks to *Wolf Hall*, more people have now heard of Thomas Cromwell, and this is a good thing. But underneath its fictionalized portrayal of Henry VIII's chief enforcer, there is a historical man, and he is one whose record for murder, looting, and destruction ought to have us apoplectic with rage, not reaching for the popcorn.

Historians rarely agree on details, so a lot about Cromwell's inner life is still up for debate. But it is a truly tough job finding anything heroic in the man's legacy of brutality and naked ambition.

Against a backdrop of Henry VIII's marital strife, the pathologically ambitious Cromwell single-handedly masterminded the break with Rome in order to hand Henry the Church, with its all-important control of divorce and marriage. There were, to be sure, small pockets of Protestantism in England at the time, but any attempt to cast Cromwell's despotic actions as sincere theological reform are hopeless. Cromwell himself had minimal truck with religious belief. He loved politics, money, and power, and the reformers could give them to him.

Flushed with the success of engineering Henry's divorce from Catherine of Aragon and his marriage to Anne Boleyn, Cromwell moved on to confiscating the Church's money. Before long, he was dissolving monasteries as fast as he could, which meant seizing anything that was not nailed down and keeping it for himself, for Henry, and for their circle of friends. It was the biggest land-grab and asset-strip in English history, and Cromwell sat at the centre of the operation, at the heart of a widely-loathed, absolutist, and tyrannical regime. When Anne Boleyn pointed out that the money should be going to charity or good works, he fitted her up on charges of adultery, and watched as she was beheaded.

As an adviser to Henry, Cromwell could have attempted to guide the hot-headed king, to tame his wilder ambitions, counsel him in patience, uphold the many freedoms enjoyed by his subjects. But Cromwell had no interest in moderation. He made all Henry's dreams come true, riding roughshod over the law of the land and whoever got in his way. For instance, we are hearing a lot about Magna Carta this year, but Cromwell had no time for tedious trials and judgement by peers. With lazy strokes of his pen, he condemned royalty, nobles, peasants, nuns, and monks to horrific summary executions. We are not talking half a dozen. He dispatched hundreds under his highly politicized 'treason' laws. (When his own time came and the tables had turned, he pleaded to Henry: 'Most gracyous prynce I crye for mercye'. But he was given all the mercy he had shown others.)

And then there is his impact on this country's artistic and intellectual heritage. No one can be sure of the exact figure, but it is estimated that the destruction started and legalized by Cromwell amounted to 90% of the English art then in existence. Statues were hacked down. Frescoes were smashed to bits. Mosaics were pulverized. Illuminated manuscripts were shredded. Wooden carvings were burned. Precious metalwork was melted down. Shrines were reduced to rubble. This vandalism went way beyond a religious reform. It was a frenzy, obliterating the artistic patrimony of centuries of indigenous craftsmanship with an intensity of hatred for imagery and depicting the divine that has strong and resonant parallels today.

It can only be a good thing that people are again thinking about Cromwell. Because as we look to the east, to the fanaticism that is sacking the cultural and artistic heritage of other ancient societies, we can all draw the same, inevitable conclusions about religious extremism in any age, whether Christian, Muslim, Jewish, Hindu, or Buddhist. None of it is pretty. All of it is real. And we, in England, are not in some way removed from it. We only have to survey the smashed up medieval buildings the length and breadth of the country, or contemplate Cromwell's record of public beheadings and other barbarous executions.

It is plain that extremists come in all shapes and sizes.

24

How Protestantism fuelled the deadly witch craze

Walpurgisnacht (May Day eve) is the annual European festival of witchcraft. Alongside Halloween six months later, it brings us face-to-face with the folk magic in our traditional culture. This piece was published to mark *Walpurgisnacht*, and to examine the tragic history of the witch craze that ravaged Europe and the New World.

In an island with such a unique and rich past, it is unsurprising that the country's leaders occasionally turn to history in times of need.

Over the last week, they have been dissecting our relationship with religion. The topic has always fired the nation up, as we wrestle to reconcile the strong and vibrant strands of paganism, Catholicism, Anglicanism, scepticism, and secularism that have dominated the last two millennia.

The Prime Minister declared that we are a Christian country; a range of intellectuals stated openly that we are not; the Archbishop of Canterbury intervened to specify that we are, historically, a Christian country; the former Archbishop of Canterbury clarified that we are, in fact, a post-Christian country; and the Deputy Prime Minister capped it all off by suggesting that the Church of England should finally be disestablished;

Meanwhile, over in Rome, an unprecedented 6,000 priests, 1,000 bishops, 150 cardinals, and two popes led the largest denomination of the largest religion the world has ever seen in a celebration of twenty-first-century Western spirituality.

This is all fascinating stuff for the historian, because prevailing religious moods are a bellwether of so many other aspects of a society.

And coincidentally, now is an interesting time for this public debate on our complex religious history, as today is *Walpurgisnacht*, one of the many northern European pagan festivals to survive, Christianized, into the modern world.

The story starts with Wealdburg, an Anglo-Saxon girl from Devon. Born around AD 710, she was sent at the age of eleven to the nuns at Wimborne, a place of calm and learning. (A fabulous later medieval chained library still survives there.) At the nunnery, Wealdburg learned the skills that would make her one of England's first female authors.

Her family was steeped in the Anglo-Saxon church and in its dangerous work to convert the pagan Saxons of Germany. Her father was St Richard the Pilgrim. Her uncle was the great St Boniface. And her two brothers were St Winibald and St Willibald. She is better known as St Walburga, the nun and missionary who ended her life as abbess at the double monastery of Heidenheim in Bavaria.

Her cult has always been slightly magical (even before J K Rowling took her name for Sirius's mother, Walburga Black). Soon after her death, she was confused with Waldborg, a pre-Christian fertility goddess, and thereafter depicted with a sheaf of corn. More magical still, when her remains were inspected in AD 893 they were found to be constantly wet. From then until today, phials of the sacred *Walburgisöl* her tomb produces are regularly distributed, and she is counted among the *Elaephori*, or 'oil-yielding' saints. Although scientific tests have demonstrated that the oil is natural water which springs up in the tomb, the contact with her bones is held by its many fans to sanctify it.

Today, people across northern Europe and Scandinavia will celebrate the eve of St Walburga's day, better known by its German name: *Walpurgisnacht*. In most places bonfires, candles, alcohol, and revelry will be on the menu, but it has a darker side, too.

As anyone who ever soaked up Dennis Wheatley's electrifying occult thrillers will know, *Walpurgisnacht* is also the foremost night for witches' sabbaths. According to legend, the most infamous and infernal of them convenes on the Brocken, the highest peak in

Germany's Harz mountains, a hundred and eighty miles from where St Walburga lies buried.

It is pure coincidence that Walburga was canonized on May Day, thus giving her name to the festivities of the night before. But it is also strangely fitting, as popular belief in the healing properties of saints' relics (and oils) is inseparable from our historical attachment to magic.

And here is where something fascinating happens. As the Reformation swept away faith in popular and largely benign Christian miracles, it instead offered belief in a much darker magic—one that would quickly lead to the horror of the witch-craze and fantastical legends like the sabbaths on the Brocken.

It is deeply ironic that the Protestant reformers, in abolishing what they saw as harmful superstitious claptrap, replaced it with terrifying magical fears that would end with the brutal and pointless murder of tens of thousands of innocent women.

Before the Reformation there had, of course, been some scattered witch trials. But the same reforming theologians who lambasted what they saw as the crude and irrational magical beliefs underpinning the cult of saints and relics rapidly convinced themselves that hundreds of towns and villages were sheltering the foulest witches and demons, whose unnatural rites jeopardized the health and salvation of Christendom. They saw them flying on diabolical beasts, covering vast distances in the blink of an eye. They found on them folds of skin used for suckling demons in the form of familiars. They accused them of sexually molesting decent folk, invading their beds as lustful *incubi* and *succubi*. They were convinced they possessed infernal powers to see the past, the present (at great distance), and the future. But above all, they feared the witches were working ceaselessly to destroy their new, rational churches.

As the reformers set about ridding the world of these devilish handmaidens, the great burnings began, peaking in the late 1500s and early 1600s, before petering out in the early 1700s. In that time, somewhere between 40,000 and 100,000 people (predominantly, but not exclusively, women) were torched alive on suspicion of practising magic.

The hysteria reached its height around AD 1600. Even King James VI of Scotland (soon to be James I of England), who later sponsored the mellifluous King James Bible, slaved over what had become his personal obsession—*Daemonologie*, a work in which he passionately set out his certainty at the existence of witches bound by unholy oaths to their infernal master.

The subject was, in fact, deeply personal for him, as he had been the victim of what he believed to be a curse which had caught his ship in fearful storms when returning from Denmark. The result was the infamous North Berwick Witch Trials, in which he personally interrogated many suspected witches at Holyrood Palace, including the healer and midwife Agnes Sampson. Under his supervision, she was stripped and shaved, a spiked witch's bridle was put into her mouth, a noose was placed around her neck, she was deprived of sleep, then repeatedly probed invasively with a pin to find the Devil's mark. Inevitably, she succumbed to the horrific torture, confessed, and was executed.

The senseless barbarity of this mass witch hysteria was not confined to Europe, but also exported to the New World. Among the many witch trials there, the best known is that at Salem in 1692, where febrile rumours of diabolic curses led to 19 people being hanged, one pressed to death, and five more dying in prison.

But how did this all happen? To bring the focus back to England, how did a society that was enjoying the fresh, new plays of William Shakespeare harbour these extraordinary beliefs about witches? And what moved the authorities to set about such extreme and brutal persecution of suspects?

The most widespread and popular view is that a sexually-repressed medieval Church became dysfunctionally obsessed with women and witchcraft, resulting in a vicious misogynistic persecution.

The evidence, though, yields a far more complex picture—not least because by the high point of the witch craze in 1550–1650, the medieval age was well-and-truly over, and the Protestant Reformation had long since killed off the monolithic nature of the one Church. The mass witch burnings took place squarely in the post-Reformation (and Counter-Reformation) 'early modern' period.

The story does, however, begin much earlier.

In many of its verses, the Bible assumes magic to be a reality—perhaps most famously when King Saul visited the Witch of Endor. It describes how he put on a disguise (as he had just, frustratingly, banned all magic in his lands) and sought out the old necromancer, whom he commanded to raise the prophet Samuel from the dead for him, which she duly did.

Yet despite the plain text of the Bible, the medieval Church took a more modern line, and categorically denied the existence of magic. Beginning with St Augustine in the AD 400s, it declared magic to be an impossibility. This view was widely followed. For instance, despite the Bible's injunction not to suffer a witch to live, Charlemagne's *Saxon Capitulary* (given at Paderborn in AD 785) ordered the death penalty for anyone who executed another for witchcraft.

The early Church's most famous formal statement on magic was in the *Canon episcopi*, a collection of canon law from *c.* AD 900, which definitively ruled that magic is not real, and that believing otherwise is an error. The *Canon* was so vastly influential that almost all medieval theology on magic used it as a starting point.

To find the origin of the idea that the medieval Church stoked the witch-craze, we need to look at two men—Heinrich Kramer and Pope Innocent VIII. Between them, they managed to advocate a short-lived minority view that has forever after been popularly seen as the official line.

The prime mover of the two was Kramer—a German Dominican and an inquisitor. In 1486, he published his notorious witch-hunters' handbook, the *Malleus Maleficarum* (The Hammer of the Witches). In it, he insisted that magic was real, and he described how inquisitors should investigate and punish witches. To beef up his credibility, he afterwards added a respected theologian, Jakob Sprenger, as a co-author. At the same time, he got Pope Innocent VIII to confirm him and Sprenger as inquisitors, and to list certain offences of witchcraft. While this papal confirmation was not a dogmatic Church statement that magic existed, it clearly showed a willingness to entertain the idea.

This was exactly what Heinrich Kramer wanted. He wished to launch himself as the pre-eminent witch-hunter, and to have his *Malleus Maleficarum* fêted as the go-to book for the wave of witch-inquisitors he hoped would follow him.

As it turned out, he failed spectacularly on both counts. Despite brandishing the papal bull in support of his views, the Church condemned his book, ideas, and methods as unethical, illegal, and theologically unsound. It wanted nothing to do with him or the *Malleus*. There would be no witch persecutions of the sort he envisaged. The Gregorian Inquisition had been established to deal with the religious matter of heresy, not the secular issue of witchcraft. Pope Alexander IV spelled this out clearly in a 1258 canon which forbade inquisitions into sorcery unless there was also manifest heresy. And this view was even confirmed and acknowledged by the infamous inquisitor Bernard Gui (immortalized by Umberto Eco in *The Name of the Rose*), who wrote in his influential inquisitors' manual that, by itself, sorcery did not come within the Inquisition's jurisdiction. In sum, the Church did not want the Inquisition sucked into witch trials, which were for the secular courts.

But fifty years before Kramer published the *Malleus Maleficarum*, Johannes Gutenburg had fired up Europe's first printing presses in Mainz, and the scandalous and titillating *Malleus Maleficarum* was soon flying off the shelves as a best seller, eagerly snapped up by a new Protestant readership whose religion was introducing them to unprecedented and violent imagery of the Christian struggle against the Devil.

In the age's new writings, the Devil became more present than ever before. Luther famously described his personal physical bouts with the Devil, whom he saw everywhere and in everything:

> *We are all subject to the Devil, both in body and goods, and we be strangers in this world, whereof he is the prince and god.*

According to Luther:

The Devil liveth, yea and reigneth throughout the whole world.

The result of this intense focus on a physical Devil was a deepening fear of evil in the every day, and of those human agents the Devil worked through. It was therefore a short step for Luther to declare that all witches were the 'Devil's whores' and to be burned. (The violence of the language was not uncommon for the period. Luther famously remarked that German peasants were 'lying, thieving hordes' and that the nobility should 'smite, slay and stay them as one would a mad dog', which led directly to a massacre of over a hundred thousand German peasants in 1525–6.) Other reforming thinkers of the time had similarly literalist views of the Bible. John Wesley saw any attempt to deny the existence of witchcraft as 'giving up' the Bible. And even into the 1700s, leading jurists like England's William Blackstone (first Vinerian Professor of Common Law at Oxford) believed that:

To deny the possibility, nay, actual existence of witchcraft and sorcery is at once flatly to contradict the word of God.

Many have theorized why Europe and the New World lost their collective reason over witchcraft for several centuries. Ideas include religious reforms, social change, misogyny, the rise of capitalism, and even an attempt to control the spread of syphilis.

Tonight, as people in numerous European countries limber up to celebrate *Walpurgisnacht* with bonfires and parties, it is the perfect opportunity to ask ourselves about our society's view of witches. With the witch-craze far behind us, we are free again to see magic— throughout the ages—as part of our historical social fabric.

Most religious traditions treasure the seasons, where a symmetry of solstices, equinoctes, and other cyclical festivals provide a framework for appreciating the circularity of life. *Walpurgisnacht* fits neatly into this pattern, falling exactly six months after Halloween, the other great pagan and witchy night of the year.

Both are ancient celebrations.

Halloween is the older, having syncretically evolved from Samhain (the Celtic liminal festival of the dead) into the Christian *triduum* of Hallowtide—All Saints Eve, All Saints Day, and All Souls Day: three days for remembering the dead.

In medieval times, alongside Hallowtide's solemn Masses and bell-ringing, regional customs saw charnel houses opened, corpses decorated with flowers, blessings and vigils in graveyards, food left out for the departed, the distribution of spiced cakes and wine, cross-dressing, troupes of revellers, mummers in masks demanding tributes, and general inversion and misrule.

The Church of England under King Edward VI and Queen Elizabeth I stamped out the Church and folk celebrations as popery, although the popular revels were never fully suppressed. They continued in rural areas throughout the 1600s and 1700s, and on occasion officials trying to stop them were beaten up. Across England, the world of the dead continued to be remembered with fires, parties, and rowdy processions, and people still knocked on doors seeking specially baked 'soul cakes' in return for saying a prayer for those in purgatory. These Samhain/ Hallowtide rituals remained a feature of English life long after the Reformation, and they continued almost wholly untouched in Ireland and Scotland, from where they were exported to the United States.

Where Halloween marks the start of winter, *Walpurgisnacht* celebrates its end (as does the Celtic Beltane, also held now). But *Walpurgisnacht* is not Celtic. It is a legacy from the pre-Christian Norse cultures of northern Europe and Scandinavia. Like Halloween, it focuses on fire, the changing seasons, the dead, and magic. But where Halloween is a time of playful mischief for remembering a historical attachment to the maverick and effervescent side of the supernatural, *Walpurgisnacht* has an altogether more sinister aspect. In the Czech Republic, for instance, *Walpurgisnacht* (*Čarodějnice*) involves the mass festive burning of straw witch effigies.

In many senses, Halloween and *Walpurgisnacht* seem to capture profoundly our ambiguity about witchcraft. There is a joy and a silliness to Halloween, with its exuberant children's storybook witches and cats. But to those who believe that history can teach nothing to our technology-fuelled age, *Walpurgisnacht* proves the contrary. With its sinister legacy of hysteria around Devilish sabbaths, and its stark reminder of the consequences of witch-hunting, it is a day to recognize—whether we are now a Christian, a post-Christian, or a secular country—that no society is ever as enlightened as it thinks it is.

25

Guy Fawkes. Islamists, converts, and terrorism: some things never change

Up and down Britain, the fifth of November is marked each year by public bonfires and burning effigies of Guy Fawkes (or in Lewes, effigies of the pope). This piece tells the story of Guy Fawkes, a Yorkshireman who became radicalized by extremists into trying to murder the king of England.

It is the 5th of November once more, which can only mean it is time to burn Guy Fawkes again (and Pope Paul V, for those in Lewes marching under their traditional 'no popery' banners). But, as the faggots are kindled tonight, it is worth remembering who Guy 'Guido' Fawkes really was.

Despite a popular belief that Fawkes was an Italian extremist, the fact is he was an entirely home-grown terrorist from the Stonegate area of York. He was baptized into the Church of England in 1570 at the beautiful St Michael-le-Belfrey by York Minster, but when his mother was widowed and married into a staunchly recusant family from the West Riding, Fawkes converted to Catholicism.

In his early twenties, he sold up his land and went to fight for his new faith in Spain's war against the Protestant Netherlands. According to a school friend, he became 'highly skilled in matters of war', yet remained devout, calm, 'pleasant of approach and cheerful of manner, opposed to quarrels and strife ... loyal to his friends'.

However, back in England, a group of extremists planning revolution desperately needed military skill. After careful enquiry, they made a beeline for Fawkes, whom they persuaded to lend his nerve and knowhow to their cause. The mastermind was Robert Catesby, a hothead who had grown angry at the treatment of England's old Catholic families under Elizabeth I and had no faith that things would improve under James I. Having failed to persuade the Spanish to invade, Catesby's new plan was simple: to bomb the Lords chamber at the opening of Parliament, kill the King and his most prominent courtiers, then stage a revolution.

However, one of the plotters sent a warning letter to Lord Monteagle, a Catholic peer: 'I would advyse you ... to devise some excuse to shift youer attendance at this parliament, for God and man hath concurred to punishe the wickedness of this tyme'. Unfortunately for the plotters, Lord Monteagle took the letter straight to court, triggering an immediate search of the vault under the Lords' chamber. In no time, the royal guard found Fawkes, matches, a watch, and 36 kegs of explosives.

Despite Fawkes's fortitude under torture—which left a deep impact on all—the game was up. Although he insisted he was 'John Johnson', they eventually found his real name. Separately, the other conspirators were rapidly unveiled, along with the enormity of their plot, which would likely have killed not only the King and his closest advisers, but everyone in the Lords that evening. Despite our obsession with burning Fawkes, he was actually sentenced to be hanged, drawn, and quartered, although he escaped the harrowing punishment by leaping off the high scaffold in Westminster's Old Palace Yard and breaking his neck.

The story is fascinating for many reasons, not least because Fawkes was a convert to Catholicism, and it is an age-old adage that converts are often among the most militant. And there are striking parallels today, where the same dynamic is again at work. One of the murderers of Fusilier Drummer Lee Rigby in Woolwich in 2013 was a convert, as was the fanatic who killed a Canadian soldier earlier this month. A former Taliban recruiter in the West, who now works for the Canadian government, has also weighed in, highlighting that today's Islamist extremists specifically target converts—they often know little about the religion and their enthusiasm can easily be subverted. No one should therefore have been surprised this summer when two jihadis from Birmingham who spent eight months fighting in Syria had bought *Islam for Dummies* and *The Koran for Dummies* as their airport reading,

Although Guy Fawkes was a minor figure in Catesby's bomb plot, history has made him its poster boy. King James I's triumphant 5th of November 'Gunpowder Plot Day' bonfire celebrations have remained enduringly popular, and Fawkes has been promoted to the central protagonist. But when we incinerate Fawkes again tonight, it is worth seeing him in context, and reflecting on the tide of young converts of all faiths who are perennially sucked into extremism.

If I was being responsible, I would end by adding that the good people of Lewes should probably now stop burning an effigy of Pope Paul V every year and put away their 'no popery' banners. These are yesterday's sentiments, and have no role in modern Britain. (If it was happening in Northern Ireland, it would doubtless be banned immediately.) But then, speaking as a deeply fuzzy and laissez-faire English Catholic, Pope-burning is a colourful, historic, and faintly hilarious English tradition, and we are losing far too much of our cultural identity nowadays. So, to all of you in Lewes tonight: burn on! And let's be thankful that these days we can laugh about it all over a mulled wine or two and a few sparklers.

26

New Year's Day is too soon after Christmas. Let's move it back to its proper place—in March

From the eleventh century, England celebrated New Year's Day on the 25th of March. This piece traces the strange story of England's calendar reforms in 1750, which not only moved New Year's Day to the 1st of January, but also implemented Pope Gregory XIII's new 'Gregorian' calendar, which England had been avoiding for over a century and a half.

Between now and New Year's Eve, you're going to hear a lot of people saying, 'It's all too much, really'. They will look fatigued and wan as they explain: 'It's the same every year. No time to recover from the Christmas liver-lashing before the onslaught of New Year's Eve.' Or words to that effect.

Well, I have a solution. We should campaign to move New Year's Day back to where it always was, from just after the time of William the Conqueror up to George II's day. For almost 700 years (arguably pretty full ones, stuffed with wool, wealth, monasteries, renaissance, empires, and so forth), the Brits managed to achieve quite a lot. And they did it with a New Year's Day at the end of March.

The man who changed it all was Philip Stanhope, 4th Earl of Chesterfield. He began in the Commons as member for St Germans (a rotten borough in Cornwall), but ended up taking his seat in the Lords, from where he sponsored a bill that changed everything. Chesterfield's Act, or The Calendar (New Style) Act, was passed by Parliament in 1750, and it had two main purposes.

The first was a Good Thing, correcting 170 years of silliness. Everyone knows that in 1752 England lost 11 days. People went to bed on the evening of the 2nd of September and awoke, troubled, on the 14th of September. Well, that was Chesterfield's doing. There probably were no rioting crowds baying 'Give us back our 11 days,' but the calendrical leapfrog must have been unsettling.

By finally pushing through the Gregorian calendar reform, Chesterfield was only acknowledging that England was very late in being modern. After all, the Julian calendar England was using at that time had been introduced in 46 BC by Julius Caesar. Unsurprisingly, by the late 1500s, it was clear that it had certain limitations. Of most concern—at least, to the people who were concerned about such things—was the fact that Easter was no longer falling where it was supposed to.

Way back in AD 325, the First Council of Nicaea (a pleasant place in western Turkey) had tied Easter to the Sunday following the first full moon on or after the spring equinox. Back then, the spring equinox fell around the 21st of March. However, by the late 1500s, the equinox was popping up around the 11th of March, and the following full moon was not behaving either. An Italian astronomer named Luigi Lilio finally sorted out the baffling tables of epacts and intercalary years, and made a calendar reform recommendation to Pope Gregory XIII in Rome.

The pope duly handed the whole thing over to a special papal Calendar Commission under a German Jesuit mathematician named Christopher Clavius. When the Commission had finished fine-tuning the details, Pope Gregory XIII announced the new calendar to the world on the 24th of February 1582. He did it in the bull *Inter gravissimas*, which chopped 10 days out of October 1582, thereby resetting the equinox and full moon, and also implementing a more accurate system for leap years to keep things under control going forward. Lilio, Clavius, and the team had clearly got a lot of it right (50 years before Galileo) as, over 400 years later, their calendar—the Gregorian calendar—remains the most widely used in the world.

But nothing is ever simple. Europe fractured into those countries which adopted the new calendar, and those which decided it was all too papist.

In England, of course, it did not go down well. By 1582, Queen Elizabeth I was coming up for a quarter of a century on the throne.

Religion was a flashpoint issue, and she offered zero tolerance on anything with a whiff of Rome. When news of Pope Gregory's calendar reached her court, the science behind it was widely admired by her foremost cartographer, astronomer, and scientific adviser—Dr John Dee (who managed to serve pro- and anti-Roman monarchs with equal zeal). Despite his later reputation as conjuror, magician, and occultist—the dividing line between these activities and science was yet to be firmly drawn—he was a brilliant scientist, whose maps and navigational calculations lay behind many of the boldest voyages of the Elizabethan period.

However, Dee was unsuccessful in persuading Elizabeth's court to adopt the new calendar.

Instead, the implementation of the Gregorian system in England was lost in the twists and turns of politics, where it remained until 1750, when it finally got through Parliament. Happily, England was not the slowest in Europe. Greece took until 1923 to introduce the 'new" calendar. So, Chesterfield's Act implemented long-overdue reforms, and that is a cause for congratulation. However, it additionally did something that was perhaps not so good, although it had also been part of Pope Gregory's 1582 reorganization.

It moved New Year's Day. Since the late 1000s, New Year's Day was widely celebrated across Latin Christendom on the 25th of March. Before that, European New Year festivities were a haphazard affair, frequently changing as different popes honoured their native traditions. Some pontiffs insisted on the 25th of December (Nativity style). Others plumped for the 1st of January (Circumcision style). The remainder preferred the 25th of March (Annunciation style). From the time of Pope Gregory VII onwards (1085), it all settled down, and Annunciation style became the norm, marking the day the Angel Gabriel visited the Virgin Mary and told her she was expecting a little miracle.

However, even though Chesterfield's Act finally pushed Lady Day off the calendar after 700 years, it still survives if you know where to look. For instance, rents due under many old land contracts are still payable on Lady Day, as well as on the three other Quarter Days:

Midsummer (the 24th of June), Michaelmas (the 29th of September), and Christmas (the 25th of December).

But perhaps more relevant: the start of the annual tax year on the 6th of April is where old Lady Day (the 25th of March) falls in the modern calendar if the missing 11 days are added back in. So, perhaps those with a love of English tradition may like to return to Lady Day for our New Year celebrations? But what will we do on New Year's Day? We can't just do ... well ... nothing.

Even in medieval England, the 1st of January was still celebrated, just as it always had been in antiquity. In Roman times, the 1st of January (the kalends) was the day when the year's new consuls took up office, and gratefully sacrificed bulls to Jupiter. It therefore quickly became a sacred day marking the start of a new civic year. As a result, it was also chosen for important events.

For instance, when the Roman Senators decided to deify Julius Caesar, they chose the 1st of January 42 BC. In time, the January kalends became the largest of the annual Roman festivals, reaching all across Europe and spanning several days of present-giving, feasting, singing, dancing, and sacrifices. So it should be no surprise that when the Church turned the 1st of January into the serious and sober feast of Jesus's Circumcision (on the octave after his birthday at Christmas), the good people of England and France decided they were going to have a party anyway.

There are many medieval records of the bawdy and 'damnable' Feast of the Fools, which took place on a range of days, but most commonly on the 1st of January. The grumpy theologians of the University of Paris even described it for us:

> *Priests and clerks may be seen wearing masks and monstrous visages at the hours of office. They dance in the choir dressed as women, panders or minstrels. They sing wanton songs. They eat black puddings at the horn of the altar while the celebrant is saying mass. They play at dice there. They cense with stinking smoke from the soles of old shoes. They run and leap through the church, without a blush at*

their own shame. Finally they drive about the town and its theatres in shabby traps and carts; and rouse the laughter of their fellows and the bystanders in infamous performances, with indecent gestures and verses scurrilous and unchaste.

At times it also seems to have been mixed in with the tradition of electing a boy chorister to replace the bishop for a while at this time of year, commonly starting on St Nicholas's day (the 6th of December). They dressed the boy in mini bishop's clothes and let him run the cathedral. In recent decades, many English cathedrals have resumed this medieval tradition.

In Salisbury, there is even a medieval stone effigy of a child bishop. Although modern killjoys insist it commemorates an adult bishop's internal organs, tradition has always maintained it is the resting place of a boy bishop who died during his short period in office. Experts still argue whether the Feast of the Fools was a survival from pagan times or a medieval invention. Still, whatever the origin of the revels, they were for many centuries traditional folk parties.

So, moving New Year's Day back to the 25th of March would allow us to celebrate the new year at a time when things really do feel new. Spring will be on the way with all the optimism that brings. And we can save ourselves the dietary hara-kiri of Christmas and New Year's Eve falling a week apart. However, for those who need a cup or two on the 1st of January, let's invite them to institute and celebrate a modern Feast of the Fools, which no doubt their ingenuity will soon turn into something richer and more interesting than tipsily singing *Auld Lang Syne* while watching Big Ben on television.

Now that Pope Francis has had a while to get his feet under the table and his nose into some of the historical manuscripts in the Vatican's collection, I think it's time we asked him to call another Calendar Commission.

THE VICTORIAN
WORLD

27

Haters back off. Lord Elgin was a hero who saved the marbles for the world

The unparalleled sculptures from the Parthenon temple in Athens displayed in the British Museum are known as the Elgin Marbles. This is because Lord Elgin brought them to England in the early 1800s. Today, celebrities enjoy backing campaigns for their return to Greece. But almost no one acknowledges that Lord Elgin saved the sculptures from destruction, and bankrupted himself to do it. This piece tells the story of how he came to rescue them.

In February 2014, while promoting his World War Two film, *The Monuments Men*, Hollywood A-List actor George Clooney declared that Britain should send the Elgin Marbles back to Greece. Despite claiming they came from the Pantheon in Rome rather than the Parthenon in Athens (and also that they had been taken by Lord 'Eljin'), he felt that returning them was now appropriate.

This was fiercely controversial territory. However, once the furore had died down, most people wrote it off as a kooky PR stunt.

Until last week, when it emerged that George Clooney's new wife, Amal Clooney, a lawyer specializing in human rights law (but not as far as we know the law of museums or antiquities), declared she was advising the Greek government on the return of the marbles to Greece.

Speaking publicly to the media about the matter, Amal Clooney said that Greece had 'just cause' to demand the return of the marbles, which she said had been taken illegally by Lord Elgin early in the nineteenth century, a fact Britain should be embarrassed about.

However, her assertion that Elgin took the marbles illegally is plain wrong, and flatly contradicts all serious histories of the marbles, as well as the reasoned findings of legal experts, and a parliamentary select committee which examined the matter in minute detail.

Furthermore, any art lover who has read up the real story will know that the collection of marbles in the British Museum simply would not exist today without Elgin because they were being systematically destroyed in Athens. If Elgin had not intervened, they would be a mere memory, like the Afghani Buddhas at Bamiyan, dynamited into oblivion by the Taliban in 2001.

The British case for ownership of the Elgin marbles is actually very simple. The sculptures were being destroyed in Athens. Elgin sought proper permission from the government in Athens to remove them. He did so with the full blessing of the Athenian authorities over a period of four years from 1801–5. He funded the entire project himself, going bankrupt in the process. His only motivation was to save these unique works of art for the world, and he made not one penny from the whole operation, but died with his estate crippled by the resulting debt. When the British government purchased the marbles from him, they did so having satisfied themselves that Lord Elgin had acted properly in all regards.

And yet Geoffrey Robertson QC, head of Amal Clooney's chambers and the senior lawyer on the team advising the Greek government, told the media last week that Elgin 'was a bankrupt. He used his diplomatic position to get a license to take the marbles and to profit personally by selling them to the British Museum. If he did that today, he would be in prison'. I hope Robertson has now fired his researchers, because that portrayal of Elgin will not last two minutes in a court, although it no doubt goes down very well in certain newspapers and with those who do not want to be troubled by the facts. It is no wonder that opinion polls demonstrate a general wish to return the marbles to Athens when the debate is so often framed with such arrant and emotive inaccuracy.

The truth is that this is a non-story. The legal position on the Parthenon marbles is unambiguously clear, and no international lawyer who has looked into the matter would say anything else—the marbles belong to Britain. So far, no advocate for the return of the sculptures has taken the argument beyond insulting Lord Elgin to actually coming up with some relevant law. And there is a reason for that, because there is no law giving Greece a right to the Parthenon marbles—not even the 1970 UNESCO convention on cultural objects or the 1995 UNIDROIT amendment to it. The legal position has been summed up succinctly by the world-leading cultural property expert, Prof John Henry Merryman of Stanford University, who concludes that the modern state of Greece has no legal, moral, or ethical case for the return of the marbles. This is why Greece has never brought a legal action for the sculptures. Instead, it wages an emotional political and media campaign, which amounts to no more than a suggestion that while the marbles may not legally belong *to* Greece, they belong *in* Greece.

It is worth starting the story at the beginning, before returning to the disingenuous historical distortions that plague the debate today.

Ancient Greek cities generally sited their municipal and religious buildings on the highest available ground, which was deemed the most fitting and mystical place for the gods to be honoured. It also made a lot of sense militarily. This area was the *akropolis*, meaning 'the high city'.

The city-state of Athens was sacred to Athena, and the people there worshipped her as the sacred Virgin (*Parthenos*), hence her great temple was the Parthenon (Παρθενών).

It was one of the world's most magnificent buildings, conceived in the mid-400s BC by the statesman and general Perikles, plum in the middle of the city's 'Golden Age'. We also know that it was designed by the architects Iktinos and Kallikrates, who incorporated many traditional techniques such as subtly bending the immense columns to enhance the perspective of the temple from different viewpoints around the city, as well as taking their art to new heights in dozens of ways. Among the many wondrous buildings of the ancient world, it marks the undoubted high point of Doric architecture.

To complete the temple, Perikles called in Pheidias, one of history's most gifted sculptors, commissioning him to fashion vast amounts of sculptural decoration out of local marble from nearby Mount Pentelikon to adorn the building's exterior, as well as to create a massive gold and ivory chryselephantine statue of the Virgin Athena to go inside the temple.

The whole was completed in 438 BC—a fitting testament to the grandeur of Athens, with its nascent democracy (although not for women, foreigners, or slaves) and immortal philosophers like Socrates, Plato, and Aristotle; playwrights like Sophocles, Aeschylus, Aristophanes, and Euripedes; and historians like Herodotus, Thucydides, and Xenophon.

Moving forward over 2,000 years to 1799, what the British ambassador to Istanbul, Lord Elgin, saw in front of him on the craggy outcrop of the *akropolis*, which by then was an Ottoman military compound, was a sorry husk.

The fabric of all the buildings was decayed, and a ramshackle mosque huddled inside the Parthenon's great pillars where once Athena's vast statue had stood. Worse still, the Ottoman forces regularly amused themselves by hacking off arms or legs of Pheidias's sculptures to sell to the tourists who had been coming in increasing numbers since around 1750. When not flogging the marble off, the Ottoman garrison fired rounds at the frieze for target practice, or simply ground the sculptures down to burn for lime they could sell.

Moving forward in time again, when Greece opened the New Acropolis Museum in June 2009, its director, Dimitris Pandermalis, called on the world's dignitaries to campaign to bring the surviving sculptures back to Athens to redress what he described as Lord Elgin's 'act of barbarism'.

The truth could not be more violently different. And it is not a question of national or political perspective. The fact is that in the early 1800s the Parthenon sculptures were being actively obliterated, and it is only thanks to the extraordinary dedication of Lord Elgin that such an amazing collection of Pheidias's unique, irreplaceable, world-class art has been preserved for people to see today.

Elgin was born Thomas Bruce in Fife in 1766. Aged five, he became the seventh earl of Elgin and eleventh earl of Kincardine. After education at Harrow and Westminster, and following university study at St Andrews and in Paris, he undertook a soldiering career in the 3rd Scots Guards, followed by a period as a representative Scottish peer. After a few diplomatic postings, in 1799, and aged only 33, he was sent as British ambassador to the 'Sublime Porte' of Ottoman Istanbul.

Before he left, he made it known in London governmental circles that he intended to use his posting to commission drawings, paintings, and casts of classical art in order to bring them home, publish the drawings, exhibit the casts, and promote the advancement of the 'Fine Arts'. He was an ardent art lover, and he wanted to make the wonders of classical art available to British artists in order to inspire and inform them. He asked the prime minister, William Pitt, if the government would fund this important work, but he was given short shrift.

Undeterred, he resolved to fund the educational venture personally. He therefore hired Lusieri, a Roman painter, two architects, two modellers, and a figure painter—and sent them all off to Athens. But when they got there, they found that not only were the local authorities wrecking the building, but the destruction had been going on for centuries.

The building had been through many changes. In the middle of the fifth century AD, Pheidias's great statue of Athena had been carted away when the temple was converted into a Christian church (dedicated, naturally enough, to the Virgin). Then, following the Ottoman conquest of Athens in 1458, the building had been turned into a mosque, with a minaret added to the southwest corner. But the low point had come on the 26th of September 1687, when Venetian forces attacking the city struck the temple with a mortar shell, igniting a gunpowder magazine the Ottomans had idiotically been storing in the building, blowing out its centre and roof, and starting a blaze that took three days to extinguish.

Once in the East, Elgin soon made his way from Istanbul to Athens, where he saw for himself the distressing condition of the Parthenon sculptures. Alarmed, he immediately applied to the Ottoman authorities for a permit (known as a *firman*) to draw and cast the sculptures in order to save some vestige of them for posterity. His timing was good, as Britain was in strong favour with the Ottomans because British troops had just expelled the French from Ottoman Egypt.

Years later, in 1816, a select committee of Parliament drew up a report of exactly what happened when Elgin was in Athens. They heard evidence from eyewitnesses, and, after deliberation, concluded that Elgin had gone through all the proper channels and correctly obtained a *firman* allowing him access to the Parthenon to make casts and drawings. However, they also heard (and saw a translation) of a second *firman* granted to him, which went much further.

It was from the acting Grand Vizier (the *Kaimakam*), who was the omnipotent Sultan's immediate deputy. It ordered the Civil Governor (the *Voivode* and the Chief Justice (the *Cadi*) to permit Elgin and his team to draw, mould, excavate, and remove any pieces of stone with inscriptions and figures.

Acutely aware of the ongoing threat to the remaining sculptures (over half had already been destroyed), Elgin did exactly what he had been granted such clear and explicit permission to do—he began rescuing the ancient artworks. There was no question of him and his men jemmying them off the building behind tarpaulins or under cover of dark. It was a fully public operation, and the witnesses before Parliament said that at no stage did any of the authorities in Athens or Istanbul take issue with Elgin's actions, complain, or intervene. Dr Hunt, a British embassy chaplain in Athens at the time, stated specifically that:

> ... *although the work of taking down and removing was going on for months, and even years, and was conducted in the most public manner, numbers of native labourers, to the amount of some hundreds, being frequently employed, not the least obstruction was ever interposed, nor the smallest uneasiness shown, after the granting of this second ferman.*

Another eye-witness, Mr Hamilton, noted that, among the native Greek population:

... so far from exciting any unpleasant sensation, the people seemed to feel it as the means of bringing foreigners into their country, and of having money spent among them.

Some years later, when the French complained (perhaps because the efforts of Monsieur Choiseul Gouffier, French ambassador to the Porte, had been slightly less successful), the Ottoman authorities issued further *firmans* confirming that they had given Elgin full authority to remove and export the sculptures, and that he had acted at all times in accordance with all applicable laws.

Entirely at his own expense, Elgin rescued 247 feet of the 524-foot frieze, 17 figures from the pediments, 15 of the 92 metopes, as well as figures from the cella, inscriptions, and various architectural features. In all, he saved about half of the carvings from the Parthenon, as well as artworks from a variety of other buildings on the *akropolis*, all of which he openly transported back to England. Dramatically, one of the ships carrying the ancient monuments went down off Cape Matapan, but Elgin paid for the two-year salvage operation personally, and oversaw the retrieval of every single piece of the sunken sculpture.

In all this, Elgin's motives shine out clearly from the written evidence and personal testimony. Although he had originally intended the drawings and casts he commissioned to be kept at his home (copies would be published or made publically available), once he had the *firman* to remove actual sculptures, he always intended the original marbles for the British Museum.

However, on heading home for Britain in 1803, Elgin and his family were captured by the French, who kept him prisoner for three years while Napoleon unsubtly suggested they might release him if he gave the Parthenon sculptures to the Louvre museum.

When Elgin finally returned to Britain in 1806 and exhibited the sculptures, they caused an overnight sensation, drawing the largest crowds the British Museum had ever seen. Elgin was hailed as a hero for saving the ancient art and for opening a window into classical Greece that captivated the nation, especially artists and writers, who had no idea such perfection had once existed on so grand a scale. Keats famously wrote a number of poems in praise of ancient Greece after seeing the marbles, and a generation of Victorian sculptors was electrified by them. Next year, the Tate in London will host an exhibition entitled *Sculpture Victorious* on the sculptures produced in Queen Victoria's reign (1837–1901), and it will visibly demonstrate the enormous influence the arrival of the marbles had on the development of British art in the period.

However, while Elgin's actions were largely celebrated, there were others who took a less rapturous view. In 1812, Lord Byron openly attacked Elgin:

> *Dull is the eye that will not weep to see*
> *Thy walls defaced, thy mouldering shrines removed*
> *By British hands, which it had best behoved*
> *To guard those relics ne'er to be restored.*
> *Curst be the hour when from their isle they roved,*
> *And once again thy hapless bosom gored,*
> *And snatch'd thy shrinking gods to northern climes abhorred!*
> *(Lord Byron, Childe Harold's Pilgrimage)*

However, this needs to be put into context. Byron was a Romantic. As such, he did not want the marbles saved, preferring the idea of them slowly decaying in a tumbledown Athens, where they could be the focus of mournful poetry on the crumbling majesty of yesteryear.

Four years later, in 1816, once the UK parliamentary select committee had confirmed that Elgin had acquired the marbles entirely lawfully, it turned to the question of whether or not the art was important enough for the nation to buy it and house it in the British Museum.

The members listened to a wide range of experts, who unanimously declared the marbles to be spectacular, of the first order, and comparable with the Apollo Belvidere, the Laocoon, and the Torso of the Belvedere, all of which were thought to be the apogee of classical sculpture. The experts categorically confirmed that the marbles were 'among the finest models, and the most exquisite monuments of antiquity'. In terms of what to do with them, the experts opined that they were 'highly fit, and admirably adapted to form a school for study, to improve our national taste for the Fine Arts, and to diffuse a more perfect knowledge of them throughout this kingdom'.

In short, the parliamentary select committee concluded that Britain was immensely fortunate to have them as objects of artistic study. They exonerated Elgin of all slanderous claims of impropriety in obtaining the marbles, and concluded that 'Lord Elgin is entitled to the gratitude of his Country'. They confirmed that Britain wanted to buy the marbles.

Parliament asked Elgin for his costs. Elgin submitted that he had spent £74,000 on the project—a colossal sum of money, a large amount of which was interest on the loans he had been obliged to take out to finance the venture. Parliament's two experts then gave wildly differing estimates of the actual market value of the marbles, ranging from £60,800 down to £25,000. By way of comparison, Parliament looked to the £20,000 paid by the British Museum for the Townley Collection in 1805, the Ægina marbles which the Prince Royal of Bavaria had snapped up for £6,000, and the Phigalia marbles which the British Museum had recently been given at a cost of £19,000. In all the circumstances, the select committee concluded that the appropriate offer to make Elgin for the marbles was £35,000, along with a position as one of the trustees of the British Museum.

Although the offer was half what Elgin had spent, and left him owing immense debts (which plagued him to his death and burdened his heirs), he nevertheless had always intended the marbles to go to the British Museum, so accepted the offer, despite higher bids from others, including Napoleon.

Sadly, the facts of Elgin's personal sacrifice to save the sculptures are not widely known among activists advocating repatriation to Greece. Instead, they assume Elgin looted them from some conquered territory in an imperialist spree of asset stripping. But nothing could be further from the truth. Britain and Ottoman Turkey were allies, and Elgin was granted full and lawful authority to take and export the marbles.

All manner of emotive and often ill-informed arguments now fly around concerning the rights and wrongs of who should own the sculptures today.

Perhaps the most widespread of all arguments is that the marbles are a unique national symbol of Greece and therefore innately belong there. But this is make-believe cultural nationalism. Modern Greece is not the same cultural entity as classical Athens, just as modern Egypt is not Pharaonic Egypt, and nor is Iran ancient Persia. Additionally, the Parthenon was only ever a building for Athenians. It was built to mark the Athenian victory over the Persians at Marathon, and was part temple, part treasure house for the tribute Athens collected from the Greek subjects of its empire. It was never sacred for all of Greece, unlike places such as Mount Olympus or the Oracle at Delphi. The marbles are breathtakingly spectacular Athenian work, but that is not the same as saying they somehow represent the whole of twenty-first-century Greece, or that the modern political entity of Greece is diminished without them.

Also, as a broader question, why do all the activists focus on the Elgin marbles alone? Large and small collections of sculpture from the Parthenon (and the wider *akropolis* area) are to be found in museums in Paris, Vienna, the Vatican, Munich, Würzburg, and Copenhagen. So why is the collection in the British Museum singled out for special anger?

More broadly, museums worldwide hold countless hundreds of thousands of artefacts originating from other countries. That is what museums do—they allow the public to learn about other cultures through their objects. In the largest 'universal' museums, the exhibition experience even allows visitors to see artefacts in their widest temporal and geographical context alongside those of neighbouring cultures.

So what do activists really want? Where is all this heading? Should all museums give back everything that does not come from a randomly circumscribed geographic radius around each museum? Should the Louvre return the Mona Lisa to Florence, even though it was purchased lawfully by the French royal family? Should the J Paul Getty Museum in Los Angeles hand back all its Greek, Roman, medieval, and European art and sculpture, including many of the world's most famous pieces? What about France returning the Bayeux Tapestry to England? Or Japanese museums sending back American rock memorabilia? Maybe Venice should give back the Horses of St Mark if we are now only allowed to see things where they were made?

These are facile arguments. Looting and criminality should be deplored and punished. But antiquities, like everything else, can be legitimately purchased or gifted, and we should celebrate museums that have quite properly acquired collections that educate and inform the visiting public.

Overarching this whole debate, the romantic notion that the marbles could simply be tacked back onto the Parthenon is deeply misguided. Even though Greece declared independence in 1832, the government left the remaining sculptures on the Parthenon to be destroyed by pollution and acid rain—and many were not taken down until 1993. Tragically, some still remain crumbling *in situ*. The result is that all the Greek ones that Lord Elgin left behind are damaged beyond recognition—blurry, fuzzy outlines like figures under a blanket, dissolved by Athens's chronic pollution (although fortunately Elgin took plaster casts of many of the ones he did not bring to England, so at least we have a record of what they used to look like). Were the Elgin marbles to be returned to Athens, they would not go back up onto the Parthenon, but would simply sit in another museum, side by side with the wrecked Greek ones. There, in Athens, far fewer visitors would see them than in London, not only because of tourist numbers, but also because—unlike the British Museum—the New Acropolis Museum charges for entry.

The saturation coverage of Amal Clooney and Geoffrey Robertson QC's visit to Greece last week clearly signals that the debate over the marbles is entering a new, media-focused phase. Those involved need to do far more research. As well as Robertson's extraordinary statement that Elgin would today go to prison for what he did, he also said that the trustees of the British Museum were 'philistines', who keep the marbles 'under bright lights, lit up as if they were corpses in a mortuary.'

Only 40 per cent are under the blue skies of Athens, where they can best be appreciated'. His researchers should have informed him that the marbles will never again—in any country—bask in the open under any kind of sky. They are fragile ancient artefacts, and it is only the care and attention shown to them by the British Museum that has kept them away from pollution and in such amazing condition into the twenty-first century.

In conclusion, despite the character assassination of Lord Elgin by those who innocently (or otherwise) view him as some sort of imperialist asset-stripping fiend, it is clear that Elgin was a hero. He carefully sought permission for all his actions from the lawful rulers of Athens (who were not some Johnny-come-lately opportunistic occupiers, but had ruled Athens for approximately 350 years), and then bankrupted himself to save the sculptures and give them to the nation and the world.

Times have changed, and we care less for culture now than we did in Elgin's day. But we should remind ourselves of what the priorities were then. For example, the 1816 parliamentary select committee could not resist the temptation to add a little epilogue to their report—and it could, in many ways, stand as testimony to the spirit that drove Elgin to such a great project and personal sacrifice:

> *Your Committee cannot dismiss this interesting subject, without submitting to the attentive reflection of the House, how highly the cultivation of the Fine Arts has contributed to the reputation, character, and dignity of every Government by which they have been encouraged, and how intimately they are connected with the advancement of every thing valuable in science, literature, and philosophy.*

However poetic that sounds, we now live in a different world. Art and culture are no longer vote winners. But it does leave one wondering why the Clooneys, with their ability to focus the entire world on any issue of their choosing, should plump for a legally nonsensical assault on the Parthenon sculptures when the world has need of help in so many areas where the Clooneys could sprinkle their stardust: the Middle East, Ebola, crippling G20 debt—the list of tricky problems needing solutions is not short. If they specifically want to focus on museum artefacts, why not highlight the help needed by the National Museum of Iraq, whose vast and priceless holding of some of mankind's oldest art, literature, and science was looted and scattered in April 2003 during the US-led invasion?

If the Greek government is about to launch a new media PR campaign for the return of the marbles, it is time to put aside the wilful misinformation and cheap innuendo that masks the genuine debt that everyone—most especially Greece—owes to Lord Elgin. The world needs to stop whipping him, and start thanking him for his Herculean efforts, *contra mundum*, in saving these wonderful sculptures for everyone.

28

Greece knows it has no legal right to the Elgin Marbles: that's why it won't sue the UK

This piece was published when the Government of Greece abandoned its legal claim to the Elgin Marbles. It explores ideas of cultural ownership, the role of the world's universal museums, and the ongoing destruction of artefacts in conflicts around the world.

The Greek government has finally acknowledged that the British Museum is the lawful owner of the 'Elgin Marbles'. That, at least, is the logical conclusion of the recent news that Greece has dropped its legal claim to the Parthenon Sculptures.

The surprise announcement came only 48 hours after Amal Clooney and the team at London's Doughty Street Chambers sent the Greek government a 150-page report admitting that there was only a 15% chance of their success in a British court, and that Greece should consider pursuing the claim at the International Court of Justice. However, quite understandably, the Greek government has decided that what Clooney is really saying is that they have no case.

The Syriza government is keenly aware that British courts are recognized the world over for their experience in resolving international disputes, including those involving British interests and institutions. So, quite reasonably, the new Greek government has concluded that an international court will probably not reach a different decision. Nikos Xydakis, culture minister, has therefore announced that Greece will drop its legal claim and pursue 'diplomatic and political' avenues instead.

This is unsurprising, as—contrary to the widespread misconception—there was nothing illegal about the way in which Lord Elgin saved the

Parthenon Sculptures from acute ongoing destruction. The mauling had started when the Greek church smashed up a large number of the ancient temple's carvings in the fifth century. The Venetians then blew up chunks of the building in 1687. And in the 1800s, when Lord Elgin arrived in Athens, the occupying Ottomans were grinding the sculptures up for limestone and using them for artillery target practice.

Elgin had intended to commission casts and paintings of the sculptures, but when he saw firsthand the ongoing damage (about 40% of the original sculptures had been pulverized), he acquired an export permit from the Ottoman authorities in Athens, and brought as many as he could back to safety in Britain. It was a personal disaster which bankrupted him, but it has meant that, since 1816, the British Museum has been able to share with its visitors some of the best-preserved Parthenon Sculptures in the world.

What is usually missing in the emotion of the Elgin Marbles debate is that the British Museum is a universal museum, which tells the story of humanity's cultural achievements from the dawn of time. In this, the work of the Ancient Greek department is world leading, and part of a network of museum classicists—including those from the New Acropolis Museum in Athens—who work together collaboratively, sharing their knowledge and passion for the classical world with the widest possible public.

Coincidentally, the British Museum (the nation's largest tourist attraction) is currently hosting a once-in-a-lifetime exhibition of Greek sculpture, drawing on its own collection and generous loans from other museums all over the world to showcase the evolution of ancient Greek ideas about beauty and the human body. In this breathtaking visual story of the march of classical ideas about aesthetics, the Parthenon Sculptures take their place, contributing eloquently to the state of sculpture in the golden age of Athenian carving under Pheidias.

The overarching misconception we need to get over is that museum objects belong uniquely to the country in which they were created. If that was so, the world should empty out its leading museums of the foreign artefacts they have purchased or been donated. Athens would be no exception in this, and would be required to return their extensive collections of Egyptian, Chinese, Islamic, and South American art.

Of course, it is an absurd idea. The world is manifestly enhanced by museums and their depth of specialized knowledge. They are, above all, educational places that enrich us all. The fact that half the surviving sculptures from the Parthenon can be seen in Athens, with the remaining half split between London, Berlin, Munich, Würzburg, Copenhagen, the Vatican, and—thanks to the British Museum—the Hermitage in St Petersburg earlier this year, ensures that the widest possible audience is able to experience for themselves the unique and bewitching ability of fifth-century Athenians to convert rough stone into warm, living flesh.

Another page has turned definitively in the story of the Parthenon Sculptures. The idea that Lord Elgin or Parliament did something illegal has finally been dropped, and not before time. Now the debate can proceed in a less antagonistic manner, and everyone can acknowledge that it is a question of politics, not looted artefacts.

As the world has recently discovered from the tragic destruction of Assyrian art at Nimrud, Mosul, and elsewhere in the Middle East, the planet's heritage does not last unless someone looks after it. And so far, in the case of the Parthenon Sculptures (and indeed its holdings of Assyrian sculpture), the British Museum continues to do the world an enormous service.

29

Did Moses read hieroglyphics? The race to translate the Rosetta Stone

The Rosetta Stone was originally found by Napoleonic French troops in Egypt. It is a code-breaker's dream, as it is inscribed with the same text in Greek, everyday Egyptian, and Egyptian hieroglyphics. This piece was published on the 215th anniversary of its discovery, and traces the story of how Thomas Young in England, and Jean-François Champollion in France, cracked it, and finally unlocked the mysterious world of Egyptian hieroglyphics.

The Bible does not give any descriptive details of the 'tablets of stone inscribed by the finger of God' (*Exodus* 31:18). It merely says that God presented the tablets to Moses on top of Mount Sinai, which raises one very major question (apart from why give a nomad heavy stone tablets), namely: which alphabet were they written in?

One simple answer may be: none. Mainstream historians do not believe the book of *Exodus*'s account of two million Hebrews being captives in Egypt before being led across the Sinai for 40 years by Moses, where God fed them on magical manna, gave them the Ten Commandments, and finally escorted them to the land of Canaan where he had once promised Abraham (an old man from modern-day southern Iraq) that his people could settle. There is no scientific evidence for any of it in Egypt or the Sinai (two million people usually leave quite a bit of stuff for archaeologists to find). Even Goshen, the place in Egypt where it is said they lived, remains unidentified. On balance, most scholars consider *Exodus* to be ancient tribal folklore—like the battling Welsh dragons, the Indian *Mahabharata*, or the Norse cosmology. Even *Haaretz*, Israel's oldest daily newspaper, has run numerous features explaining that the account of the Egyptian slavery, the Exodus, and delivery into the promised land as told in the Bible is legend, not hard history.

The Ten Commandments may be further evidence of this mythos, as there are, in fact, three different sets of the Ten Commandments in the Bible, which all tend to get jumbled up as *Exodus* and *Deuteronomy* repeat themselves. Interestingly, the only one that is explicitly called 'The Ten Commandments' (*Exodus* 34) leaves out 'You shall not kill' and replaces it with the splendidly eccentric, 'You shall not boil a kid in its mother's milk'.

Anyway, assuming for the moment that there was someone called Moses, and that he did have stone tablets with ten laws on them at some stage, then which alphabet were they carved in?

The biblical story of Moses leading the Hebrews lout of Egypt is usually considered to be set in the middle of the second millennium BC. However, the book of *Exodus*, which tells the story, is normally placed around 500–400 BC. And the oldest known manuscript fragments of *Exodus* and the other writings of the Torah date from later still, *c.* 150 BC–AD 70. Interestingly, in each of these distinct periods, Hebrew was written with a different alphabet. Classifications vary, but basically the first paleo-Hebrew alphabet that emerged *c.* 900 BC mutated several times until it settled into the modern 'square' alphabet by *c.* 300 BC. However, crucially, none of these alphabets was around *c.* 1500 BC when Moses received the Ten Commandments.

So what did the Ten Commandments look like?

According to the Bible, Moses was abandoned as a baby by the Hebrew slaves in Egypt. He was then found beside the river Nile by Pharaoh's sister, who took him in and raised him at the royal court of Egypt. So the first question is: what language did he learn when growing up? No one knew he was a Hebrew, and the whole court would have spoken Egyptian. So there is no reason why they would have taught him the language of the Hebrew slaves. He would have spoken (and, if he was educated, read) Egyptian.

The same may also be true of some of the other Hebrews in Egypt, as they had been there for 430 years (*Exodus* 12:40–1), which is long enough to have learned the local language. This needs to be seen in the context of the later Babylonian captivity in the sixth century BC, when many Hebrews were carried off by Nebuchadnezzar from Judah in modern-day southern Israel to Babylon, 50 miles south of modern-day Baghdad. Even though their captivity lasted only 60 years, during that time they definitively abandoned Hebrew and switched permanently to the Babylonian language of Aramaic, retaining Hebrew only as a liturgical and scriptural language until its revival in modern times. (Hence in the New Testament Jesus and everyone else speaks Aramaic, not Hebrew.)

So, if the Hebrews had been in Egypt for over 400 years at the time of the Sinai wandering, might the Ten Commandments have been written in Egypt's sacred alphabet—hieroglyphs (Greek: *hieros*, sacred, *glyphe*, carving)?

Moving forward in time, today is the 215th anniversary of the discovery of the Rosetta Stone—the unique artefact that allowed eighteenth-century scholars finally to unlock the baffling enigma of ancient Egyptian hieroglyphs, whose meaning had been lost to the world for over 1,500 years.

The Rosetta Stone is an unassuming, irregular piece of granite, 112 by 76 by 28 cm. It was found in 1799 by French Napoleonic troops near Fort Saint Julien at the Egyptian town of el-Rashid (Rosetta), 40 miles east of Alexandria in the Nile delta. When the French in Egypt surrendered to the English in 1801, the Treaty of Alexandria required the handover of all looted antiquities, following which the Rosetta Stone made its way to the British Museum back in London, where it has been on permanent display since 1802—save for a short stint in a postal railway tunnel 50 feet under Holborn in 1917 to protect it from aerial bombardment, and a trip in 1972 to the Louvre.

What makes the Rosetta Stone so unique for Egyptologists is that it is carved with the same text in two languages and three alphabets (Greek, formal Egyptian hieroglyphs, and day-to-day Egyptian demotic), In 1999, the dirty black stone was fully cleaned, removing centuries of finger grease, printers' ink, protective carnuba wax, and even white paint that had been used to fill the letters to make them legible. The object that emerged was a beautiful grey flecked with pink.

Soon after the stone arrived in London in 1802, two men—one in England and one in France—set about trying to unlock its coded mysteries. As their starting point, they looked to the three alphabets carved into the stone. Hieroglyphs were the Egyptian priests' sacred language, demotic was the country's ordinary day-to-day script, and Greek was the official language of the Ptolemys' administration. Both men hoped that the presence of all three alphabets would allow them to use the stone to unravel the ever elusive hieroglyphs.

In England, Dr Thomas Young (1773–1829), a polymath, polyglot, physician, and scientist made the first breakthrough. While holidaying in Worthing with an image of the stone's inscriptions, he made two startling discoveries.

Most significantly, he shattered the widely held myth that the hieroglyph pictures had meanings. Instead, by focusing on a series of names enclosed in stylized oval borders known as 'cartouches', he succeeded in reading the name 'Ptolemy' phonetically. In other words, he saw that each symbol of the hieroglyphs represented a phonetic sound, just like in English and most alphabets today.

With this breakthrough, he was able to read the first words in hieroglyphs in a millennium and a half. This phonetic revelation also led him to his second discovery—that the writing should be read in the direction the animals in the text were facing.

Based on these two discoveries, he went on to find other names in cartouches. However, he also believed that his phonetic approach only applied to the names of non-Egyptians like the foreign Ptolemy dynasty from Macedonian Greece. He still imagined, along with everyone else, that all other hieroglyphs were picture writing.

Young, in fact, had a truly amazing mind. Although he described his work on the Rosetta Stone as 'the amusement of a few leisure hours', he went on to compile a dictionary of over 200 hieroglyphs, as well as giving his name to the 'Young's modulus' theory of elasticity, discovering astigmatism, working on colour vision, and making advancements in the wave theory of light. As Young left off, across the Channel in France, Jean-François Champollion (1790–1832) was just beginning his hieroglyph studies in earnest. He was a very different kind of scholar to Young. Aged 10, he had become captivated by the mystery of hieroglyphs, and vowed that one day he would crack them. He was obsessive about it.

Building on Young's work, he found that even the most ancient Egyptian royal names in cartouches (and not just those of later invaders) were spelled phonetically. He also discovered that some hieroglyph symbols operated on the rebus principle, in which, for example, in English, a picture of a cat requires the reader to make the sound 'cat' rather than think of a physical cat. Champollion made this breakthrough by applying his fluent knowledge of ancient liturgical Coptic (his preferred language when writing in his personal journal). He knew that in Coptic the word for sun was 'ra', and realized that a picture of the sun in the hieroglyph text required the reader to make the sound 'ra', as at the start of the name 'Rameses'.

It was 1823, and putting this all together with Young's phonetic discoveries, Champollion had finally cracked it. The hieroglyphic alphabet was a mix of phonetic characters and characters based on the rebus principle, with the underlying language being Egyptian, traces of which survived in liturgical Coptic.

Now Champollion had the key, the world could see that the Rosetta Stone was a proclamation by the priests of Memphis affirming the religious cult of the 13-year-old Pharaoh Ptolemy V Epiphanes (205–180 BC).

> *Whereas King Ptolemy, living forever, the manifest god whose excellence is fine, son of King Ptolemy and Queen Arsinoe, the father-loving gods, is wont to do many favours for the temples of Egypt and for all those who are subject to his kingship, he being a god, the son of a god and a goddess, and being like Horus son of Isis and Osiris, who protects his father Osiris, and his heart being beneficent concerning the gods, since he has given much money and much grain to the temples of Egypt ... (R Simpson, Demotic Grammar in the Ptolemaic Sacerdotal Decrees, 1996)*

It is fairly formulaic and turgid stuff, but formal royal proclamations of any culture are rarely light reading.

So, should the plaudits for cracking the Rosetta code go to Young or Champollion?

Both men have their supporters and detractors. It was an age of intense Anglo-French rivalry, and, not surprisingly, their work was quickly viewed as a competition of national intellectual prowess. Young was humble by nature and congratulated Champollion on his discoveries, but he also wanted Champollion to acknowledge his original breakthrough. Champollion refused, claiming to have solved it all entirely by himself, dismissing Young's claims with a certain inimitable Gallic swagger:

> *The Briton can do as he pleases—it shall be ours: and all of old England will learn from young France to spell hieroglyphs by a totally different method. (Champollion, letter to his brother from Thebes, 1829)*

However, both men undoubtedly deserve the laurels. Young had the initial eureka moment and made the connection that had eluded the world's savants for centuries. As his tomb in St Andrew's Chapel, Westminster Abbey records, it was he who:

> *... first penetrated the obscurity which had veiled for ages the hieroglyphicks of Egypt.*

But it was Champollion who worked assiduously to unravel the whole alphabet and develop a rigorous understanding of the entire system of hieroglyphs. Where Young was almost an accidental Egyptologist alongside his career as a physician and experimental scientist, Champollion was fiercely driven by the baffling world of hieroglyphs to the exclusion of all else. They were his life's work. Once he had solved them, he took to his bed for five days with exhaustion.

The world's 1,500-year loss of understanding of Egyptian hieroglyphs is a reminder of the impermanence of even the most monumental empires and their legacies. Where once hieroglyphs boldly adorned a thousand walls, the last known example was finally incised on the island of Philae in AD 394. Although Egyptian continued to be spoken, Egypt's new Christian authorities soon outlawed hieroglyphs as pagan, and replaced them with the Greek Coptic alphabet. Several centuries later, when Egypt fell to Islam, the chain was finally broken as Coptic gave way to Arabic. The process of forgetting was complete.

Around the time Young published his revolutionary findings on the Rosetta Stone in the supplement to the fifth edition of the Encyclopedia Britannica's entry for 'Egypt', the English poet Shelley summed up the romance of the lost, sandy, transient world of the Pharaohs:

> *I met a traveller from an antique land*
> *Who said: 'Two vast and trunkless legs of stone*
> *Stand in the desert. Near them, on the sand,*
> *Half sunk, a shattered visage lies, whose frown,*
> *And wrinkled lip, and sneer of cold command,*
> *Tell that its sculptor well those passions read*
> *Which yet survive, stamped on these lifeless things,*
> *The hand that mocked them and the heart that fed:*
> *And on the pedestal these words appear:*
> *'My name is Ozymandias, king of kings:*
> *Look on my works, ye Mighty, and despair!'*
> *Nothing beside remains. Round the decay*
> *Of that colossal wreck, boundless and bare*
> *The lone and level sands stretch far away.'*
> *(Percy Bysshe Shelley, Ozymandias, 1818)*

So, back to Moses, the Ten Commandments, and whether the tablets might have been written in hieroglyphs. Honestly? Who knows. Who knows if he was even there. But it can be said for certain that in the second millennium BC, in the Sinai desert, the hieroglyph alphabet was well known, whereas biblical Hebrew was still a thousand years off.

As the unrest in the Middle East again endangers the priceless holdings of the region's museums, just like during the 2003 war, when thousands of artefacts were looted, the anniversary of the discovery of the Rosetta Stone is a poignant reminder of the value of every artefact from the past—especially the ones whose value we do not yet understand.

30

Ada Byron, Countess of Lovelace: coding pioneer a century before Alan Turing

An increasing number of films and programmes credit Alan Turing with inventing the 'drum machine' type of computer used to crack the Nazi's Enigma code. In fact, it was invented a hundred years earlier, and its first programmer was Ada, Countess of Lovelace, also famous as Lord Byron's daughter. She was the first computer programmer, and this piece was published on her birthday.

Benedict Cumberbatch's portrait of a halting, frustrated, brilliant Alan Turing in *The Imitation Game*, 2014 has beamed the Cambridge mathematician's unique contributions to modern digital computing onto the Hollywood big screen.

However, the impression it leaves of Turing as the visionary who dreamed up an unprecedented, futuristic machine of computational cogs and wheels is misleading. The story of groundbreaking English 'drum' computers started over a hundred years earlier.

Mechanical machines have, of course, been performing complex computational functions for centuries. In 1901, divers pulled a rusty box of cogs from the depths of the Aegean near the island of Antikythera. International experts have deduced from the oddity's 30-something gearwheels and countless astronomical inscriptions that it was part of a precisely engineered machine for crunching the mind-boggling mathematics needed to model the positions of the sun and moon and to predict solar eclipses. According to research published in the last few weeks, the Antikythera Mechanism dates to 205 BC, over 1,200 years before mechanical clocks appeared in Europe.

Today is the 199th anniversary of the birth of Ada Byron (1815–82), Countess of Lovelace, only legitimate child of the poet Lord Byron. When she was 19, she met Charles Babbage (1791–1871), the Devonian genius who arguably invented computers. Their partnership was perhaps the true birth of computer science, as he invented the hardware, while she has gone down in history as the first programmer. (The US Defence department's computer language is called Ada, after her).

Like Turing, Babbage was a Cambridge mathematician. Turing was a fellow at King's, while Babbage was the Lucasian Professor, a post held by both Sir Isaac Newton and Stephen Hawking.

Babbage's first foray into mechanized mathematics was his Difference Engine, a calculating machine cranked by a handle. He was never able to build more than a seventh of it (which worked magnificently), but in 1991/2002 the Science Museum managed it, using materials from the 1820s. It weighs five tons, and operates exactly as Babbage predicted.

But Babbage's major scientific leap came in 1834, when he started work on a steam-powered machine to perform an infinite variety of programmable operations. He called it his Analytical Engine, and it is recognizably the first modern digital computer. Like the Polish 'Bombe' machine that Turing took as his starting point at Bletchley, and like Turing's subsequent designs for the 'Universal Turing Machine' and 'Automatic Computing Engine', Babbage's computer used vast banks of rotating drums. The design was truly unprecedented and visionary, allowing it to store 1,000 numbers, each stretching to 40 decimal digits. Just like a modern computer, it incorporated a separate processor and memory bank, looping, and conditional branching. It even had a printer. Sadly, Babbage only had funding to assemble a few parts of it.

Interestingly, away from designing computers, Turing and Babbage had something else in common: both were covert government code-breakers. From 1938–45, Turing was at the Government Code and Cypher School at Bletchley Park, where he first ran Hut 8 (Naval and U-boat cyphers), before eventually becoming consultant to all Bletchley's operations. Babbage's wartime role is not so well-known, but during the Crimean War he cracked the enemy's Vigenère's autokey cypher, although the British government never allowed it to be known for fear of losing the intelligence advantage.

Ada Lovelace collaborated with Babbage (he called her his 'enchantress of numbers'), and it was the most significant work of her short life. She was taught mathematics by her mother, who hoped to keep her well away from poetry. Ada was clearly gifted, and when she met Babbage he asked her to translate an Italian account of his Analytical Engine written by the future Prime Minister of Italy. The work engrossed her, and her fame rests primarily on one of the many notes she added for Babbage, in which she proposed an algorithm for the Analytical Engine to calculate a sequence of Bernoulli numbers. This algorithm is arguably the first true piece of computer code.

English innovations in computing have not slowed since Babbage, Lovelace, and Turing. In June, a chatbot called 'Eugene Goostman' won a competition at the Royal Society marking the 50th anniversary of Turing's death. Its simulation of a 13-year-old Ukrainian boy was hailed by many as the first programme ever to pass the 'Turing Test', a sacred benchmark in artificial intelligence requiring a computer to deceive more than 30 per cent of its human judges into believing it to be human for a period of five minutes.

But not everyone views all modern computing developments positively. Tim Berners-Lee, English inventor of the World Wide Web, has spent much of 2014 being increasingly concerned with what the internet has become. Understandably so. He could never have foreseen the criminality, terrorism, and nation-sponsored cyber warfare now travelling through its servers. And, on the more theoretical side, in a moment of uncharacteristic pessimism, last week Professor Stephen Hawking dramatically predicted that the development of full artificial intelligence could spell the end of the human race.

As no civilization or technology lasts indefinitely, perhaps one day, far in the future, a diver will find a hard drive containing the code for the Eugene Goostman chatbot, and be as baffled by it as we are by the Antikythera Mechanism.

WORLD WAR ONE

31

Fritz Haber: the horror story of the man who invented poison gas

Fritz Haber, the German scientist who won the Nobel prize for the Haber-Bosch process which 'made bread out of air', was also the mastermind behind industrially killing enemy soldiers with chlorine gas in the trenches of World War One. This piece traces his extraordinary and infamous contributions to chemistry and mankind.

Michael Gove, Nick Clegg, and Boris Johnson have fired the opening salvos in the 2014 political battle for the moral high ground over World War One. But for all their ire and passion, it is an intellectually sterile, formulaic, and redundant debate.

No soundbite stereotypes can adequately package the brain-numbing complexity of the escalation of World War One, or the varying sentiments of those who suffered four years of industrialized death on barbed wire and icy ocean floors.

But the tub-thumpers will not be deterred, I am sure. We will see a lot more of this type of silliness as the year unfolds. Let's hope we get some more interesting analysis from other quarters.

For example, what about the role of scientists in World War One? This comes to mind, as today marks the anniversary of the death of one of the best known of them: the physical chemist Fritz Haber—a man who put his deep scientific learning to work in the cause of killing.

It's an inescapable fact that wars are fought with technology. From Greek fire and longbows to the payload of the Enola Gay and unmanned drones, the military has always demanded innovative science.

Scientists and engineers fight wars as surely as armed forces. From the quiet hum of their laboratories and workshops, they develop everything from military food rations and armour to field medicine, weapons, and munitions.

With the occasional exception—like Bishop Durand of Albi, who invented a fast-repeating trebuchet for attacking the Cathars of Montségur in 1244—we do not know a lot about who invented weapons back in the mists of time.

But nowadays we have names, and individual scientists are fully credited with their contributions to warfare.

For instance, Louis Fieser developed napalm for the US military. Oppenheimer and the others of the Manhattan Project were tasked with making the nuclear bombs that eventually laid waste to Hiroshima and Nagasaki. And Sir Barnes Wallis was engaged to perfect the first 6- and 10-ton bunker-busters, as well as bouncing bombs to take out the Ruhr valley dams in Operation Chastise.

Scientists have been at the heart of warfare and their contributions have often been decisive. As Sir Ian Jacobs, Churchill's wartime military secretary, famously remarked on the influx of refugee scientists (including 19 Nobel laureates), 'the Allies won the [Second World] War because our German scientists were better than their German scientists'.

Science is now, irreversibly, the handmaiden to war.

It is impossible to conceive of a militarized nation that does not pour money into scientific weapons research. (This is especially interesting in a Dawkins-esque context, in which one of the reasons given for science's inherent superiority over religion is that religion is labelled as history's chief facilitator of war.) As Oppenheimer mused in July 1945 after overseeing the first ever nuclear test explosion in New Mexico, 'I am become death: the destroyer of worlds'.

Science can be used for good or ill. And today marks the death, 80 years ago, of a man who lived that choice more starkly than perhaps anyone else in the twentieth century.

In the early 1900s, Europe was running into serious problems fertilizing its crops. The vast shipments of bird droppings from South

America were drying up, and there was no obvious alternative.

Enter the extraordinary physical chemist, Fritz Haber.

He was born on the 9th of December 1868 in Breslau (now Wrocław, Poland), and studied first at Heidelberg under Bunsen (of Bunsen Burner fame), then in Berlin. Once qualified, he worked in Zurich, Jena, and Karlsruhe, before finally settling back in Berlin-Dahlem.

Knowing that the air around us is 78.09 per cent nitrogen by volume. Haber discovered that it could be 'fixed' with hydrogen using high pressure, medium temperature, and a catalyst. The result was synthesized ammonia, from which fertilizer could be made.

It was one of the most significant scientific discoveries in modern history. Together with Carl Bosch from the chemicals giant BASF, he perfected the Haber-Bosch process, and they rolled it out at the BASF plant in Ludwigshafen.

The direct impact on the world's ability to fight famine and feed itself was staggering. In 1900 the global population was 1.6 billion. It is now 7.2 billion thanks, in large part, to Haber and Bosch, who 'made bread out of air', as the publicity of the day said. Today, it is estimated that more than 50 per cent of the nitrogen atoms in the average human body derive from the Haber-Bosch process.

In recognition of his pioneering work, Haber received the 1918 Nobel Prize for chemistry (awarded in 1919).

Last November saw the one hundredth anniversary of the launch of the Haber-Bosch process, and scientists from all over the world gathered in Ludwigshafen to assess its extraordinary legacy.

But nothing comes at zero cost, so as well as celebrating the science of Haber-Bosch, the delegates also looked openly at the damage it had done. Not only is there the immediate environmental impact of a global population of over 7 billion humans, there are also the direct consequences of pouring and pumping unprecedented amounts of nitrates into the earth's water and air.

That said, a hundred years ago, Haber could not have foreseen these consequences. He can have had no inkling of the environmental impacts of his discovery.

One choice he did have to make, though, was in relation to his country's war effort, which badly needed nitrates for explosives. But it was a simple decision for him—a patriot—to allow his process to be militarized so Germany could again fill its empty cartridge cases and bombs.

So neither of these issues were direct ethical choices he had to make about scientific innovation.

The one that was put before him (or, rather, that he gave himself), was whether or not to use his knowledge and intellect to take a major scientific step towards mass industrialized killing.

And, without wavering, he did.

He can confidently be identified as the person who first suggested the battlefield use of clouds of air-dispersed chlorine gas as a weapon of mass destruction.

The idea got the green light, and he personally arranged and organized its deployment. On the 22nd of April 1915, he oversaw the opening of 6,000 cylinders of chlorine gas at Ypres, awaking the world to a new terror.

In less than 10 minutes on a Belgian Spring day, 1,000 French and Algerian soldiers lay dead, with a further 4,000 wounded.

Haber kept going. Over the course of the month, he released 500 tons of the fatal gas.

His wife, Clara Immerwahr, was also a gifted chemist—the first woman to be awarded a PhD from the University of Breslau. However, unlike her husband, she was a pacifist. Despite Fritz's belief that death by gas was no worse than any other form of wartime killing, his guiding hand in the chemical carnage of the trenches destroyed her.

When he returned triumphantly home after Ypres to celebrate his promotion to Captain, she challenged his work. Unable to sway him, and overwhelmed with shame, she took his service revolver and shot herself. The next day, Fritz abandoned his grieving 13-year-old son, Hermann, and returned to the front line and his gas deployments, this time in the East against the Russians. (Years later, aged 44, Hermann also committed suicide at the shame of his father's work.)

Although the battlefield use of poison gas was manifestly in breach of international treaty obligations, the genie was out of the bottle, and all sides now piled in. Back in Germany, Haber was promoted to head the Chemical Warfare Service.

To be fair, Haber had not started the battlefield gas attacks in World War One. That honour goes to the French, who first deployed tear gas (xylyl bromide), leading to an escalation. But Haber's unique, early, and defining contribution to trench warfare was to up the ante, replacing irritant gases with fatal clouds of WMDs.

After so long, it is hard to know what really motivated Haber. His claim that he believed chemical attacks would bring the war to a speedy and decisive end does not explain why he kept at it for years, long after it was clear that there would be no swift and immediate resolution.

There is a suggestion that his zeal lay in an unusually strong love of his country as he was, along with most of Europe in the early 1900s, fervently patriotic. In the face of rising anti-Semitism, he had even become a Christian to deepen the Germanness he felt so passionately. This intense nationalism is the usual explanation for his willing contribution to the war effort—but it seems a little simplistic. Many people love their countries profoundly without developing weapons of mass destruction. Maybe his mother's death while giving birth to him affected him in ways that no one diagnosed in the late 1800s and early 1900s. We shall probably never know.

After the war, he continued trying to use science to assist his country. Conscious of the crippling reparations imposed by the Treaty of Versailles, he set about trying to extract gold from seawater to help Germany pay the impossibly unrealistic fines. To his intense frustration, he failed.

All the while, he continued his work on toxic gases. Then, one morning in 1933, his world collapsed when he was refused admission into the Berlin Institute he oversaw. Despite having changed his religion years earlier, he had run foul of the new racial laws, and was no longer welcome.

Broken, he left the country he idolized.

Ironically, a scientist at Cambridge University offered him a laboratory. Haber duly came to England. Although he was pleased to be working again, he soon found the damp weather aggravated his health. He left, and died the following year in Switzerland en route to British Palestine. He therefore did not live to witness what use was made of Zyklon B, a hydrogen-cyanide-based gas product he had been developing. Neither did he see how many members of his own immediate family were killed with it.

To put Haber into the context of his time, he was by no means the only scientist willing to develop chemical WMDs. If he had not done it, the chances are someone else would, and that person could just as easily have been from one of the other combatant countries. As it was, in 1915, the governments of France, England (and eventually the US) all managed to find their own willing scientists to brew up a variety of horrific lethal killing smogs.

What had started with exchanges of chlorine soon moved on to phosgene, and eventually mustard gas. The British army even had dedicated Royal Engineer Special Gas Companies in charge of deploying the chemical weapons on the battlefield. All sides worked hard at the technology. Take William Livens, for instance, an English soldier and engineer (Oundle and Cambridge) who vowed to exterminate as many of the enemy as he possibly could. His successes included chemical mortars, flame fougasses, and petroleum throwers that filled enemy trenches with flaming oil.

In any event, by the end of World War One, after all sides had gone resolutely chemical, over 124,000 tons of military gas had been produced, resulting in an estimated 90,000 deaths and 1.3 million casualties.

These deaths were all, technically, in breach of international treaty obligations banning the use of battlefield poisons and gases, but war is war—and the niceties of international law are often left for the victors to pick over afterwards.

It is, though, odd that Haber should have been awarded a Nobel Prize. Odd because Alfred Nobel specifically instituted the prize to polish up his own reputation, tarnished from a lifetime of developing explosives. Having one day seen his premature obituary in a French newspaper under the banner, '*Le marchand de la mort est mort*' (The merchant of death is dead), he decided to work on his legacy by instituting a prize to celebrate the best in human achievement.

Haber's work on synthesizing ammonia was a singular accomplishment. If the Nobel Committee had presented him a prize in 1913 when he first made his nitrogen fixation breakthrough, he would have been warmly applauded.

But in 1918, with the world's most horrific war drawing to a close, Fritz Haber was identifiably the man most directly responsible for unleashing one of its defining terrors:

> *Gas! Gas! Quick, boys!—An ecstasy of fumbling,*
> *Fitting the clumsy helmets just in time;*
> *But someone still was yelling out and stumbling,*
> *And flound'ring like a man in fire or lime …*
> *Dim, through the misty panes and thick green light,*
> *As under a green sea, I saw him drowning.*
> *(Wilfred Owen, Dulce et Decorum Est, 1917)*

An award like the Nobel Prize survives on the quality of its laureates. Perhaps in recognition of this, of the 1,380-word biography of Fritz Haber on the Nobel Prize website, only one sentence mentions his work on poison gases.

Large numbers of diplomats and scientists boycotted his award ceremony in Stockholm. They were not disputing that he was a gifted scientist. But he made choices. And they were ones that many people did not agree with.

Rewarding infamy is a dangerous precedent. I rather suspect that had Alfred Nobel been looking down at the award presentation, he would have agreed with the nays. For all his genius, in 1919 Fritz Haber could not really be said to rank among those who 'have conferred the greatest benefit on mankind'.

32

When Churchill got it very wrong: Gallipoli

The Gallipoli campaign in Turkey was one of World War One's most notorious military disasters. Churchill was its chief architect, and the outcome cost him his job. This piece tells the story of the ill-starred operation, the bravery and suffering of the soldiers, and how it unexpectedly gave birth to the modern identities of Australia and New Zealand.

Three of Britain's most illustrious warships grace Portsmouth's historic dockyard: Henry VIII's Mary Rose, Nelson's HMS Victory, and the groundbreaking ironclad HMS Warrior.

Now, nestling among them, they have a more modest cousin.

HMS M33 was launched on the 22nd of May 1915. She was so insignificant she did not even warrant a name: just 'M' for monitor class and a number. Yet now she is famous as the only naval survivor of the 1915 Gallipoli campaign.

In this centenary year of Gallipoli, M33 has opened today in Portsmouth as a museum for the public to experience what life was like for her 72 men. As well as offering a fascinating insight into naval warfare a century ago, it provides a moment to reflect on what happened at Gallipoli, and why it matters.

The campaign's objective was simple but bold: to take Ottoman Turkey out of the war completely. The plan was to launch a naval attack and amphibious landing to secure the Gallipoli peninsula and open up the Dardanelles strait. Allied vessels would then pass through the strait and on to Istanbul, where they would take the city and cripple the Ottoman war effort. The campaign's main advocate was a 41-year-old Winston Churchill, First Lord of the Admiralty in Asquith's Liberal government.

On the 19th of February 1915, the naval bombardment began hammering the Ottoman coastal defences, and minesweepers started clearing the mouth of the Dardanelles. However, the area turned out to be surprisingly well defended, and casualties were unexpectedly high. Three British warships were lost, with three more heavily damaged. Meanwhile, amphibious units under General Ian Hamilton had left Egypt for Lemnos, and at 0600 on the 25th of April, in broad daylight, they landed on five beaches along the western shore of the strait at Cape Helles.

Unfortunately, the prolonged naval bombardment had given the Ottomans time to anticipate troop landings and make preparations. Accordingly, the unsuspecting attack units waded ashore directly into mined trip wires in the shallows, barbed wire, sniper fire, and heavy machine guns.

Fighting was intense, and called for immense courage. On W Beach alone, the Lancashire Fusiliers earned six VCs before breakfast.

French troops landed at Kum Kale on the eastern side of the strait, while the Australian and New Zealand Army Corps (ANZACs) beached 12 miles north of Cape Helles at Ari Burna, or ANZAC Cove. Two days later, the Zion Mule Corps also landed in support.

Ottoman defences turned out to be so strong that by the 28th of April there was a frustrating stalemate. The Allies had succeeded in establishing beachheads, but were unable to advance beyond them. Even the addition of Indian infantry and Gurkha Rifles on the 1st of May at Sari Bair failed to break the deadlock. The commander of the Ottoman troops at Ari Burna was jubilant. (He would later become famous as first president of the new Republic of Turkey: Mustafa Kemal 'Atatürk'.)

Back in Britain, a political storm erupted. On the 15th of May, Lord Fisher resigned. He was First Sea Lord and arguably the most important British admiral since Nelson. He had long argued against the viability of the campaign, and been highly critical of Churchill's obsession with it.

As spring turned to summer, the British staged a further landing on the 6th of August at Suvla Bay, just north of ANZAC Cove. Among the ships participating was the brand spanking new M33: a 568-ton M29-class, built in just seven weeks with two oversize six-inch guns and a shallow draft specially designed for close coastal bombardment. However, to everyone's frustration, this landing also ended in another small beachhead and a stalemate.

There appeared to be no way forward.

In September, Lt General Charles Munro took command and recommended abandoning the whole venture. In November, Lord Kitchener, the Secretary of State for War, visited Gallipoli and agreed. The order was given, and all troops were extracted by the 9th of January 1916.

The lack of success was blamed on poor strategy and planning, along with inadequate equipment and munitions. Churchill was stripped of his position as First Lord of the Admiralty. He resigned from politics in defeat, and went to fight in France. Asquith's reputation was fatally damaged, and he eventually resigned, to be replaced by David Lloyd George.

The Allies had lost around 52,500 men. The aim of crippling the Ottomans had failed. And yet, the campaign came to be defined by the bravery of the Allied forces. Britain's soldiers and sailors won 12 VCs, Australia's nine, and New Zealand's one. In Australia and New Zealand, the 25th of April 1915 is still commemorated annually as ANZAC Day, when the 'ANZAC spirit' of grit and determination was born: a baptism of fire that transformed the two dominions into nations.

So, in Portsmouth's historic dockyard, is there an unflattering comparison between Nelson's Victory and M33's defeat?

The answer is no. The Allies may not have secured the Dardanelles or taken Istanbul. But they did tie up a vast amount of Ottoman firepower, which undoubtedly achieved the secondary objective of relieving the pressure on Grand Duke Nicholas's Russian forces fighting the Ottomans in the Caucasus.

Visiting the diminutive M33 in Portsmouth provides an excellent opportunity to reflect on the fact that military science requires the study of operations that go well and those that do not. Gallipoli may not have succeeded in its primary goal, but it provided vital lessons about amphibious landings, many of which were applied directly in planning the decisive Allied landings in Normandy on D-Day June 1944.

All told, the little M33 represents just as rich a slice of British history as HMS Victory or the Mary Rose. It is a mark of totalitarian regimes to insist only on honouring those who fall in burnished victories. The 72 men of M33, and those who fought at Gallipoli, served to the utmost of their ability in what they were tasked to do. In putting M33 next to Victory, we are saluting them all.

WORLD WAR TWO

33

Agent Garbo: the amazing Spanish spy who took on Hitler and saved D-Day

Juan Pujol García invented 27 pro-German spies dotted around Britain and led a one-man deception campaign against the Nazis, feeding them made-up reports from these fictitious agents. Hitler trusted García's reports so much that the false information he fed the Germans about D-Day changed the course of the battle. After the war, García was decorated by both sides. This piece tells his extraordinary story.

On the 6th of June 1944, President Franklin D Roosevelt solemnly declared, 'You don't just walk to Berlin'.

He was speaking at a White House press conference, where he had just announced that Allied troops had landed in northern France.

The gathering was a homely affair, with none of the bombast associated with similar events today. In fact, it was an occasion of masterly understatement. What he could have said was that the largest naval invasion in the history of the world was finally under way. But as he gave the assembled journalists the anodyne update, what he had no way of knowing was quite how successful the operation would be. Within a year, the war with Germany would be over, and Hitler would have a bullet in his head.

The long-awaited amphibious invasion of France was not a secret, and it came as no surprise to German High Command. Stalin's armies had been scything ever deeper into Hitler's forces in the east, where victories like those at Stalingrad and Kursk were definitively pushing the Germans west, out of Russia. But everyone knew that Hitler's hold on most of mainland Europe was strong and not likely to be shaken.

Stalin had therefore been urging the Allies to open up a second front in France to overstretch Germany's war economy and troops. So Hitler and his generals knew it was coming.

Preliminary plans for a European invasion had been drawn up by the Americans in 1942 (Operations Roundup and Sledgehammer), but they were derailed by Churchill's preference for military activity in North Africa, Sicily, and Italy to clear the Mediterranean. Finally, at a meeting in the Russian embassy in Tehran, Roosevelt and Stalin ganged up on Churchill, forcing him to abandon plans for a southern invasion in the Balkans, and securing his commitment to Operation Overlord, a full-frontal invasion of mainland France in May 1944.

At around this time, 2,600 miles west of Tehran, an unlikely part of the story had also begun to take shape.

Juan Pujol García was a native of Barcelona. His experiences in the Spanish Civil War—in which he fought for both sides without ever firing a bullet—had given him a deep loathing of both fascism and communism. At the outbreak of World War Two, he was horrified at the increasing power of the Nazis, and approached the British authorities in Spain and Portugal to enquire if he could help for 'the good of humanity'. Finding his offer repeatedly rebuffed, García decided on a more unorthodox route. He approached German intelligence in Madrid, and told them (quite untruthfully) that he was a Spanish official who regularly travelled to England. He explained that he was fanatically pro-Nazi, and just wanted to do his fascist duty.

The German authorities snapped him up, gave him some basic training, codenamed him 'Alaric Arabel', and sent him off to gather information on his next trip to England.

However, instead of heading for London, García made for Lisbon, where he began one of the most extraordinary and significant subterfuges in espionage history.

Not content with being an agent himself, he used a Blue Guide to England, a book on the railways, a few reference manuals, and a couple of old magazines to invent a handful of completely fictitious agents roaming England. He dreamt up lives and adventures for each of his agents, fabricated intelligence reports from them, and solemnly passed the information back to his German handlers in the *Abwehr*, where the communications were received with earnest appreciation.

Despite his enthusiasm for fiction, García's ignorance of Britain did lead to a few close shaves, like when he reported that men in Glasgow 'would do anything for a litre of wine'. But fortunately the cultural gaffe went unnoticed, as it seems those reading his reports had similarly scant knowledge of Scotland.

Throwing himself into his new life, and armed with his platoon of fake agents, García set about wrong-footing German intelligence wherever he could. And month by month, his handlers' confidence in him grew.

Before long, British intelligence intercepted his messages, and was at first alarmed that there appeared to be a highly active enemy agent in Britain. But when they uncovered that he had significant German naval resources tied up in a hunt for a non-existent convoy, they realized he was, unbelievably, working a one-man disinformation campaign against Hitler. British intelligence quickly brought him to England, where they paired him up with Spanish-speaking MI5 officer, Tomás Harris, and set the two to work.

Under Harris's guidance, García (now codenamed Garbo by MI5) increased his network of fictitious agents to 27 entirely made up people. The cast list included several military personnel, a disgruntled NAAFI storeman, the Welsh nationalist fascist leader of the Brothers of the Aryan World Order, an Indian poet, a Venezuelan student in Glasgow, and even one known just as 'a low grade spy'.

To further strengthen García's credibility with Berlin, MI5 allowed him to pass some genuine information, too. For instance, he reported that one of his agents on the Clyde had seen a warship putting to sea painted in Mediterranean colours. The ship was, in fact, taking part in Operation Torch in North Africa, but García's information was purposefully sent too late to be damaging to the campaign. Nevertheless, the report had the desired effect, boosting his profile in Berlin even higher, where it was viewed as a 'magnificent' piece of espionage.

As D-Day approached, the intelligence services were preparing for the invasion alongside the military. All planners wanted to capitalize on Hitler's belief that the inevitable invasion would come across the narrowest part of the Channel, from Dover to the Pas-de-Calais (150 miles east of the actual landing site).

So began Operation Fortitude South—a mindboggling plan to create a ghost invasion army—a vast American force of 11 divisions (150,000 men) known as the 'First US Army Group', commanded by the tank whizz General George S Patton.

Endless phony radio traffic was generated to give the impression of intense troop mustering activity in Kent and Essex. Acres of dummy wooden aircraft and inflatable tanks were moved into the south-east to be spotted by German reconnaissance and spies. And British intelligence was all the while intently monitoring German reactions through the Ultra project at Bletchley Park, which was able to intercept and decipher all enemy communications. In intelligence terms it was a perfect 'closed loop'—that rare creature in the world of subterfuge in which one side is able to introduce disinformation and then see precisely what reaction it triggers.

As D-Day approached and Operation Fortitude South progressed, Tomás Harris of MI5 brought García into the great deception plan. Fired up with the mission of bombarding the Germans with false invasion information, García dutifully filed voluminous reports from his 'agents' reporting on the build-up of the fictitious First US Army Group in the south-east of England. He passed over 500 messages—at times four transmissions per day—all giving detailed intelligence about General Patton's non-existent army in Kent, together with its plans to invade across the Straits of Dover.

German High Command lapped up García's reports. They were so impressed with the quality of his information that they made almost no other efforts to develop alternative intelligence sources in England, leaving García the undisputed man of the moment. His intelligence was nectar to Hitler, who saw it as an affirmation of his belief that the Allies would soon storm the Pas-de-Calais.

In preparation for the landings, Hitler had appointed the highly-experienced 'Desert Fox', Field Marshal Erwin Rommel, to oversee coastal defence against the invasion. Rommel's last major command had been with the *Afrika Korps*, where his leadership and respectful treatment of prisoners of war had won the admiration of all sides. On the north of the Channel, the Allies were ranged under future US president General Dwight D Eisenhower, who brought in as commander of the land invasion the English General Bernard 'Monty' Montgomery, Rommel's old adversary from the deserts of North Africa.

Rommel's new task was by no means straightforward. As early as 1942, Hitler had called for a defensive Atlantic Wall to be built along the coastline of Europe, from the north of Finland to the Spanish border. The task was clearly impossible, and therefore only implemented patchily. When Rommel took over responsibility, he found the defences in a sorry state, so focused on beefing up the Wall in strategic places with pill boxes and artillery, as well as laying mines, underwater obstacles, and antitank devices on the beaches. Inland, he laid over a million '*Rommelspargel*' (Rommel's asparagus)—four- to five-metre high posts linked to wires, mines, and grenades, designed to counter aerial landings. Unlike Hitler, he suspected a Normandy beach assault, and tried to bring tanks up to the Normandy coast. However, his commander, General Von Rundstedt, disagreed, preferring to place the armour closer to Paris, from where it could be more widely deployed as needed. Rommel was convinced this would lead to the tanks' destruction by Allied planes as they rumbled to the beaches, but Hitler intervened to give some tanks to each of them, with the remainder kept under his personal control—a chaotic Hitlerish decision which happily crippled Rommel's ability to use the armour effectively.

The Allied preparations had been intense. They already enjoyed overwhelming air superiority, and took full advantage of it in the five days before D-Day. Over 11,000 Allied aircraft flew 200,000 missions to drop 195,000 tons of explosives on surrounding French infrastructure, demolishing artillery, roads, railways, bridges, and radar, isolating the landing zone to slow down the German response. Additionally, they focused heavily on the Pas-de-Calais in an effort to give the false impression that the invasion would be coming there. Over 2,000 aircraft were lost in these sorties, but the objectives were achieved. At the same time, London and the BBC coordinated the French resistance in a massive programme of covert sabotage and disruption to the rail network, electrical facilities, and communication lines.

Shortage of landing craft meant that the original plan for a 1st of May invasion was delayed until June. The moon had to be full, and the tide half in. The next available date, the 4th of June, was also abandoned owing to bad weather, but, spotting a small window, Eisenhower finally gave the green light for the 6th of June.

With an immense stroke of luck, Berlin's meteorologists had predicted unceasing terrible weather for two weeks. Many of the soldiers in Normandy had therefore been given leave, while their officers had been sent to Rennes for wargames exercises. Rommel was also absent, having taken the opportunity to nip back to Germany for his wife's birthday and to try to challenge Hitler over the question of where to deploy the tanks. He was therefore nowhere near Normandy when the invasion began just after midnight on Tuesday the 6th of June 1944.

Over 2,200 British and American bombers unleashed the offensive with a pounding from the air, while minesweepers cleared the Channel approaches. A swarm of 822 aircraft (some towing gliders) then dropped US paratroopers to the west of the landing zone and British paratroopers to the east to secure the perimeters. All in all, around 13,000 Allied aircraft were airborne before dawn.

After a choppy hundred-mile crossing, the first troops began wading ashore at 6.30am. The American forces landing on Omaha beach faced heavy defences and took over 2,000 casualties (as depicted in Spielberg's graphic 1998 film, *Saving Private Ryan*). By contrast, US and Free French troops on Utah beach, British troops on Gold and Sword beaches, and Canadian troops on Juno beach, were all slightly more fortunate in facing less resistance.

Even as D-Day dawned, the Operation Fortitude South intelligence deception plan was still in full swing. At the same time as the 7,000 invasion craft headed across the Channel for the Normandy beaches, Allied aircraft dropped vast quantities of tin foil strips known as 'window' to fool the radar on the French coast into thinking a massive invasion fleet was steaming out of Dover.

García's hotline into the *Abwehr* was needed now more than ever, and he duly sent a barrage of messages from his 'agents' to assure German High Command that the Normandy landings were merely a diversion. His reports were littered with detail (e.g., weary troops being issued with vomit bags) and worked so well that Hitler kept two armoured divisions and 19 infantry divisions back in the Pas-de-Calais throughout June, July, and August, and it is certain that had these units not been held back, the Allies would have faced a far bloodier landing. Even as late as the 29th of July, Hitler remained so convinced that García was on his side that he personally awarded him the Iron Cross for 'extraordinary service'. By the time anyone realized there was no invasion force bound for Calais under General Patton, it was too late.

Once over their initial disarray, Rommel's troops put up sustained heavy resistance, resulting in non-stop fighting until the 12th of June, when all five beaches were finally connected into one 50-mile united beachhead.

Despite the fierce fighting, the invasion rapidly settled into a stalemate, with the Allies largely pinned down. Way behind schedule, the Americans did not manage to break west and secure the Cherbourg peninsula until the 28th of June.

By this stage, Allied morale was low, but the same was also true of the German troops. On the 17th of July Rommel was injured by fire from a British plane. And when Von Rundstedt unguardedly told Hitler that all was lost and they should make peace, he was promptly fired. The malaise was, in fact, widespread across the entire battle-weary German army, triggering the 20th of July Plot—the army's failed attempt to blow Hitler up in order to end the war. In the wake of the botched assassination, Hitler had almost 5,000 people executed. Rommel was the most senior plotter, but owing to his fame and popularity, Hitler could not risk having him arrested and murdered by the Gestapo. Instead, he forced Rommel to commit suicide with a cyanide pill in return for an assurance his family would not be harmed under the *Sippenhaft* laws which permitted execution of offenders' relatives.

Needing to maintain the momentum, the Allies continued the assault on France in Operation Dragoon, another massive and successful beach invasion on the 15th of August—this time in the south, around Saint-Tropez and Saint-Raphaël.

Finally, the tide started turning. The Germans in the north began retreating, and on the 24th of August Paris fell to the Allies and the Free French—although, shamefully, the Americans, with no British complaint, refused to allow the black Free French soldiers from Africa (over two thirds of the Free French forces) to take part in the liberation march through Paris, insisting it be staged as an 'all-white' event. (It was a startling piece of racism in a war fought, at least in part, in combat racism—although perhaps not surprising given the segregation in the American army at the time, and General Montgomery's later public support for apartheid in South Africa.)

Allied troops were at the German frontier by September, and in January 1945 the full-scale assault on Germany began, culminating in the Soviets under Zhukov taking Berlin in April, with British. American, and other Allied troops firmly established 60 miles to the west of the city.

Back in England, García stepped down after D-Day for his own safety. In December, the Director General of MI5 awarded him the MBE, thus making him perhaps the only person to have been decorated by both sides in World War Two. Having done his part 'for the good of humanity', García slipped away, and nothing was heard of him until he faked his own death in Angola in 1959. But he was subsequently traced and invited back to England, where he met with HRH the Duke of Edinburgh at Buckingham Palace, was reunited with a group of wartime MI5 officers, and was taken on an emotional tour of the Normandy battlefields. He then retired to a quiet, anonymous life in Venezuela, dying peacefully in Caracas in 1988.

Juan Pujol García's incredible imagination and extraordinary bravery saved many thousands of lives during the invasion of France. Anthony Blunt (who worked in MI5 during the war and knew Tomás Harris very well) confided that one of the Allies' highest commanders said García's contribution to D-Day was worth an entire armoured division. More broadly, García undoubtedly facilitated the overall success of the Normandy landings, which were the beginning of the end of the world's bloodiest war. So perhaps, rather than erecting memorials to divisive figures like Arthur 'Bomber' Harris, how about a memorial to the creative genius of Juan Pujol García, who did more for Britain and a peaceful Europe than most people will ever know.

34

Noor Inayat Khan: a gutsy British World War Two hero, a woman, and a Muslim

Noor Khan was a dreamy children's writer who became one of Britain's most important underground radio operators in Nazi-occupied Paris. Her extreme courage and resilience make her improbable and tragic story read like a film. This piece was published 70 years after her death.

On Friday the 26th of September, Parliament voted for military action in Iraq. Many suspect it is the opening phase of what will become the third Iraq war in the space of 25 years. In the Commons debate, a number of Muslim MPs spoke of the Muslim community in Britain, shining a light into what must be a difficult time as they face the inevitable upsurge in anti-Islamic feeling that can already be seen on the streets, in the social media, and plastered across the comments sections of online newspapers.

Of course, it is simply not possible to categorize an entire section of the British public as definitively one thing or another. There are certainly no straightforward classifications of Islam in Britain, where it has a long and rich history, drawing on an immense number of cultures. Although we again see and hear the usual extremist spokespeople denigrating Britain on television and radio, no one seriously imagines they represent anything other than a tiny minority view.

Moderate opinion is not newsworthy, so it is rarely heard. But it is important to remember that it is there. For example, in the last century alone, hundreds of thousands of Muslims volunteered to fight for Britain—in notably large numbers during World Wars One and Two—with many sacrificing their lives, as recorded on war memorials in all the main theatres of battle. At a time like this, perspective can be sobering.

This year marks the 70th anniversary of the death of one British war hero—who happened to be a woman and a Muslim. Given the endless current debates about Britain and Islam, it is a good time to tell her story again.

Noor Inayat Khan was an Indian princess through her father's side—a direct descendant of Tipu Sultan, the legendary eighteenth-century 'Tiger' ruler of Mysore.

Her father, Inayat Khan, was a Sufi Muslim intellectual, who made his living as a musician and philosopher of mystical Islam. Her mother was an American, and the two fell in love after a lecture he gave on mysticism at an ashram in San Francisco. They married in London in March 1913, and set up house in Bloomsbury.

Inayat Khan's work took him abroad for lengthy periods, and for a while he temporarily relocated the family to Moscow, where Noor was born in the Vusokopetrovsky monastery just over a mile from the Kremlin. After moving back to London briefly, the family eventually settled in France, where Noor spent most of her childhood.

By the time she finished school, Noor was fluent in English and French, much influenced by her father's mysticism and pacifism, fascinated with stories and music, and by all accounts gentle and dreamy.

On leaving school, she enrolled in the École Normale de Musique in Paris to study piano and harp, and the following year began a degree in child psychology at the Sorbonne. When she graduated, she turned to writing for children, publishing a number of successful books, and penning stories for the children's page of the Sunday *Figaro* newspaper, a number of which were also broadcast on Radio Paris and later the BBC.

When World War Two broke out, she unhesitatingly signed up for the French Red Cross, and received training in nursing and first aid. But as the Germans broke through into France and advanced on Paris, she made a decision that would change her life forever. Although her father had instilled in her a firm Sufi Muslim belief in non-violence, she nevertheless knew that she could not sit by and watch the horrors of modern warfare, especially the atrocities against civilians, women, and children. So she headed to England to join the war effort.

Burning to do as much as she could, she applied to join the Women's Auxiliary Air Force (WAAF), a corps of women created to perform the support functions needed by the Royal Air Force in order to free the men for direct combat roles. When she was rejected because she had been born near Moscow, she sent a passionate letter back insisting that as a British Protected Person she be allowed to serve her country. She was immediately accepted, and on the 19th of November 1940, aged 26, she joined the WAAF as an Aircraftswoman Second Class, number 424598.

There was little science in which tasks individual WAAFs were trained in. Noor was selected to be a wireless operator, and promptly packed off to Harrogate for a month's basic military training. Despite her small size—she was five foot three inches tall and weighed less than eight stone—she nevertheless passed all the physical exercises. After the discipline of the parade ground and the barracks, which she passed with an A grade, she was sent to Edinburgh for six months with 34 (Balloon Barrage) Group, where she received instruction in wireless telegraphy. Again, her instructors scored her with A grades.

In June 1941 she was promoted to Aircraftswoman First Class and posted to RAF Bomber Command at Abingdon in Oxfordshire, where by the end of the year she was promoted to Leading Aircraftswoman.

However, unknown to her, a shadowy group was watching her from its headquarters deep in the Ermin Street Hotel in London's fashionable St James's district. They were the men of the Special Operations Executive (SOE), and they had decided they wanted to meet her. So, on the 10th of November, she was called to an interview in Room 238 of the scruffy Hotel Victoria on Northumberland Avenue off Trafalgar Square. There, in a shabby room furnished only with a kitchen table, two hard chairs, and a naked light bulb, she was interviewed by the SOE's chief recruiter, 'Captain' Selwyn Jepson.

The organization Noor was being interviewed by was new—the brainchild of Winston Churchill, who wanted a fifth column to work behind enemy lines in Nazi-occupied territory specializing in sabotage and helping the resistance movements. This clandestine secret service was separate from MI5 and MI6, and drew heavily on the lessons learned from the IRA's highly effective guerrilla warfare against the British in Ireland. The SOE would, in Churchill's words, be 'the Ministry of Ungentlemanly Warfare' tasked to 'set Europe ablaze'.

The nature of SOE's cloak-and-dagger work meant it needed all sorts of covert equipment. Workshops at the Victoria and Albert Museum, the National History Museum, and the Thatched Barn at Barnet invented a cornucopia of sabotage gear: explosives secreted in dead rats, tropical fruit, horse droppings, pens, milk bottles, nuts and bolts; concealed radios in logs and petrol cans; shoes that laid false trails; and—most famously—exploding Buddhas for sale by street hawkers to Japanese troops. There were also a whole range of spy gadgets: spectacles with microfilm dots, miniature compasses in buttons, diminutive saws for escape, maps on silk scarves. The ingenuity was endless. Today, there is even a blue plaque at the Natural History Museum commemorating the 'toy shop' where many of these devices were made—a workshop which provided the inspiration for the character of Q in Ian Fleming's James Bond books, as Fleming had worked closely with SOE when he had been in Naval Intelligence.

The SOE department taking an interest in Noor was F Section, which specialized in recruiting fluent French speakers. Because of the nature of SOE work, Jepson was looking for people 'with real guts' who were willing to go up against the *Abwehr* (German military intelligence) and the collaborating French *Milice*. Courage and bluff were more important than anything else, as if the agents were discovered behind enemy lines, they would not have the protection given to uniformed forces under international law, but would face certain torture and death at the hands of the *Gestapo*.

Noor was one of the first women invited to interview by the SOE, as it was only in April 1942 that the War Cabinet had reached the decision to authorize SOE to employ women agents in the field. As Captain Selwyn Jepson (who recruited Noor) later recalled:

I was responsible for recruiting women for the work, in the face of a good deal of opposition, I may say, from the powers that be. In my view, women were very much better than men for the work. Women, as you must know, have a far greater capacity for cool and lonely courage than men. Men usually want a mate with them. Men don't work alone, their lives tend to be always in company with other men. There was opposition from most quarters until it went up to Churchill, whom I had met before the war. He growled at me, 'What are you doing?' I told him and he said, 'I see you are using women to do this,' and I said, 'Yes, don't you think it is a very sensible thing to do?' and he said, 'Yes, good luck to you.' That was my authority!' (interview with the Imperial War Museum)

Jepson usually interviewed potential recruits two or three times. But in Noor's case there was something so sincere about her that it only took one meeting. After he offered her the job, she replied by letter to confirm her acceptance. Although she had real concerns about leaving her family (with whom she was always immensely close), and despite the fact she was very much in love and had recently become engaged, she had come to an important life decision:

I realise how petty our family ties are when something in the way of winning this war is at stake. I shall therefore accept gratefully the privilege of carrying out the work you suggested.

Behind the scenes, the reason for SOE's interest in Noor was the dire shortage of covert radio operators in occupied France. Each SOE/Resistance network comprised an organizer, a courier, and a radio operator to send the messages back to London. Because the radio operators had to keep the large radios with them, they were especially vulnerable, and the *Gestapo* was keenly aware that capturing the radio operator neutralized the entire cell. As a result, the average life expectancy of an SOE radio operator in France was six weeks.

Now that Noor had accepted, the first step was for her to be discharged from the WAAF and enrolled in the First Aid Nursing Yeomanry—a volunteer organization which would, uniquely, train women in firearms and other military skills. (In total, of the 50 women sent into France by the SOE, 39 were members of the First Aid Nursing Yeomanry.)

After intensive training at Wanborough Manor, an Elizabethan pile in Surrey, Noor (now Nora Baker) was sent to the spy's finishing school at Beaulieu in the New Forest, where the SOE put her through harsh lessons in survival behind enemy lines. (The SOE's access to dozens of large English country houses for its training courses led to its nickname as 'Stately 'Omes of England'.) The instructors who ran the training at the country house and around the grounds of the ruined medieval Cistercian abbey were seasoned and demanding—Kim Philby had finished his role as an instructor there only a short time earlier.

It turned out that Noor was not a natural at any of the activities she was being taught, but her instructors consistently noted her diligence, conscientiousness, and calm resolve. Weapons, explosives, and sabotage training clearly frightened and upset her—they were, after all, a world away from Sufi meditation and writing children's books—but she persevered.

At Beaulieu, part of the training involved being hauled out of bed in the middle of the night and subjected to mock interrogations by men wearing *Gestapo* uniforms. The sessions were rough and ruthless (although not overly physically violent), but their purpose was important. If the trainee cracked, it was better to know that before sending them behind enemy lines where they could endanger others. If the trainee held out, then it gave everyone concerned—especially the trainee—a boost in confidence. Noor did not break, but was palpably terrified by the sessions. She vowed that if ever she was caught, she would simply just never say anything.

Her final report was highly positive, as were the comments on her character.

She is a person for whom I have the greatest admiration. Completely self-effacing and un-selfish. The last person whose absence was noticed, extremely modest, even humble and shy, always thought everyone better than herself, very polite. Has written books for children. Takes everything literally, is not quick, studious rather than clever. Extremely conscientious. (Lance Corporal Gordon, lead instructor)

The next stage was advanced SOE signals training at Thame Park (another former Cistercian abbey) just outside Oxford, where Noor was the first woman ever to be put on the course. But as the grind of the instruction wore on, behind the scenes events were moving quickly. Paris needed a new wireless operator, and Noor—even though her training was unfinished—was the only person with the required profile.

When asked if she would go even though she was not fully trained, she agreed without hesitation. As a final preparation, she was quickly put through a crash survival course in Bristol, where she had to rent rooms, find a job, set up and use cut-outs to deliver messages, and survive an arrest and interrogation by the police.

As her departure date drew closer, a number of SOE individuals began to voice their concerns about her suitability. No one doubted she was diligent and committed, but she was often identified as emotional, and many believed she had inherited a certain impractical dreaminess from her father. Some even thought she was too beautiful and exotic to go unnoticed. Later, Yvonne Cormeau, one of her fellow trainee agents at Beaulieu who survived, said she was a 'splendid, vague dreamy creature, far too conspicuous—twice seen, never forgotten' who should never have been sent to France. One unimpressed instructor said that the 'potty princess' had radically split opinions at Beaulieu, and that she was utterly unsuitable. Referring to the influence her father had over her, he complained, "Do you know what the bastard taught her? That the worst sin she could commit was to lie about anything." The interrogation by the Bristol police had not gone too well, either. The superintendent had reported back to the SOE saying, 'If this girl's an agent, I'm Winston Churchill'.

Nevertheless, Paris desperately needed a 'pianist' (code for telegrapher), and there was no one else. With her training cut short,

Noor was fitted for French-made clothes, and given French ID papers and a ration card. Her only spy equipment apart from a Webley pistol was a knock-out pill, a Benzedrine pill for energy, a pill to induce a stomach disorder, and a cyanide pill that could be safely swallowed but would kill if bitten.

She had been assessed as unsuitable for parachute jumping, so at the next full moon, wearing a green oilskin coat, she boarded a Lysander from 161 Squadron at Tangmere near Chichester and, after a swift Channel crossing, was dropped at a covert landing strip north-west of Angers.

As she stepped back onto French soil, she was no longer Noor Inayat Khan or Nora Baker, but now Jeanne-Marie Renier, a children's nurse, codenamed MADELEINE after a character in one of her books. It was the 16th of June 1943, and she was the first woman wireless operator to be inserted behind enemy lines. Shortly before she landed, the BBC World Service broadcast the message: 'Jasmine is playing her flute' to let the reception committee know she was flying in.

The first thing she did on landing was bury her Webley pistol, as it would be too incriminating if found during the many searches all residents of Paris suffered daily.

Noor quickly found her contacts in the PROSPER/CINEMA network of SOE/Resistance fighters and was up and running in no time,

One of the greatest dangers in her role was the wireless unit itself. The Mark II crystal set she operated weighed 30 pounds and filled an entire suitcase. It was not easy to hide, and nor was the 70 foot aerial she needed to rig up for each broadcast. However, the 400 strong team of women from the First Aid Nursing Yeomanry staffing the SOE's listening post at Grendon Underwood soon began to receive vital information from agent MADELEINE.

Noor had been in Paris for only five days when, after years of trying but failing, the *Gestapo* finally penetrated the PROSPER network and began arresting its agents. Within only 3 days, they had all the main people rounded up and in custody. Noor's world had collapsed. Miraculously still free, she broke the devastating news to London, who told her it was too dangerous for her to stay on her own and that she would be extracted as soon as possible. However, aware that she was now the only radio operator left in Paris, she declined, saying she would rather stay. She knew she was now the only connection with London, and she wanted to keep them informed of events while simultaneously trying to rebuild the blown network.

For a little under three months, Noor used every skill she had been taught at Beaulieu to evade arrest. Aware the *Gestapo* had her description and she was top of their wanted list, she changed her hair colour and style frequently, and kept moving around the city. She carried her wireless set with her at all times, travelling daily between a network of bedsits and rooms she rented or borrowed. On one occasion, some German soldiers in the same *Métro* carriage asked what was in her suitcase and she happily showed them, explaining it was cinematic equipment.

As the only radio operator in Paris, she also began sending messages for other sections, including directly to De Gaulle's office in England. While on the run, she arranged the escape of 30 Allied airmen, the return of a number of agents to England, four sets of false papers for other agents, and the delivery of significant amounts of money and weapons to the Resistance.

When London finally convinced her that another radio operator was being sent to replace her, she agreed to be flown home on the 14th of October. As she went around saying her goodbyes, a Frenchwoman named Renée, who was on the periphery of Noor's circle, presented herself at *Gestapo* headquarters on the Avenue Foch and offered to sell them Noor's whereabouts for 100,000 francs.

As the net closed on the day before her planned extraction, Noor shook off a group of *Gestapo* hoods sent to pick her up, but when she later returned to one of her rooms, she found a French *Gestapo* officer waiting for her inside. After a struggle, she was subdued and taken to *Gestapo* headquarters at 82–6 Avenue Foch. At the first opportunity, she climbed out of a bathroom window five floors up, but was immediately caught and brought in again.

For a month and a half she was held in the headquarters and refused to reveal anything. Hans Kieffer, the station head, later confirmed that she yielded no information and they had been unable to make a single arrest from interrogating her.

While there, she made contact with two other prisoners, and together they hatched a plan to escape. They procured a screwdriver and managed to break out of the barred skylights in their individual cells and onto the roof. But an air raid sounded immediately, and the rooftops were suddenly ablaze with searchlights. They were quickly found missing from their cells, and a hasty cordon thrown around the building found them once they had climbed down to ground level and were trying to make a break for it.

When asked to sign an assurance that she would not try and escape again, Noor refused to lie, and said it was her duty to try at every opportunity. As a result, she was branded 'highly dangerous', and on the 25th of November was transferred to Pforzheim prison, making her the first SOE agent to be sent back to mainland Germany. She was now being held under the dreaded *Nacht und Nebel* (night and fog) regulations. People who disappeared into *Nacht und Nebel* were gone, and no further information was ever provided to family or other enquirers.

At Pforzheim, she was treated barbarously, chained in solitary confinement on minimum rations for 10 months, during which time she resolutely provided her *Gestapo* interrogators with no information at all. Meanwhile, London had no idea she had been taken as the *Gestapo* were using her radio set to transmit phony information back to the SOE. Unknown to Noor, she was awarded the George Medal in February 1944 for her extraordinary bravery and heroism in fighting on.

Finally, on the 11th of September, Pforzheim prison received a message direct from Berlin to move Noor. She was reunited with three other SOE women and put on a train south to Dachau. Forced to walk the last two kilometres on foot, she entered the infamous *Arbeit macht frei* gate into the concentration camp around midnight. She was immediately taken to a cell where she was savagely beaten and kicked until the small hours. Then, as dawn came, she was shot in the back of the head, before her body was taken to the crematorium and incinerated.

She was 30 years old.

The same gruesome fate ultimately awaited most captured SEO agents. Himmler's orders were that they were to be interrogated without mercy, then killed to prevent information about their interrogations or the workings of the *Gestapo* being reported back to London. Of over 200 agents from SOE's French section who were caught, only 26 survived.

In honour of Noor's extraordinary personal courage and sacrifice for Britain, she was posthumously granted an MBE and awarded the George Cross—the civilian equivalent of the Victoria Cross, with which it ranks equally in precedence. In memory of her sacrifice for France, she was given the highest French award for civilian bravery: the *Croix de Guerre* with Gold Star, and every Bastille Day a French military band plays outside the family house in the Parisian suburb of Suresnes where she grew up. There are also tributes to her in Dachau, and on numerous military and SOE memorials.

In London. HRH the Princess Royal unveiled a bust of Noor in Gordon Square in November 2012, commenting that the life of the 'spy princess', while truly remarkable in its own right, also 'has a real connection to our modern era'.

Noor's story is powerful, as sacrifice for a greater good always is. She gave her young life—as did millions of others—to gift posterity the world she wanted to have. So as opinions harden about Britain's role in the Middle East, it is worth remembering that the society we live in today was bought in part, unquantifiably but surely, by Noor's courage, loyalty, and blood, in the field, and in the lonely, dawn terror of Dachau.

Her story should end with the recollection of Captain Selwyn Jepson, the SOE's chief recruiter who met her that fateful winter day just off Trafalgar Square when he recruited her:

> *I see her very clearly as she was that first afternoon, sitting in front of me in that dingy little room, in a hard kitchen chair on the other side of a bare wooden table. Indeed of them all, and there were many who did not return, I find myself constantly remembering her with*

a curious and very personal vividness which outshines the rest ... the small, still features, the dark quiet eyes, the soft voice, and the fine spirit glowing in her.

35

Dresden was a civilian town with no military significance: why did we burn its people?

As World War Two was coming to a close, between 25,000 and 35,000 German civilians were incinerated in the firestorm bombing of Dresden. This piece was published on the 70th anniversary, recounts the history of the bombing, and asks what military rationale there was for the slaughter?

Today marks the 70th anniversary of 'Operation Thunderclap', one of the twentieth century's most controversial military actions.

From the 13th to the 15th of February 1945, British (and some American) heavy bombers dropped 2,400 tons of high explosives and 1,500 tons of incendiary bombs onto the ancient cathedral city of Dresden. In just a few hours, around 25,000 to 35,000 civilians were blown up or incinerated.

Victor Gregg, a British para captured at Arnhem, was a prisoner of war in Dresden that night who was ordered to help with the clear up. In a 2014 BBC interview he recalled the hunt for survivors after the apocalyptic firestorm. In one incident, it took his team seven hours to get into a 1,000-person air-raid shelter in the Altstadt. Once inside, they found no survivors or corpses: just a green-brown liquid with bones sticking out of it. The cowering people had all melted. In areas further from the town centre there were legions of adults shrivelled to three feet in length. Children under the age of three had simply been vaporized.

It was not the first time a German city had been firebombed. 'Operation Gomorrah' had seen Hamburg torched on the 25th of July the previous year. Nine thousand tons of explosives and incendiaries had flattened eight square miles of the city centre, and the resulting inferno had created an oxygen vacuum that whipped up a 150-mile-an-hour wind burning at 800 Celsius. The death toll was 37,000 people. (By comparison, the atom bomb in Nagasaki killed 40,000 on day one.)

Chief of the Air Staff Charles Portal had calculated that bombing civilians could kill 900,000 in 18 months, seriously injure a million more, destroy six million homes, and 'de-house' 25 million, creating a humanitarian crisis that, he believed, would speed up the war.

This thinking was not trumpeted from the rooftops. But in November 1941 the Commander-in-Chief of Bomber Command said he had been intentionally bombing civilians for a year. 'I mention this because, for a long time, the Government, for excellent reasons, has preferred the world to think that we still held some scruples and attacked only what the humanitarians are pleased to call Military Targets. I can assure you, gentlemen, that we tolerate no scruples.'

The debate over this strategy of targeting civilians is still hotly contentious and emotional, in Britain and abroad. There is no doubting the bravery, sacrifice, and suffering of the young men who flew the extraordinarily dangerous missions: 55,573 out of Bomber Command's 125,000 flyers never came home. The airmen even nicknamed their Commander-in-Chief 'Butcher' Harris, highlighting his scant regard for their survival.

Supporters of Britain's 'area bombing' (targeting civilians instead of military or industrial sites) maintain that it was a vital part of the war. Churchill wrote that he wanted 'absolutely devastating, exterminating attacks by very heavy bombers from this country upon the Nazi homeland'. In another letter he called it 'terror bombing'. His aim was to demoralize the Germans to catalyse regime change. Research suggests that the soaring homelessness levels and family break ups did indeed depress civilian morale, but there is no evidence it helped anyone prise Hitler's cold hand off the wheel.

Others maintain that it was ghastly, but Hitler started it so needed to be answered in a language he understood. Unfortunately, records show that the first intentional 'area bombing' of civilians in the World

War Two took place at Monchengladbach on the 11th of May 1940 at Churchill's orders (the day after he dramatically became prime minister), and four months before the Luftwaffe began its Blitz of British cities.

Not everyone was convinced by city bombing. Numerous military and church leaders voiced strong opposition. Freeman Dyson, now one of Britain's most eminent physicists, worked at Bomber Command from 1943–5. He said it eroded his moral beliefs until he had no moral position at all. He wanted to write about it, but then found the American novelist Kurt Vonnegut had said everything he wanted to say.

Like Gregg, Vonnegut had been a prisoner in Dresden that night. He claimed that only one person in the world derived any benefit from the slaughterhouse—him, because he wrote a famous book about it which pays him two or three dollars for every person killed.

Germany's bombing of British cities was equally abhorrent. Germany dropped 35,000 tons on Britain over eight months in 1940-1 killing an estimated 39,000. (In total, the UK and US dropped around 1.9 million tons on Germany over 7 years.)

Bombing German cities clearly did have an impact on the war. The question, though, is how much. The post-war US Bombing Survey estimated that the effect of all allied city bombing probably depleted the German economy by no more than 2.7 per cent.

Allowing for differences of opinion on the efficacy or necessity of 'area bombing' in the days when the war's outcome remained uncertain (arguably until Stalingrad in February 1943), the key question on today's anniversary remains whether the bombing of Dresden in February 1945 was militarily necessary—because by then the war was definitely over. Hitler was already in his bunker playing out his final absurd fantasies. The British and Americans were at the German border after winning D-Day the previous summer, while the Russians under Zhukov and Konev were well inside eastern Germany and racing pell-mell to Berlin.

Dresden was a civilian town without military significance. It had no material role of any sort to play in the closing months of the war. So, what strategic purpose did burning its men, women, old people, and children serve? Churchill himself later wrote that 'the destruction of Dresden remains a serious query against the conduct of Allied bombing'.

Seventy years on, fewer people ask precisely which military objective justified the hell unleashed on Dresden. If there was no good strategic reason for it, then not even the passage of time can make it right, and the questions it poses remain as difficult as ever in a world in which civilians have continued to suffer unspeakably in the wars of their autocratic leaders.

THE MODERN
WORLD

36

The dark, deep roots of Britain's fascination with witchcraft

In 1944, Helen Duncan and Jane Yorke were convicted in London under the Witchcraft Act. This piece tells their story, and looks at Britain's wider fascination with witchcraft, from Halloween to Harry Potter and Gandalf.

As the cinema queues form again for our seasonal dose of hobbits, wizards, and strangely aggressive dwarves, there seems to be a big question hanging in the air—larger even than whether the intrepid hairballs will reach the next unpronounceable town.

It is this. What does our fascination with watching them yomp to-and-fro across Middle-earth tell us about Britain's beliefs today? More precisely, what does it reveal about our attitude to magic and the supernatural?

To put the question in context, in 1937 J R R Tolkien published his neo-medieval epic, *The Hobbit or There and Back Again.*

Its magic-fuelled adventure was an instant hit.

Yet in 1944, only seven years later, juries at London's austere Old Bailey were still gamely convicting women under the ancient Witchcraft Act 1735.

Moving ahead six years, in 1950 Tolkien's friend and fellow don C S Lewis enchanted the public with his witchy goings on in Narnia. Hot on its heels, in 1954 Tolkien unleashed the great *Lord of the Rings* trilogy, which was instantly acclaimed by a loyal and expectant readership.

So how did the same public coo with delight at Gandalf's nonchalant command of the magical realm, yet look on with equanimity as Helen Duncan and 72-year-old Jane Yorke were subjected to full criminal trials for talking to spirits? The same readers of Tolkien and Lewis watched as both women were convicted by jury, fined in the case of Yorke, and carted off to Holloway Prison in the case of Duncan.

Fortunately, the offence was no longer capital, and there was never any question of hanging—although it would be another 11 years before the gallows trap was finally shut in Britain. The honour of being the last witch to be burned in the British Isles went to Janet Horne in Scotland, who was sent to the stake in 1727 for riding her daughter to the Devil, where he shod her. At least, as far as the presiding sheriff was concerned, this seemed the only explanation for her unfortunate daughter's deformed hands and feet.

So how, in Blitz-scarred London, were two women found guilty under witchcraft legislation at a time when Tolkien and Lewis were stamping out wizards and witches by the kilo?

Whoever reads the (refreshingly) short Witchcraft Act 1735 quickly finds that it is tragically misnamed. It should really be called the Abolition of the Idea of Witchcraft Act.

The previous Witchcraft Acts had been built on the unshakable certainty that witches—who wantonly consorted with foul demons and undermined upstanding members of society—needed to be put to death.

King Henry VIII (1542), Queen Elizabeth I (1562), and King James I (1604) all passed Witchcraft Acts to reinforce this view. In fact, James I was so dippy about the subject, he took up his pen in 1597 and sweated over a small treatise he called *Daemonologie*. It begins:

> *The fearefull aboundinge at this time in this countrie, of these detestable slaues of the Deuill, the Witches or enchaunters, hath moved me (beloued reader) to dispatch in post, this following treatise of mine, not in any wise (as I protest) to serue for a shew of my learning & ingine, but onely (mooued of conscience) to preasse thereby, so farre as I can, to resolue the doubting harts of many.*

Not long after, of course, he commissioned the King James Bible, which remains, for many, the gold standard of Bible translation, despite its strong grounding in the politics and beliefs of the day.

But it was all to change just over a century later under the Germanic influence of King George II. His Witchcraft Act of 1735 put an end to all the previous broomstick mumbo-jumbo. It rejected completely the idea that witches existed, and instead targeted fraudulent witches.

Therefore, what Helen Duncan and Jane Yorke were actually convicted of in 1944 was fraud. The Act put it like this:

> IV. ... *if any Person shall ... pretend to exercise or use any kind of Witchcraft, Sorcery, Inchantment, or Conjuration, or undertake to tell Fortunes, or pretend, from his or her Skill or Knowledge in any occult or crafty Science, to discover where or in what manner any Goods or Chattels, supposed to have been stolen or lost, may be found, every Person, so offending, being thereof lawfully convicted on Indictment or Information ... shall, for every such Offence, suffer Imprisonment by the Space of one whole Year without Bail or Mainprize, and once in every Quarter of the said Year, in some Market Town of the proper County, upon the Market Day, there stand openly on the Pillory by the Space of One Hour.*

Still, the subtle legal distinction was probably lost on the two women. In the grey newspapers of war-tired London, Helen Duncan and Jane Yorke went down in sensationalist legend as Britain's last two witches—a notoriety that still dogs them.

Duncan was, it was claimed, manifestly a fraud, repeatedly shown to be regurgitating cheesecloth, egg white, rubber gloves, and all manner of other fabricated 'ectoplasm'. Yorke's séances were less dramatic, but there was a suspicion that she, like Duncan, might be preying on the war bereaved.

In Duncan's case, there was additionally a whiff of intrigue. She revealed in a séance that a missing sailor had gone down on HMS Barham. This caused something of a stir, as knowledge of Barham's sinking in November 941 was tightly restricted to Whitehall and the families of the bereaved. With the D-Day Normandy landings only three months away, it has been suggested that some in government believed it was safer to confine Duncan to Holloway until after the summer offensive.

So why were the two women indicted under the Witchcraft Act? Both could as easily have been charged with deception, or offences under Section 4 of the Vagrancy Act 1824 which covered fraudulent fortune telling, astrology, and spiritualism.

Churchill, prime minister at the time, was troubled by the use of the witchcraft charges, which he called 'obsolete tomfoolery' in a letter he fired off to the Home Secretary immediately after Duncan's conviction.

But the fact the trial was specifically sensationalized by the government's law officers through linking it to the ancient witchcraft laws hints at something much deeper in the British psyche.

The answer lies, at least in part, in the same fascination that keeps us returning for our annual silver-screen wizard fixes.

We are, as a nation, fascinated by the magical.

Of course, ever since George II's Witchcraft Act of 1735, we do not believe in magic any more. We tone it down wherever possible. Even the institution at the historical heart of our cities and villages that was built on a belief in magic is a bit shuffly on the subject. Their special word for magic, 'miracles'—which exists only to distinguish Christian magic from other less classy sorts—is pretty far down the agenda these days.

But still the British take to their sleeping bags to lie outside barricaded bookshops until opening time to get the latest book redolent of wise ones in pointy hats.

The fact is that our fascination seems to be longstanding. Although we can rightly celebrate the British learning behind the World Wide Web, the Higgs Boson, and a host of other national achievements, our scientific prowess seems unable to shake our collective fascination with the manifestly irrational and supernatural—the idea there is a little magic somewhere, if we only know where to look for it.

And we do not just indulge this fetish on the screen.

On the 31st of October each year, the nation gets routinely pagan.

Regardless of the modern commercialization of Halloween, the country is carrying on the rites of the pre-Christian people of these Islands—tipping fancy dress moon-studded hats to the age-old winter festivals of the living and the dead.

And only five days later, on the 5th of November, we gaze deeply into the wintry fires of our forebears, in a rite that has everything to do with Celtic and Anglo-Saxon traditions.

Yet it's not just in winter that we acknowledge our magical past.

Local Mayday traditions abound, as spring returns and nature reawakens. Take Maypole dancing. Despite centuries of stern disapproval—starting with the Commonwealth of the mid-1600s, which castigated the revelry as idolatrous—it remains firmly anchored in many villages, towns, and cities. Every spring, poles are still strung with ribbons, and the zesty dance around them in honour of long-forgotten seasonal rites.

Once you start thinking of Britain as steeped in millennia of the magical and supernatural, you start to see it everywhere.

For example, there are the legions of bizarre Green Men festooning our medieval churches and cathedrals, emerging from, spewing out, or interbred with billowing foliage. Their magical oneness with nature has no basis in Christianity, but would have fitted into Tolkien's imaginary world without a ripple.

If that all sounds too genteel and you like your magic to have more teeth, then consider Britain's place as the home of modern magical practices. And I do not mean Paul Daniels or Derren Brown. According to the world expert Professor Ronald Hutton, modern pagan witchcraft (or Wicca) is the only world religion made in England.

It is worth realizing that Wicca (from the Anglo-Saxon *wicca*, witch) was only taken public by the former civil servant Gerald Gardner once the coast was well and truly clear following the repeal of the Witchcraft Act in 1951.

In fact, there is a vast amount in this area that is uniquely British.

Modern druidry, the Golden Dawn, and even Aleister Crowley's Thelema, are all successful British magical exports. They may sound fringe now, but in their heyday they attracted adherents like the Nobel Prize winning poet W B Yeats and Constance, Oscar Wilde's wife, who all dressed up and performed high society ancient magical rituals.

Among other notable Victorian supernatural organizations, the most famous is perhaps The Ghost Club, founded by fellows from Cambridge University to investigate the paranormal. Over the years, its elite membership has included Charles Dickens, Sir Arthur Conan Doyle (a keen spiritualist), and Siegfried Sassoon.

So. Back to Bilbo, Harry, Dumbledore, Aslan, Hagrid, Gandalf, Hermione, Galadriel, and the great roll call of the rest, who have now been assimilated into British winter as readily as *Stollen* and Christmas markets.

Even though the 2011 census shows a drop in organized religion and a rise in more flexible alternatives, it seems we are far from embracing a systematic secularism. Instead, we are, in our droves, transfixed by mythical figures who straddle the large space in our minds for wonder and the irrational.

The final question is: why Britain? What makes Britain so rich in writers and audiences who flock to these themes?

This time, the answer is as clear as looking out of the window at the British landscape, while remembering that the word 'pagan' comes from *pagani*, meaning people from the countryside.

The inescapable reality is that these islands battle with elemental weather, giving us a visceral awareness of the drama of the changing seasons. Coupled with the long dark nights of winter and the euphoria of summer light, the British have always had an innate awareness of the proximity of the natural world, and its power to make or break us in any year.

The result is an understandable fascination with the behaviour of nature. It is therefore no wonder that we have always been transfixed by figures who command the forces that the rest of us can only watch.

And there is nothing new in that. Cnut the Great—all powerful king of England and much of Scandinavia—can have been thinking of little else when he pitched his chair on the shore to show his toady courtiers that even he, for all his magnificence, could not command the tide.

At least his fun was not spoiled by any Witchcraft Acts.

37

How German is the Queen?

During World War One, in a move to look less German, the British royal family changed its name from Saxe-Coburg-Gotha to Windsor. When the Queen travelled on a state visit to Berlin, this piece unravelled the age-old connections between Germany and the British royal family.

'Elizabeth the Second, by the Grace of God, of the United Kingdom of Great Britain and Northern Ireland and of Her other Realms and Territories Queen, Head of the Commonwealth, Defender of the Faith.'

You can't get more British than that, really.

Yet as the Queen prepares for another state visit to Germany, idle minds again turn to questions about the connections between our two countries, and not least the Teutonic heritage of the Royal Family.

So, to put it in a nutshell, how German is the Queen?

The obvious place to start is the family tree, although unfolding it is enough to make even the most seasoned genealogist reach for a stiff drink. Yet what comes across very clearly—and very quickly—is that there is a lot of German in it.

There is no real starting point, but we may as well begin with 1714. Queen Anne died, and her direct Stuart line came juddering to a halt. This caused a thorny problem because her 50 (or thereabouts) closest suitable relatives were all Catholic, so distinctly non grata. They were passed over, and in the end Georg Ludwig, the Protestant Prince Elector of Hanover, got the job, and our royal house changed from Stuart to Brunswick-Lüneburg-Hanover, bringing with it a wealth of connections to the ancient royal houses of Welf and Este.

It is worth pausing to note that, until recently, members of the Royal Family had no surname. They customarily used first names and the name of their house, which was inherited from the father (Richard the Lionheart was a Plantagenet, Henry VIII was a Tudor, George I was a Hanover).

Accordingly, the House of Hanover ended with Queen Victoria, and her descendants took the dynastic name of her husband, Prince Albert, which was also German: Saxe-Coburg-Gotha, a branch of the eminent House of Wettin.

Simple. But it does not end there.

When World War One bred increasing anti-German sentiment in Britain, astute observers noted that Kaiser Bill was Queen Victoria's grandson and our King George V's first cousin. In recognition of the delicacy of the position, George V changed the name of his royal house from Saxe-Coburg-Gotha to Windsor, after the castle. At the same time, he also took the modern step of adopting Windsor as a surname for his family.

On her accession, Queen Elizabeth II chose to keep the name Windsor, and in 1960 the Queen and the Duke of Edinburgh announced that they wanted their descendants who do not have an HRH title to be Mountbatten-Windsor. (Mountbatten is the Duke of Edinburgh's adopted name. His German-Danish-Greek royal lines are Schleswig-Holstein-Sonderburg-Glücksburg on his father's side, and Battenberg on his mother's.)

Well, so much for the German genealogy—not to mention customs. The Royal Family still opens its presents on Christmas Eve, following the German tradition, which Prince Albert was particularly keen on following.

On the other hand, there's no point overstating it. The Queen is also directly descended from over a thousand years' worth of Britain's royal houses, including the Stuarts, Tudors, Plantagenets, Angevins, Normans, and Wessex.

It is, in fact, worth remembering that the word 'English' is derived from the Angles, of Anglo-Saxon fame. When the Romans cleared out of Britain in AD 410, a range of German, Danish, and Dutch tribes that we sloppily call the Anglo-Saxons moved in from across the Whale Road. That's not forgetting the Vikings either, who brought Danish, Norwegian, and Swedish blood to swathes of Britain. So, to be honest, if we scrutinize the Royal Family's connections with the Fatherland, we should take a long look at our own, too, and acknowledge that this country has had the most profound and close genetic and cultural ties with the people of Germany and Scandinavia for over 1,500 years.

To put it in perspective, the Queen's family have lived in Britain for many centuries. She speaks English as her first language and French fluently. Not German. She was born in Bruton Street, Mayfair. She grew up largely at 145 Piccadilly, Richmond Park, and Windsor Great Park. She served in the war as a mechanic and driver with the Women's Auxiliary Territorial Service. She is unostentatious, supremely diplomatic, and often seen laughing. She rides without a hat, enjoys playing the Nintendo WII, and is fond of racing pigeons. Most especially of all, she is known throughout the world for her keen love of dogs and horses.

How much more British could HM be? Seriously?

FIRST PUBLISHED

Chapter 1. 'Flavius Josephus, the Roman destruction of Jerusalem, and two millennia of bloodshed in the Middle East' **was first** published in *The Daily Telegraph* on 5 August 2014 as 'Two millennia after the sack of Jerusalem, what does history tell us about violence in the Middle East?'

Chapter 2. 'Theodosius I: the forgotten man who turned Christianity into a global religion' was first published in *The Daily Telegraph* on 27 February 2014 as 'This is the man who turned Christianity into a global religion. Do you even know his name?'

Chapter 3. 'Rome was not civilized and the 'Dark Ages' were not dark' was first published in *The Daily Telegraph* on 18 February 2014 as 'Why the so-called 'Dark Ages' were just as civilized as the savage Roman Empire'.

Chapter 4. 'The Vikings were no worse than the Anglo-Saxons' was first published in *The Daily Telegraph* on 14 January 2014 as 'The Vikings were no worse than the Anglo-Saxons. Let's celebrate this rich immigrant culture'.

Chapter 5. 'Alfred the Great, king of Wessex, was a Roman Catholic' was first published in *The Daily Telegraph* on 20 January 2014 as 'King Alfred was a Roman Catholic. Let's bury him in Westminster Cathedral'.

Chapter 6. 'King Harold's England was multicultural and decidedly European' was first published in *The Daily Telegraph* on 6 January 2014 as 'As the Euro elections loom, let's remember the coronation of our last Anglo-Saxon king'.

Chapter 7. 'The battle of Hastings (1066) wasn't such a big deal' was first published in *The Daily Telegraph* on 14 October 2014 as 'The true story of the Battle of Hastings, today in 1066'.

Chapter 8. 'The cult of Magna Carta is historical nonsense: Oliver Cromwell called it 'Magna Farta" was first published in *The Daily Telegraph* on 17 June 2014 as 'The cult of Magna Carta is historical nonsense: no wonder Oliver Cromwell called it 'Magna Farta".

Chapter 9. 'The Magna Carta barons were guilty of treason' was first published in *The Daily Telegraph* on 31 July 2015 as 'Magna Carta trial: The barons' treason must be exposed'.

Chapter 10. 'Save the Statute of Marlborough (1267): our oldest law' was first published in *The Spectator* on 15 June 2015 as 'In praise of charming but pointless laws—like the Magna Carta'.

Chapter 11. 'Medieval cathedrals are bursting with colour again' was first published in *The Daily Telegraph* on 24 December 2014 as 'Cathedrals are bursting with colour again'.

Chapter 12. 'Richard the Lionheart and Saladin: chivalry and atrocities' was first published in *The Daily Telegraph* on 4 April 2014 as 'Cruel, anti-English and almost certainly gay: meet the real Richard the Lionheart'.

Chapter 13. 'Saladin and the fateful battle of Hattin (1187): lessons for the modern Middle East' was first published in *The Daily Telegraph* on 2 July 2014 as 'What the Crusades tell us about shifting borders in the Middle East'.

Chapter 14. 'Forget the *Da Vinci Code*: this is the real mystery of the Knights Templar' was first published in *The Daily Telegraph* on 19 December 2013.

Chapter 15. 'A stain on history: the burning of Jacques de Molay, Grand Master of the Knights Templar' was first published in *The Daily Telegraph* on 18 March 2014 as 'A stain on history: the burning of Jacques de Molay, Grand Master of the mysterious Knights Templar, 700 years ago today'.

Chapter 16. 'The Turin Shroud is one of the greatest medieval artworks ever created' was first published in *The Spectator* on 27 April 2015 as 'If the Turin Shroud is the work of a medieval artist, it's one of the greatest artworks ever created'.

Chapter 17. 'Regicide and ambition: Richard III and the death of the 'princes' in the Tower' was first published in *The Daily Telegraph* on 18 February 2015 as 'How bad a guy was Richard III?'

Chapter 18. 'Reburying Richard III: is it the right body?' was first published in *The Daily Telegraph* on 21 March 2015 as 'Richard III: we're burying the wrong body'.

Chapter 19. 'Medieval al-Andalus: tolerance and totalitarianism' was first published in *The Daily Telegraph* on 2 January 2014 as 'Today is the anniversary of the fall of Moorish Spain. Was it really such a wonderful place?'

Chapter 20. 'Savonarola and Mary Queen of Scots: the bloody underside of the 'civilized' Renaissance' was first published in *The Daily Telegraph* on 17 February 2014 as 'The bloody underside of the 'civilized' Renaissance'.

Chapter 21. 'Columbus, greed, slavery, and genocide: what really happened to the American Indians' was first published in *The Daily Telegraph* on 2 September 2014.

Chapter 22. 'How the Tudor spin machine hid the brutal truth about the English Reformation' was first published in *The Daily Telegraph* on 23 May 2014 as 'How a Protestant spin machine hid the truth about the English Reformation'.

Chapter 23. 'Thomas Cromwell was the Islamic State of his day' was first published in *The Daily Telegraph* on 22 January 2015.

Chapter 24. 'How Protestantism fuelled the deadly witch craze' was first published in *The Daily Telegraph* on 30 April 2014 as 'How Protestantism fuelled Europe's deadly witch craze'.

Chapter 25. 'Guy Fawkes. Islamists, converts, and terrorism: some things never change' was first published in *The Daily Telegraph* on 5 November 2014.

Chapter 26. 'New Year's Day is too soon after Christmas. Let's move it back to its proper place—in March' was first published in *The Daily Telegraph* on 30 December 2013.

Chapter 27. 'Haters back off. Lord Elgin was a hero who saved the marbles for the world' was first published in *The Daily Telegraph* on 21 October 2014 as 'Amal Clooney should back off. Lord Elgin was a hero who saved the marbles for the world'.

Chapter 28. 'Greece knows it has no legal right to the Elgin Marbles: that's why it won't sue the UK' was first published in *The Daily Telegraph* on 14 May 2015.

Chapter 29. 'Did Moses read hieroglyphics? The race to translate the Rosetta Stone' was first published in *The Daily Telegraph* on 15 July 2014 as 'What does the Rosetta Stone tell us about the Bible? Did Moses read hieroglyphs?'

Chapter 30. 'Ada Byron, Countess of Lovelace: coding pioneer a century before Alan Turing' was first published in *The Daily Telegraph* on 10 December 2014 as 'Ada Lovelace paved the way for Alan Turing's more celebrated codebreaking a century before he was born'.

Chapter 31. 'Fritz Haber: the horror story of the man who invented poison gas' was first published in *The Daily Telegraph* on 29 January 2014 as 'The man who invented poison gas: a horror story'.

Chapter 32. 'When Churchill got it very wrong: Gallipoli' was first published in *The Daily Telegraph* on 6 August 2015 as 'We must mark failures like Gallipoli alongside our successes'.

Chapter 33. 'Agent Garbo: the amazing Spanish spy who took on Hitler and saved D-Day' was first published in *The Daily Telegraph* on 6 June 2014 as 'The spy who saved D-Day'.

Chapter 34. 'Noor Inayat Khan: a gutsy British World War Two hero, a woman, and a Muslim' was first published in *The Daily Telegraph* on 8 October 2014 as 'A gutsy British Second World War hero—a woman, and a Muslim, Have you ever heard of her?'

Chapter 35. 'Dresden was a civilian town with no military significance: why did we burn its people?' was first published in *The Daily Telegraph* on 12 February 2015.

Chapter 36. 'The dark, deep roots of Britain's fascination with witchcraft' was first published in *The Daily Telegraph* on 31 December 2013.

Chapter 37. 'How German is the Queen?' was first published in *The Daily Telegraph* on 24 June 2015.

ALSO BY
CRUX PUBLISHING

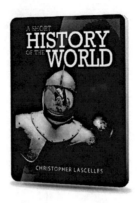

A Short History of the World

by Christopher Lascelles

*"A clearly written, remarkably comprehensive guide to the
greatest story on Earth - man's journey from the earliest
times to the modern day. Highly recommended."*
**Dan Jones, author of The Plantagenets:
The Kings Who Made England**

There is an increasing realisation that our knowledge of world history – and how it all fits together – is far from perfect. *A Short History of the World* aims to fill the big gaps in our historical knowledge with a book that is easy to read and assumes little prior knowledge of past events. The book does not aim to come up with groundbreaking new theories on why things occurred, but rather gives a broad overview of the generally accepted version of events so that non-historians will feel less ignorant when discussing the past.

While the book covers world history from the Big Bang to the present day, it principally covers key people, events and empires since the dawn of the first civilisations in around 3500 BC. To help readers put events, places and empires into context, the book includes 36 specially commissioned maps to accompany the text. The result is a book that is reassuringly epic in scope but refreshingly short in length. An excellent place to start to bring your historical knowledge up to scratch!

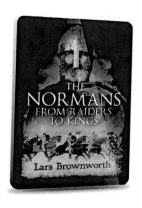

The Normans: From Raiders to Kings

by Lars Brownworth

"An evocative journey through the colourful and dangerous world of early medieval Europe"
Jonathan Harris, author of Byzantium and the Crusades

There is much more to the Norman story than the Battle of Hastings. These descendants of the Vikings who settled in France, England, and Italy - but were not strictly French, English, or Italian - played a large role in creating the modern world. They were the success story of the Middle Ages; a footloose band of individual adventurers who transformed the face of medieval Europe. During the course of two centuries they launched a series of extraordinary conquests, carving out kingdoms from the North Sea to the North African coast.

In *The Normans*, author Lars Brownworth follows their story, from the first shock of a Viking raid on an Irish monastery to the exile of the last Norman Prince of Antioch. In the process he brings to vivid life the Norman tapestry's rich cast of characters: figures like Rollo the Walker, William Iron-Arm, Tancred the Monkey King, and Robert Guiscard. It presents a fascinating glimpse of a time when a group of restless adventurers had the world at their fingertips.

CPSIA information can be obtained at www.ICGtesting.com
Printed in the USA
LVOW10s0533100316

478563LV00025B/442/P